# YOUR SPACIAL OFFICE

USING THE VISION PRO AND MACBOOK TO TRANSFORM YOUR WORKSPACE

## SCOTT LA COUNTE

ANAHEIM, CALIFORNIA

www.RidiculouslySimpleBooks.com

**Disclaimer**: *Please note, while every effort has been made to ensure accuracy, this book is not endorsed by Apple, Inc. and should be considered unofficial.*

# Table of Contents

# INTRODUCTION

**Unleash your virtual office!**

Are you ready to work and play in a whole new dimension with the Apple Vision Pro? This book is the ultimate resource for anyone who wants to learn how to use this amazing device to turn their space into a virtual office.

The Vision Pro is not just the best TV you'll probably ever have. It is a powerful workstation that lets you interact with digital content in three-dimensional space. You can use it to create, collaborate, communicate, and entertain in ways that were never possible before.

But how do you get started with this revolutionary device? And what are the best apps and tools to use with it?

This book answers all these questions and more. It covers everything you need to know about the Vision Pro, from its hardware and software to its accessories and settings.

In this book, you will learn:

- **What is spatial computing and how to use the Vision Pro**
- **How to connect Bluetooth devices like keyboards and trackpads to help you work more efficiently**
- **How to connect your Mac and use macOS and its apps on the big screen**
- **How to use the Vision Pro for video calls and conferencing**
- **How to customize your virtual office with spatial computing**
- **Tips and tricks to optimize your productivity and creativity with the Vision Pro**
- **How to use macOS**
- **And much more!**

This book is a practical and informative guide that will help you unleash the full potential of the Vision Pro. Whether you are a professional, a student, a hobbyist, or a casual user, this book will show you how to work and play better with the Apple Vision Pro.

*Note: This guide is crafted with the aim of enhancing your Vision Pro experience. While not officially endorsed by Apple, Inc., it offers a wealth of knowledge and tips to help you make the most of your device.*

# [1]

# Getting to Know the Vision Pro

## WHO IS THIS THING FOR?!

The Vision Pro is a revolutionary device. Putting it on for the first time is... it's an experience beyond words. I could extol its immersive and lifelike qualities endlessly, but words simply can't capture its essence. It's nothing short of incredible. When I first used it, all I could think about was how, in a few years, my child might use this technology in school, potentially transforming education. Imagine not even needing to attend school physically—students could interact and see their peers as if they were right there with them.

So, it's for everyone, right? Well, sort of, but not quite yet. If you have $3,500 to spare, then sure, why not purchase it? You might as well get one for your less fortunate friend too! However, for the vast majority of us, the Vision Pro remains just out of reach—for now. It's on the horizon; much like the iPhone revolutionized our daily lives, the Vision Pro is set to do the same. It will become more affordable and lighter. It's already excellent, but there's always room for improvement.

To be clear, the Vision Pro isn't a beta product. It's a polished device that outperforms any other of its kind. It's not even a fair comparison to other headsets.

But who is it actually for? There are numerous applications. Developers, for instance, are a primary audience; if you're looking to be at the forefront of a technology that will reshape our work and interactions, then the Vision Pro is essential. It's a must-have for understanding and creating for this new platform. For those who travel frequently, the Vision Pro is a game-changer, offering a vast virtual office space when physical space is limited. This is equally true for remote workers without a dedicated workspace; it enables focus in less-than-ideal environments—just make sure you have a comfortable chair to avoid neck strain, which can occur even with good support. It's also the ultimate entertainment device for movie enthusiasts; it promises an experience superior to any television you might own, though it does come with a caveat of isolation—you can't share a movie on the couch with someone unless they have their own headset.

If you're concerned about migraines and motion sickness, rest assured that these issues are less about the experience and more about the device's weight causing muscle strain. While individual experiences may vary, most agree that the motion sickness associated with other headsets is not an issue with the Vision Pro. You might feel a bit odd the first few times you remove it, but this is largely due to the level of immersion—your brain is adjusting to new experiences. It's important to ease into it gradually. Don't rush into active movement; instead, sit back, relax, and acclimate to this novel experience. I would recommend doing no more than 20 or 30 minutes at a time when you first start using it; and I know it's going to be really tempting to push the limits because of how fun it is.

We are on the brink of a technological revolution, and as new applications are developed daily, the Vision Pro will only improve. If you're not convinced that the Vision Pro is for you, that's understandable; but consider revisiting it in a few years.

## WHAT IF I HAVE A MEDICAL CONDITIONS

So maybe the Vision Pro is for you, but what if your prone to get migraines, your pregnant, or have another health condition? It may or may not be for you. How can you be sure: talk to your doctor before using it.

If you get the green light from your doc, here are some pointers:

- Start seated and ease into less immersive experiences.
- Keep your sessions short and sweet, with plenty of breaks.
- If you feel any discomfort, dizziness, or eye strain, it's time to take a break.

For those with medical devices like pacemakers, hearing aids, or defibrillators, your new tech buddy, the Vision Pro, could be a bit too magnetic. So, again, it's best to consult your doctor or the device manufacturer before using Vision Pro.

If all's well, remember:

- Keep a safe distance between your Vision Pro and any medical devices.
- If you notice any interference with your device, it's better to stop using the headset.

Here are some clear signs to take a break or seek medical advice:

- Any symptoms related to your medical condition pop up.
- You're all clear from your doctor but still feel physically uncomfortable, dizzy, or visually strained.
- You notice any skin irritation, swelling, or itchiness during or after use.

Using the Apple Vision Pro can be a blast, but your health should obviously be the top priority. Always consult with your healthcare provider to ensure a safe and enjoyable experience.  It's always better to be safe than sorry.


## APPLE VISION PRO WITH PRESCRIPTION LENSES

What if you think the Vision Pro is for you, but your like lots of other people: you wear glasses. Good news! You can't wear your glasses with the Vision Pro directly (you can wear contacts, however), but there's a solution: Zeiss Optical Inserts. These are specially designed for the Vision Pro, catering to a wide range of prescriptions, including those for astigmatism. Sadly, if your glasses have a prism value, these inserts aren't yet an option.

Do you need them? I only need glasses for far away, so I didn't think I'd spend $149, but I'm glad I did. It's right on my face, so why bother?

Because the depth of the picture can be far away. I've tried it with and without it and it's enhanced with it.

To get these inserts, you'll need a prescription that includes your full name, date of birth, and the details of your eye care professional. Remember, it should cover both your distance and near correction needs and shouldn't be expired. And here's a tip: contact lens prescriptions won't do the trick here.

If you're a fan of progressive or bifocal lenses, you're in luck, as these inserts cater to most such needs. After you send in your prescription, you'll hear back within a day about the availability of your custom inserts. It took me less than 5 hours, and even though it said it would take three weeks, they were at my doorstep at launch.

If your eyewear is more about catching up on the latest bestseller, you can opt for Zeiss Optical Inserts – Readers. They come in various strengths to match your reading glasses. But, if you find yourself squinting or feeling uneasy while using the Vision Pro, it might be time to consult an eye care professional for a more suitable prescription.

If you use soft single vision contacts, you're good to go without any additional inserts. However, hard lens users might face challenges with eye tracking. In such cases, consider the Zeiss Optical Inserts or an alternative control method, like Pointer Control.

What if you've had monovision surgery or use monovision contacts? You'll want to switch to Zeiss Optical Inserts based on an eyeglass prescription.

Vision Pro is a tech marvel that uses your gaze to navigate. But if you have conditions like eyelid drooping, strabismus, or nystagmus, this feature might not work as smoothly. Don't worry, though. The Vision Pro's Accessibility features come to the rescue, allowing you to navigate using wrist, head movements, finger gestures, or voice commands.

## BATTLE OF VR

I'm sure when you heard about the Vision Pro, one of the first things you said was, "That's a lot of money! More than almost any other VR headset out there." Apple will tell you, "Well, this isn't a VR headset–

it's spatial computing." But that doesn't stop the comparison from other devices. In this section, we'll take a look at three headsets: the Meta Quest 3 (arguably the most popular), the PSVR 2 (for gamers), and the HoloLens 2 (Microsoft's answer to mixed reality and one of the best headsets out there for enterprise), and we'll see how they stack up against the Vision Pro.

## META QUEST 3

When it comes to VR, the one everyone usually jumps to is the Meta Quest. The headset has been turning heads for several years with each generation of the device. Let's take a look at how the two compare.

### Price and Affordability

- Meta Quest 3: Priced at $499, the Meta Quest 3 is positioned as a more affordable option in the VR market. This pricing strategy suggests an aim to attract a broader consumer base.

- Apple Vision Pro: At $3,499, the Vision Pro is a high-end device targeting a niche market. Its premium price point reflects its advanced features and is likely aimed at professionals or enthusiasts seeking the best possible VR/AR experience.

### Operating System and Ecosystem

- Meta Quest OS: The Quest 3 runs on the Meta Quest OS, a platform that has evolved from the Oculus ecosystem, known for its robust library of games and applications.

- visionOS: Apple's Vision Pro operates on visionOS, which offers seamless integration with other Apple products and services. This Quest OS is not unituitive, but Vision OS proves a more unified and potentially more user-friendly experience, especially for existing Apple users.

### Control Mechanisms

- Meta Quest 3: Utilizes updated Touch controllers, maintaining a form of physical interaction that is familiar to many VR users.

- Apple Vision Pro: Offers a controller-free experience, leveraging eye tracking and hand gestures. This advanced approach gives it a more immersive and intuitive user experience.

## Display Quality
- Meta Quest 3: Features an LCD with a resolution of 2064x2208 per eye, providing a clear and vivid visual experience.
- Apple Vision Pro: Boasts dual 4k micro-OLED displays, which is crucial for professional applications and high-end gaming.

## Processing Power
- Meta Quest 3: Powered by the Snapdragon XRGen 2 processor, ensuring smooth performance in standard VR applications.
- Apple Vision Pro: Equipped with the Apple silicon chip M2, known for its efficiency and power, indicating potentially better performance, especially in more demanding applications.

## Design and Comfort
- Meta Quest 3: Offers a refreshed Quest form factor, 40% lighter and slimmer than its predecessor, focusing on user comfort during extended use.
- Apple Vision Pro: Adopts a premium, lightweight ski-goggle design; the Quest is slightly lighter, but both are heavy devices that take a little getting used to. Apple's straps do feel much more premium, however.

## Sensor Technology
- Meta Quest 3: Employs front cameras for AR and tracking, which is sufficient for general VR experiences.
- Apple Vision Pro: Incorporates over a dozen cameras for advanced AR, iris scanning, which all offer a more sophisticated approach to user interaction and environment mapping.

## Audio Experience
- Meta Quest 3: Includes onboard speakers and a 3.5mm jack, offering standard audio capabilities.

- Apple Vision Pro: Features advanced spatial audio with high-fidelity speakers, enhancing the immersion and realism of the VR/AR experience.

## IPD Adjustment

- Meta Quest 3: Utilizes a physical adjustment dial, allowing users to manually set the interpupillary distance for comfort and clarity.

- Apple Vision Pro: Lenses adjust automatically, providing a more user-friendly experience and potentially better visual quality for a wider range of users.

## Tracking Capabilities

- Meta Quest 3: Focuses on controller and some hand-tracking, sufficient for most current VR applications.

- Apple Vision Pro: Offers full-body motion capture via cameras, a feature that could revolutionize VR interactions and open new possibilities in various applications.

## Storage Options

- Meta Quest 3: Starts at 128GB, with a 512GB version rumored, providing ample space for games and apps.

- Apple Vision Pro: the Vision Pro comes in 256GB, 512GB, and 1TB.

## Passthrough Camera Quality

- Meta Quest 3: Features full-color passthrough, enhancing the AR experience.

- Apple Vision Pro: Offers incredibly high-resolution passthrough, setting a new standard in the clarity and realism of AR applications. The Meta Quest passthrough is grainy in lowlight situations; it's enough to know where you are in a room, but not at all like the HD on the Vision Pro.

## Battery Life and Portability

- Meta Quest 3: Offers 2 to 2.5 hours of battery life, which is typical for current VR headsets.

- Apple Vision Pro: Provides up to 2 hours of usage, which, given its advanced features, is reasonable. The Vision Pro weigh about 1.3 pounds, which is slightly heavier than the Quest 3.

The Meta Quest 3 and Apple Vision Pro cater to different segments of the VR/AR market. The Quest 3 offers an affordable, user-friendly experience suitable for gaming and general VR applications. In contrast, the Vision Pro is a premium device that pushes the boundaries of VR/AR technology, aimed at professionals and enthusiasts seeking the most advanced experience possible.

Many people suggest that if the Vision Pro is out of your budget, the Quest 3 serves as a good alternative. However, I believe this comparison isn't quite apt. For those who are primarily interested in gaming and perhaps fitness, and are seeking a genuine VR experience, the Quest 3 can be a decent option if the Vision Pro is unaffordable.

On the other hand, if you're like me and require a headset for both work and productivity, with the added bonus of occasional entertainment, then the Quest 3 might not be the best purchase. Given the significant investment required for a Vision Pro, it's understandable if it's beyond your budget. In such cases, I would advise waiting for the next iteration of the Vision Pro or considering the Quest 4, depending on its specifications, which have yet to be released at the time of this writing.

While working on the Quest 3 isn't out of the question, it doesn't offer the same ease of use as the Vision Pro. It is fairly quick, especially for Windows users, since it's compatible with the operating system, unlike the Vision Pro. The main issue with the Quest 3 is the awareness that you're using it—the visuals are somewhat blurry and lack sharpness. In contrast, the Vision Pro provides an immersive experience; if it weren't for the weight of the headset, you might even forget you're wearing it.

## PSVR 2

Meta Quest isn't the only game in town—especially if you want a gaming headset. PSVR 2 is designed for the PlayStation, so you'll need a PS5 to use it. But how do they stack up? Let's find out:

## Display and Visual Fidelity

- Apple Vision Pro: Boasts an impressive display with 23 million pixels per panel, exceeding the resolution of most 4K TVs. This feature promises unparalleled clarity and detail in visual content.

- PSVR 2: Features two 2000 x 2040 OLED displays, along with 4K HDR capabilities. While this is impressive, it seems the Vision Pro might have an edge in terms of sheer pixel density and clarity.

## Integration and Usability

- Apple Vision Pro: Offers versatility with its mixed-reality capabilities, allowing users to blend apps with their environment. The device can be used plugged in or powered by a battery pack, providing 2 hours of runtime. Additionally, it includes an external screen displaying the user's eyes, enhancing the sense of presence.

- PSVR 2: Integrates seamlessly with the PlayStation 5, connecting via a USB C cable. This integration ensures a hassle-free setup for gamers, with no concerns about battery life.

## Design and Interaction

- Apple Vision Pro: Sports a futuristic ski-goggle design with a sleek and thin profile. It features a plush band for comfort and a stylish silvery hue. Interaction with the device is facilitated through voice, eye movements, and hand gestures, offering a controller-free experience.

- PSVR 2: While not as aesthetically sleek as the Vision Pro, it is designed for comfort. The PSVR 2 requires the use of tactile, light, and user-friendly Sense Controllers for navigation and gameplay.

## Price Point

- Apple Vision Pro: Positioned as a premium product, the Vision Pro is priced at a steep $3,499, reflecting its advanced technology and mixed-reality capabilities.

- PSVR 2: More affordable at $549, the PSVR 2 is significantly cheaper than the Vision Pro, making it a more accessible option for VR gaming enthusiasts.

The Apple Vision Pro and PSVR 2, while both offering immersive experiences and high-resolution graphics, cater to distinct audiences and purposes. The Vision Pro is a high-end, mixed-reality device suited for those seeking a comprehensive and versatile AR/VR experience, particularly for streaming, viewing, and professional applications. In contrast, the PSVR 2 is a dedicated VR gaming headset, ideal for PlayStation 5 users looking for an immersive gaming experience.

You can play games on the Vision Pro–there's thousands to pick from when you consider all the iPad apps brought in to the ecosystem; but PS5 was built for gaming, so it's not going to surprise anyone when I say the games on the PSVR 2 are superior.

## HOLOLENS 2

Finally, if you thought the Vision Pro was the only $3500 headset, then you must have forgotten about the HoloLens. Don't worry! So has everyone else! The HoloLens is Microsoft's answer to mixed reality. And I know what you are thinking: Microsoft has MR?! Yes! And it's actually really cool. They've been working in this space for years and actually have the lead on Apple in a lot of ways. Is it a superior device? Let's find out!

### Design

- Apple Vision Pro: The Vision Pro sports a sleek, stylish design akin to a pair of ski goggles. Made of aluminum with a curved glass display, it exudes a modern, consumer-friendly aesthetic. This design choice reflects Apple's focus on creating a device that is not only functional but also fashionable.

- HoloLens 2: In contrast, the HoloLens 2 has an industrial look with a visor-like form factor, constructed primarily from plastic. This design is more utilitarian, emphasizing functionality and durability, which is important for business and industrial applications.

### Features

- Apple Vision Pro: Designed primarily for consumers, the Vision Pro boasts a wider field of view than the HoloLens 2, potentially offering a more immersive AR experience. Its comfort is also a key feature, making it suitable for extended use. The Vision Pro's "spatial computer" powers are another highlight, promising innovative interactions with the digital world.

- HoloLens 2: Targeted towards businesses, the HoloLens 2 excels in advanced tracking capabilities and seamless integration with the Microsoft ecosystem, including various enterprise applications. This focus on professional use cases gives it an edge in environments where robustness and precision are crucial.

### Price

- Apple Vision Pro: The Vision Pro is priced at $3,499. This price point positions it as a premium product, reflecting its advanced technology and design.

- HoloLens 2: The HoloLens 2 is currently available at $3,500 and $4,500 for the enterprise edition. This pricing strategy underscores its focus on professional and industrial markets, where the investment can be justified by the device's utility in specialized applications.

The Apple Vision Pro and the HoloLens 2, while both powerful AR headsets, serve different purposes and audiences. The Vision Pro is an excellent choice for consumers who value style, comfort, and a wide field of view in an AR headset. Its capabilities are geared towards immersive experiences in personal entertainment, gaming, and perhaps light professional work.

On the other hand, the HoloLens 2 is ideally suited for businesses and professional environments. Its advanced tracking features, robust build, and integration with Microsoft's suite of enterprise tools make it a practical choice for industries like manufacturing, healthcare, and education.

## PURCHASING A VISION PRO

The Vision Pro is one of the most unique buying experiences Apple has ever offered. For the best fit, you can go to any Apple Store with an appointment, and get measured. If you don't want to do that, you can also do it on your iPhone or iPad (you can use your computer, of course, but you'll be referred to your iPhone or iPad to do the measurements). My advice: use an iPhone. I tried it on an iPad Pro, and found the process a little more frustrating–I was turning my head in all kinds of different ways trying to get it to scan.

The other thing I highly recommend is doing the scan two or three times. The first time I tried it, I got a medium. The next two times, small. The Light Seal also measured at at 21W and 23W. If going into the store is not an option, then you might want to pick up both, and then return the one that doesn't fit.

When you start the checkout, you'll be greeted with a page to scan your face first. It's a quick process, but make sure you have plenty of light. This isn't going to work in a dimly lit room. I had to switch rooms the first time I tried it.

If you have ever did Face ID on your Apple device, the next steps are pretty similar. You'll scan your face by looking in different directions. (note: forgive my picture below–I'm on the West Coast, so ordering the Vision Pro was a 5AM wake up call!)

After you do it once, you'll do the exact same thing a second time.

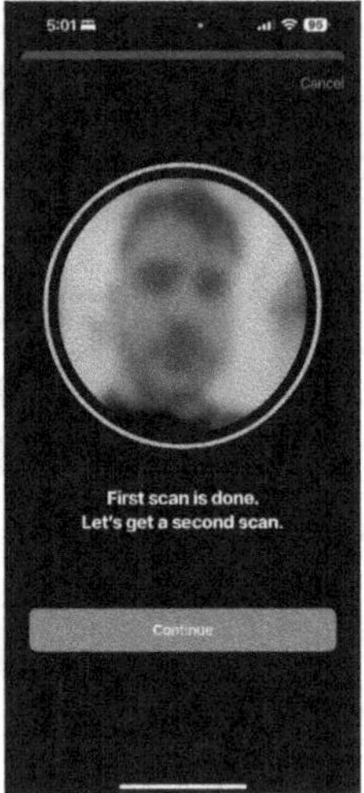

Once the scan is complete, you'll get a screen saying your face has been measured. You'll need to scroll a little to get to the next part, which is the prescription lenes.

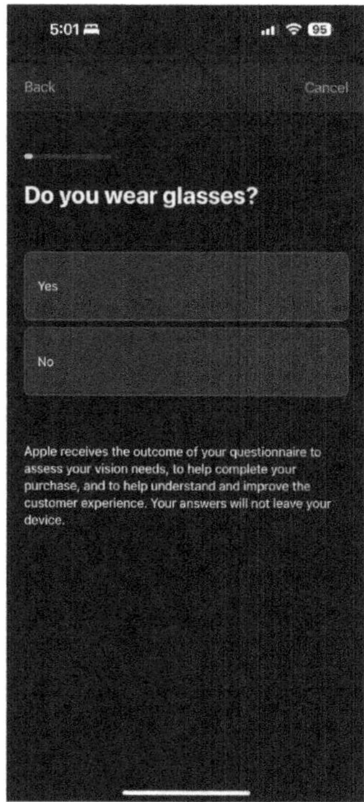

The next part of the buying process is easier–just a handful of questions about if you wear glasses, contacts, or have ever had corrective eye surgery. This will help determine if the ZEISS lenses are ideal for you.

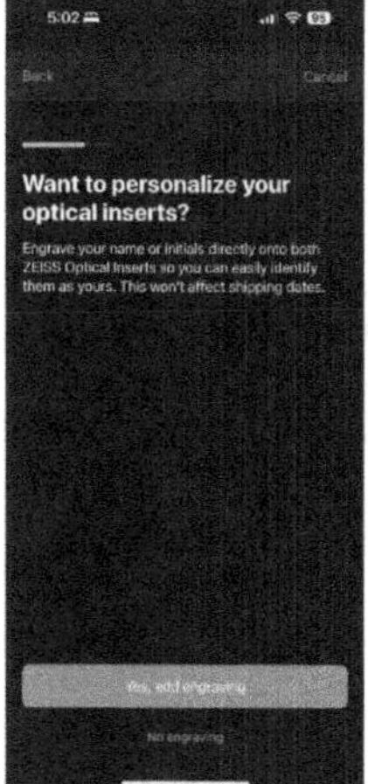

Once this questionnaire is done, it will either tell you that you don't need the lens add-on, or it will tell you to upload your prescription. You don't need your prescription to put in an order. You can skip it and then come back and add it in later.

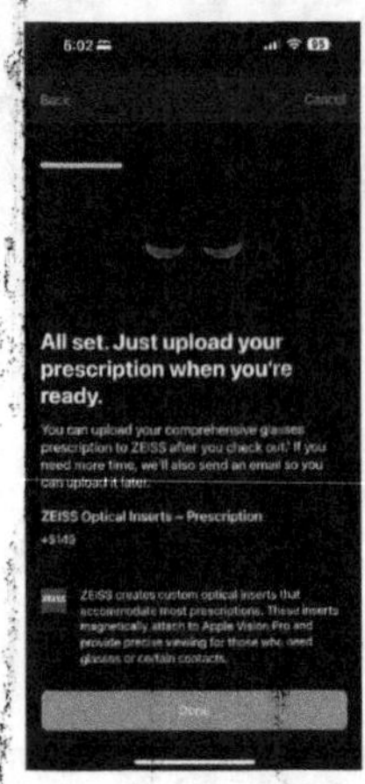

The rest of the buying is pretty standard. It will ask if you want to do payment plans, if you want Apple Care+ (skip to the section on Apple Care+ if your on the fence about this–hint: repairs without it can cost over $2,000!), and if you want to pick it up at a store or ship it to you. Once you do all that, you can put in your order, and your all set! The entire process will take about 5 to 10 minutes.

## UNBOXING

I don't typically do unboxing when I publish how to books; the Vision Pro is not the typical product, however, so I'm doing things a little differently. This section will walk you through how it's packaged.

The first thing that might surprise you is how big the box is. It's over 5 pounds and is bigger than the box for a MacBook.

To give you an idea of how big it is, let me show you the Belkin battery pack accessory (this is an optional extra purchase), and then I'll show it next to the box.

Here's the front side of the Belkin battery pack holder; it can either be clipped to you or you can use the lanyard to carry it around your next.

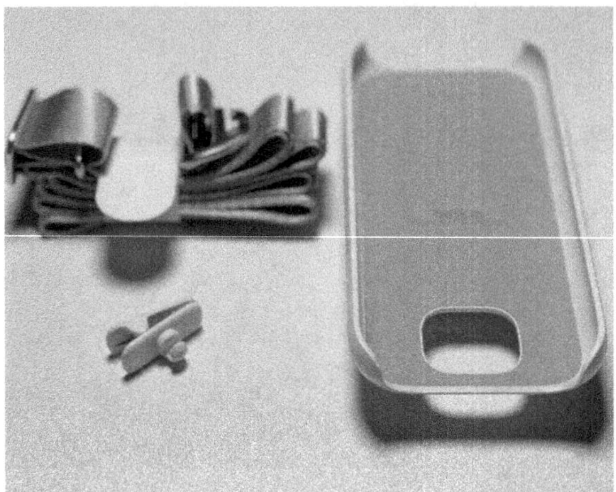

Below is the front side; and to give you an idea for how large the Vision Pro battery is; it's about the same size and weight as an iPhone Pro Max.

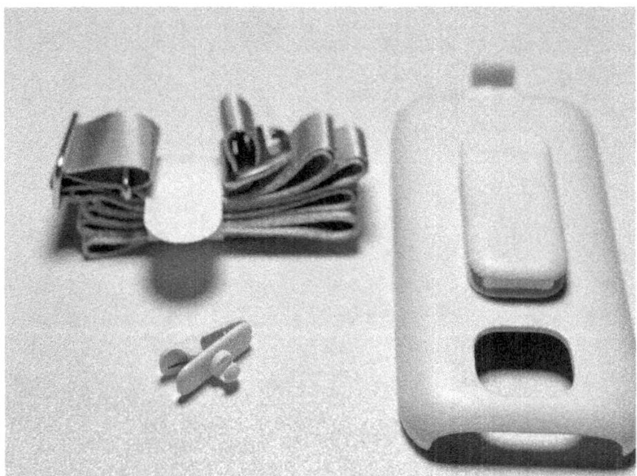

And here it is next to the Vision Pro box.

Once you peal back the easy to peel sticker attached to each side of the box, you lift the box and see the Vision Pro in all it's beauty. Some people have commented that the box can double as a nice stand. I'd agree with that, but personally prefer the travel case, which protects it if it happens to somehow fall. You'll also notice that there's a front cover; you should use that anytime you're not using the device to protect it from dust and scratches.

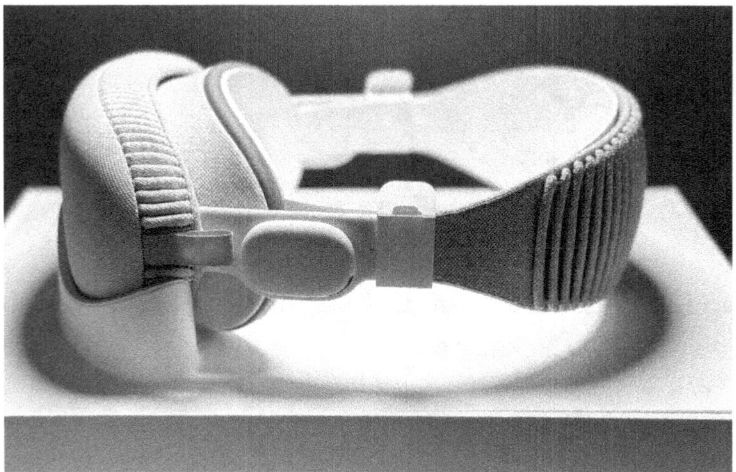

Life up the Vision Pro and you'll find the battery. A lot has been said about the battery pack; I found it to be very well build, not that heavy, and easy to either attach to you or set to the side. I didn't notice it was even there. The battery charges with an included USB-C adapter; you can charge it while you are using the Vision Pro.

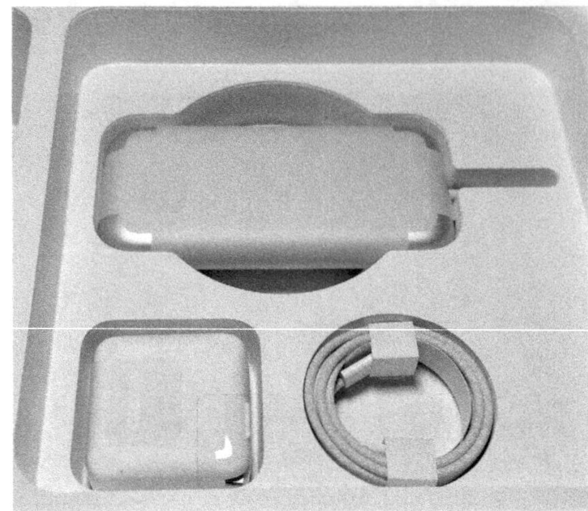

Also at the top of the box is the Light Seal Cushion. There's already a cushion magnetically attached to the Vision Pro; this one is a little bit thicker

. If you are using the Zeiss lens inserts, then you'll probably want to swap it out with this slightly thicker one.

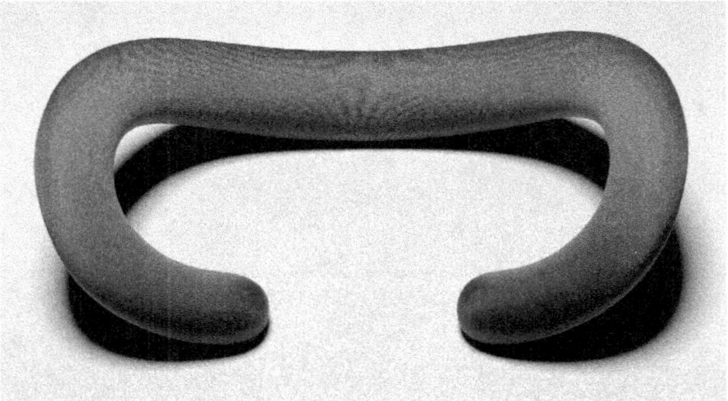

Under the Light Seal is a polishing cloth.

I recommend using this to clean your Vision Pro over something else you might have.

Under the cloth is the Dual Loop band.

The Dual Loop band helps distribute the weight more evenly, and many people prefer it over the softer single band.

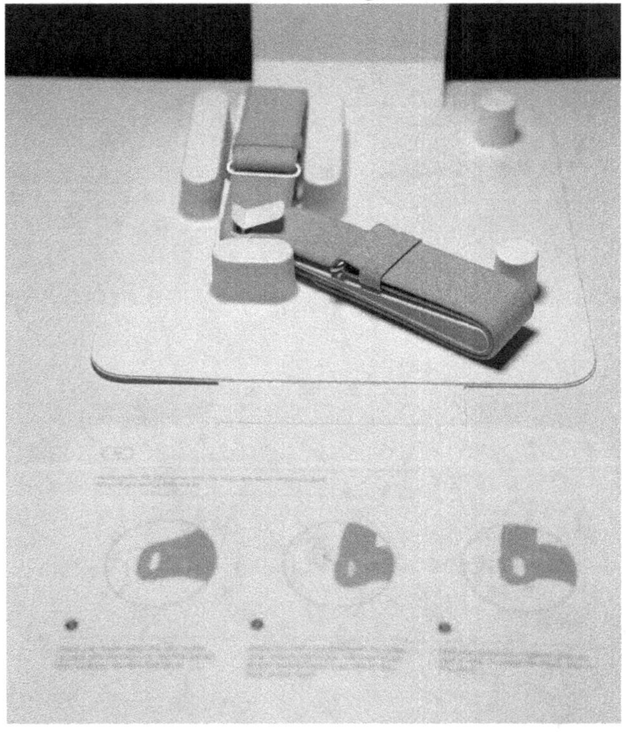

And finally, you have something not seen in and Apple Product in a very long time—something not included in most products anymore: a get started manual!

It's not at all comprehensive but covers the basics—such as removing the straps and battery; it's a very thick paper, full color and excellent quality. A part of you might want to put it on your bookshelf!

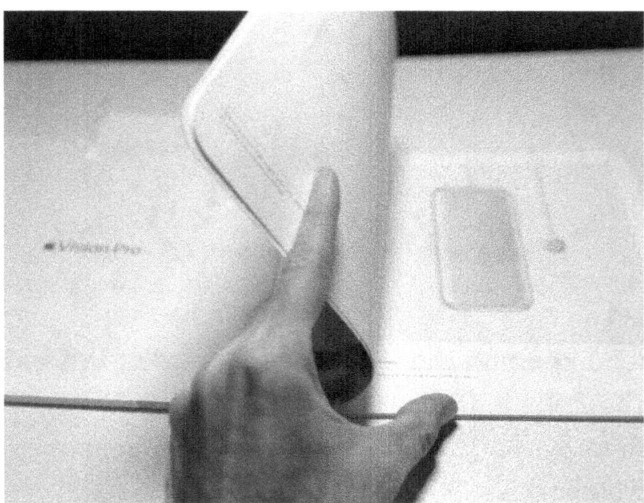

Below are a few things not included in the box, but you might want to pick up. First is the Zeiss lens inserts.

Even though this is from another company, the packaging is very much Apple, and you can tell they worked closely with Zeiss on this partnership.

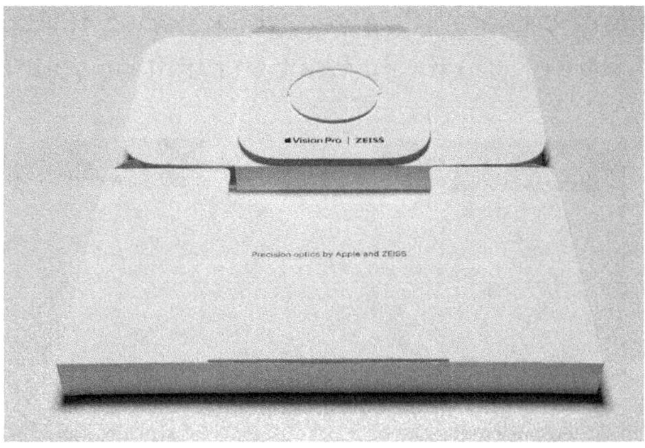

I recommend keeping the box it came in; as of this writing, there is no case for the Zeiss lens inserts; if other people use your Vision Pro, you'll have to take the inserts out and keep them somewhere that they won't get scratched.

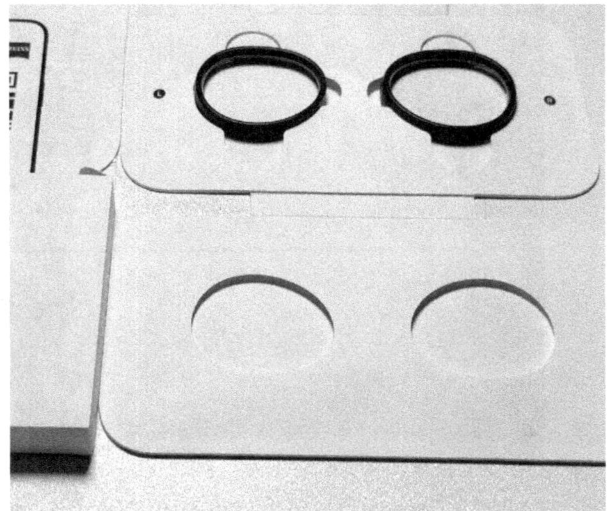

Something else I recommend buying is a spare Light Seal cushion; it's $29 and handy when someone else is using your Vision Pro. It attaches magnetically to the headset and can be swapped out in seconds.

Finally, there's the Apple Vision Pro travel case. It's $199 and one of the few cases out there, as of this option. It's your best option if you're travelling with the Vision Pro, but also a great option for storing your headset when not in use. There are two things I don't like about the case: one, it's a bit big, so if you are travelling with it, you can't really pack it in a backpack; two, the zippers are a bit stiff—it doesn't unzip as easy as I'd like.

## PRE-INSTALLED APPS

If you have used anything Apple (from Macbooks and iPads to iPhones) then the Vision Pro will have a lot of very familiar apps. Below are the apps that come installed with the Vision Pro. Some (like Capture and Encounter Dinosaurs) are exclusive to the Vision Pro; most are the apps you already know, but enhanced for the Vision Pro.

Apps enhanced for the Vision Pro:

- App Store
- Encounter Dinosaurs
- Files
- Freeform
- Keynote
- Mail
- Messages
- Mindfulness
- Music
- Notes
- Photos

- Safari
- Settings
- Tips
- TV

Apps installed but not optimized for the Vision Pro:
- Books
- Calendar
- Home
- Maps
- News
- Podcasts
- Reminders
- Shortcuts
- Stocks
- Voice Memos

What does installed but not optimized mean? Many apps that will be on the Vision Pro–both from developers and from Apple–will merely be iPad apps that are ported over to the Vision Pro. They work fine, but there's nothing special about them.

This book was written when the Vision Pro first came out; expect Apple to add more apps later.

# [2]
# GETTING STARTED

With the Vision Pro out of the box, let's take a look at using the Vision Pro for the first time.

## THE BATTERY

Before you can use the Vision Pro, you have to plug it in—there is zero battery on the Vision Pro; unlike a laptop, if you unplug it, you'll still have a few hours of use, the Vision Pro will instantly shut off if you remove it.

To attach the battery, you line up the circle on the battery connector with the circle on the side of the Vision Pro (the circle that is unfilled); once it's lined up, you twist to line it up with the filled circle. To remove the battery, just follow those steps in reverse.

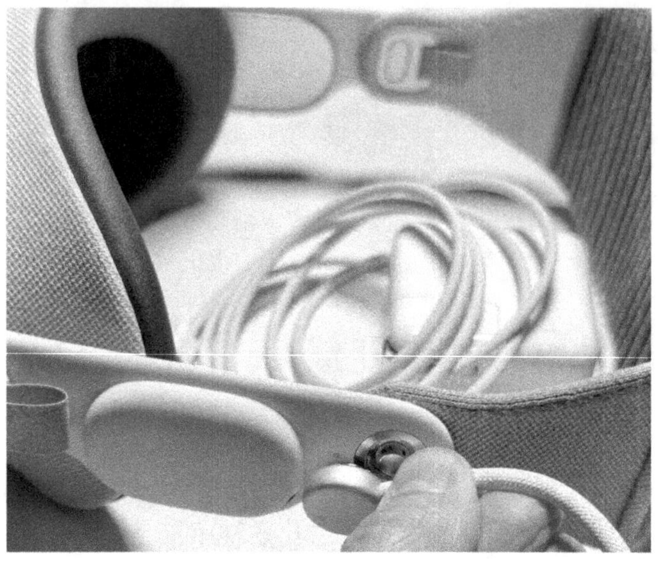

### How to charge the Apple Vision Pro battery

The Vision Pro comes with a USB-C Charge cable and USB-C power adapter; it's recommended that you use the charging unit it came with.

### What the battery's light means

The battery light has different light indicators. Let's look at what they mean. If you have the charging cable plugged in, these are the different indicators:

- **Green**: the battery is full.
- **Amber**: the battery is not full, but it has enough charge for you to use Apple Vision Pro.
- **Amber blinking slowly**: the battery is too low to run your Apple Vision Pro. Charge the battery for 10 minutes, or until the light is amber and not blinking when you tap the battery.

If you have the battery unplugged, here's the light indicators you'll see:

- **Green**: the battery is more than half full.
- **Amber**: the battery is less than half full.
- **Amber blinking slowly**: the battery is too low to run your Apple Vision Pro. Charge the battery for 10 minutes, or until the light is amber and not blinking when you tap the battery.

# WEARING THE VISION PRO AND ADJUSTING THE STRAPS

Here's one of the most important things to know about getting started with the Vision Pro: it's heavy and fitting it wrong is going to make it feel heavier. Part of having a comfortable experience is adjusting the bands properly.

When I first started hearing people review the headset, I kept hearing about the weight and was a little nervous; I wanted this for productivity and to work while I wasn't in my office. How was I going to do that with a brick on my head?!

To my relief, it was a little lighter than expected; even better, adjusting the straps really does help.

The Vision Pro comes with two headbands (and the headbands come in different sizes): the Solo Knit Band and the Dual Loop Band. The Solo Knit Band is already attached to your Vision Pro, but you can switch to the Dual Loop Band anytime you want. Just take off the Solo Knit Band and snap on the Dual Loop Band.

Most people will probably find the weight is distributed more evenly with the Dual Loop Band, which goes over the head, but my advice is try both for a little bit of time.

### WEARING THE VISION PRO WITH THE SOLO KNIT BAND

Grab your device by the frame with one hand and the Solo Knit Band with the other. Don't pick up Vision Pro by the Light Seal, Straps, or power cable; these can come loose and cause you to drop the Vision Pro.

Put the device close to your face and slide the Solo Knit Band over the back of your head. Depending on your hairstyle, you might find it easier to put the head band on first and then pull the device over your eyes.

Once you have the device on, turn the Fit Dial clockwise to make the Solo Knit Band tighter and counterclockwise to make it looser. You want the Vision Pro to be snug. You can also move the back higher or lower to see if it distributes the weight better.

When I bought the Vision Pro, it said to get the medium; I ended up getting the small as well to be safe, and found that the small was more comfortable. So if you don't like how it feels, it could be you have the wrong strap size.

If your headband is too tight, it might irritate your skin, make you feel uncomfortable, or leave marks on your face. The marks will go away pretty quick.

If your headband is too loose or not in the right position, you probably will see a message that says that the device is too high or too low. Just move it up or down until it feels right.

### WEARING VISION PRO WITH THE DUAL LOOP BAND

Pick up the device, and again, remember to hold your Vision Pro by the frame, and not the Light Seal, straps or cable.

Put the device close to your face and slide the Dual Loop Band over the back of your head.

Hold Vision Pro to your face with one hand, making sure it's evenly supported on your forehead and cheeks.

While you're holding Vision Pro to your face, use your other hand to tighten the lower strap first, then the upper strap.

### REMOVING THE STRAP

To remove the strap, hold the headset with one hand, and with the other, pull upward on the orange tab; it slides off easily. To put it back in, just slide it in.

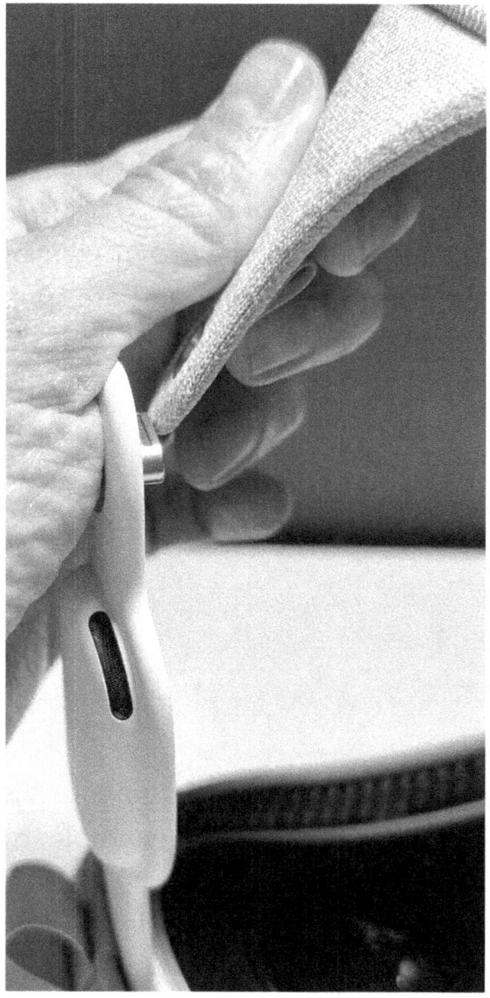

### HOW TO TAKE OFF APPLE VISION PRO

Make the headband looser before you take it off. For the Solo Knit Band, just turn the Fit Dial to the left. For the Dual Loop Band, just pull the tab on the lower strap away from your head.

Take off the device by holding the frame.

When you put down your device, don't let the cover glass touch any hard surfaces, like a table or countertop. They might scratch it. Put the battery next to Vision Pro when you're not using it so the power cable doesn't get tangled with other stuff.

When you're done with Vision Pro, put the cover on to keep it safe.

**HOW TO MAKE VISION PRO FIT PERFECTLY**

As much as possible, you want the Vision Pro to feel balanced on your face. It should be snug, but not tight.

If the head band is too tight, turn the Fit Dial to the left and pull the device by the frame away from your face.

If your eyelashes touch your Vision Pro or your eyes are too far away, then you will see a message that your eyes are too close to the screens; try using the Light Seal Cushion with a "+" on it that came in your box. If that doesn't work, you might need a different size Light Seal.

## CLEANING

Cleaning is an important part of keeping your Vision Pro working as intended. Dirty or smudgy cameras, for example, might affect how hand tracking work.

First: **don't** use isopropyl alcohol, Windex, Clorox, or similar stuff to clean surfaces of the Vision Pro. Clean your Vision Pro with a dry cloth, a little wet cloth, or ideally, the cloth that came with the Vision pro.

Make sure your Apple Vision Pro Polishing Cloth is clean and keep it in a clean bag. Backpacks, handbags, pockets, and other places might have things that could scratch your device.

**CLEANING THE GLASS COVER**

If the cover glass gets dirty, wipe it with a clean, dry microfiber cloth — like the one that came with your Apple Vision Pro.

If you see any loose things on your cover glass, wipe them with a clean, dry microfiber cloth.

## THE SETUP

The Vision Pro setup is very easy; unfortunately, I could not capture it, but I'll do my best to explain the steps below:

### Step 1

Place the headband on your head and turn the dial on the right side of the headband to adjust the fit. The display will tell you to press and hold the digital crown and gaze at the floating glasses to adjust your view.

### Step 2

You need an iPhone or iPad to set up the Vision Pro. The headset will ask you to bring your phone close to your face and unlock it. Your phone will display a QR code that you need to scan with the headset to continue.

### Step 3

Hand gestures are the first main way you'll interact with VisionOS, so the headset needs to recognize your hands. It will ask you to extend your arms in front of you and show your palms to the headset. Then it will ask you to turn your hands over.

### Step 4

Eye tracking is the second way you'll be interacting with your environment, so the headset needs to track how your eyes move. It will ask you to look at a dot, then at six dots in a circle, and tap your finger as you look at each one. Then it will brighten the screen and do the circle again, then brighten it more and do it one last time.

### Step 5

You can skip this step if you want and do it later. I'll show you how in the book. The Vision Pro will ask you to remove it and point the Vision Pro at your face. The display on the front will glow and show you some circles with your face in them. The speakers will ask you to look at the headset, then tilt your head left, right, up, and down. Then it will record your facial expressions by asking you to smile with your mouth closed, smile with your teeth, close your eyes, and raise your eyebrows. These eight actions are enough for the Vision Pro to create what's called a Persona—I'll cover this a bit more later.

This was the most frustrating part of the setup for me. The first time I tried it, it kept telling me to look down and left, then it said the setup failed. The second time I tried with better lighting, and it succeeded. It should be noted, that this feature is in Beta.

### Step 6

The Vision Pro uses Optic ID instead of Face ID. This means it scans your eyes to confirm your identity—that way you don't have to type in your password. After you set up your FaceTime persona, the Vision Pro will ask you to look at a symbol. After a few seconds, Optic ID will be set. That's it. As a backup, the Vision Pro will also ask you to set up a six-digit passcode (you can also switch it to four-digit). You'll need to use the passcode whenever the Vision Pro restarts.

If you lose your passcode you will have to bring the headset to an Apple Store to recover it, so make sure you pick something you remember.

### Step 7

You're almost there. The the Vision Pro will show you a quick tutorial on how to use the basic gestures and functions, like selecting items, resizing windows, and opening quick menus.

That's it. You're all set. The whole process is very easy, but it takes about 10 minutes. I didn't show you here how to set up the Zeiss inserts. You can do that during the setup or later. I'll show you how in the book.

## USING VISION PRO WITH ZEISS INSERTS

If you didn't add your Zeiss inserts during the setup, you can quickly do it at any time after you start using the device by following these steps.

With the on the Vision Pro, attach the optical inserts; they'll snap right in—just make sure you are snapping them into the correct side.

Remove the cover, then put on the Vision Pro. It will automatically detect the inserts and walk you through the setup process; part of the process will be scanning a code that came with your inserts, so make sure you don't through away the box!

You can also pair new inserts at any time, by going to Settings > Eyes & Hands, and then tapping on Setup Up New Optical Inserts.

# [3]

# Navigating Around the Vision Pro

Now that you've learned what the Vision Pro is (and isn't) and seen what the setup is like, let's learn how to move around the device.

## GESTURES

Before getting into the OS itself, let's talk about gestures.

Gestures are probably the first thing that will completely blow you away when you use the Vision Pro; yes, it's a stunning display and the apps can be addictively fun. But it's really how sophisticated the gestures are that reveal how much tech is inside this thing. It's intuitive and when you get used to it, it's faster than using a mouse.

Before I go into the different gestures, here are a few things to keep in mind:

- It may seem like some kind of magic, but it's actually all the cameras that make gestures work; that means you need to keep the cameras clean and have enough light for the cameras to see you. If it's having difficulty registering what your hands are doing, it could be you need more light or the camera is dirty.
- You don't have to lift your arm up when you use Apple Vision Pro. You can keep your hand relaxed on your desk or in your lap when making most gestures. The first time, your hands will probably instinctively raise up, but just remember that they don't have to.
- Make sure Apple Vision Pro can see your hands, and not hide them under a desk or a blanket.

- If you wear gloves, it's probably not going to read your gestures–if it does, it's not going to be as accurate.
- Don't cross your hands. It won't know you're right from your left.

So let's look at the gestures:

### Touch

You can touch some things in visionOS directly with your fingers. For example, when the visionOS virtual keyboard shows up, you can type by touching the keys directly with one finger on each hand.

### Tap your fingers together

To pick something in Apple Vision Pro, look at it and tap your thumb and index finger together.

Tapping your thumb and index finger together is like tapping something on your iPhone or clicking something on your computer — use this gesture to pick an app.

### Pinch to see more options

Pinch and hold something in Apple Vision Pro to see more options. Look at something, tap your thumb and index finger together, and hold. When you see more options, let go and then tap to pick the option you want.

### Pinch and drag

To move things around in Apple Vision Pro, look at something and then pinch your thumb and index finger together. Keep your thumb and finger together as you move it where you want it, then let go. This can be things like Windows or menus.

### Pinch and flick your wrist

To move or scroll fast through stuff, pinch your thumb and index finger together, flick your wrist up or down, then let go in one smooth move.

# BUTTONS

The Vision Pro has two buttons:

1. **The Digital Crown** that controls the amount of the environment that is showing and brings up the Home button
2. **The Top button**, which is what you use to take photos—it's the one on the left side of the headset.

The buttons can also be used for another of shortcuts, as you can see below.

## SCREENSHOTS

I'll show you how to do screen recording in the section on Control Center; if you want to capture a still screenshot of your screen press the Digital Crown and Top button at the same time. You'll hear a camera sound and the screen capture will be stored in your library.

## FORCE CRASH APP

If an app isn't responding Press and Hold the Top button and Digital Crown at the same time until a window comes up asking you what you want to force close.

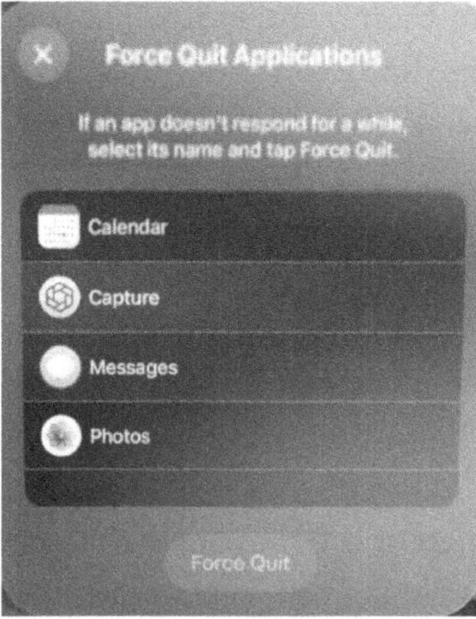

## POWER VISION PRO OFF

There is no power button on the Vision Pro, but you can still power it down. Do the same steps as above (press and hold the Digital Crown and Top button), but continue to hold longer. A message will come up to power the Vision Pro off.

## RECALIBRATE TRACKING

If you want to recalibrate your vision tracking, press the Top button 5 times.

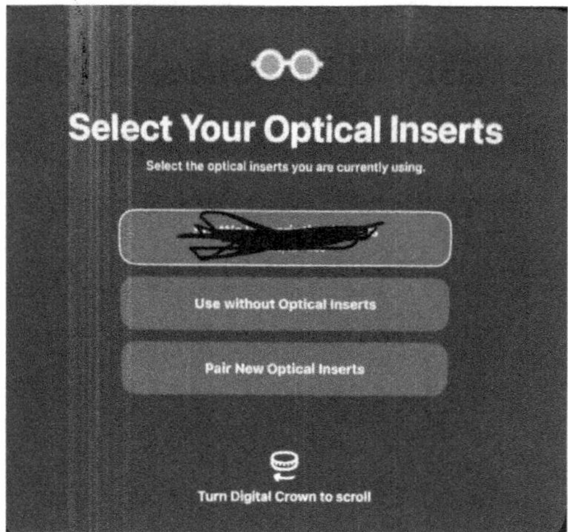



## GUIDED ACCESS

Guided Access is an accessibility featured that you can turn on by triple pressing the Digital Crown. With Guided Access, you can lock your Vision Pro to one app only, and choose what you can do in that app. This way, you won't get distracted by other stuff.

## RECENTER WORKSPACE

Press and hold the workspace and your windows will be recentered to your new position. For example, if you turn around in your chair, you can move all your windows to the new spot.

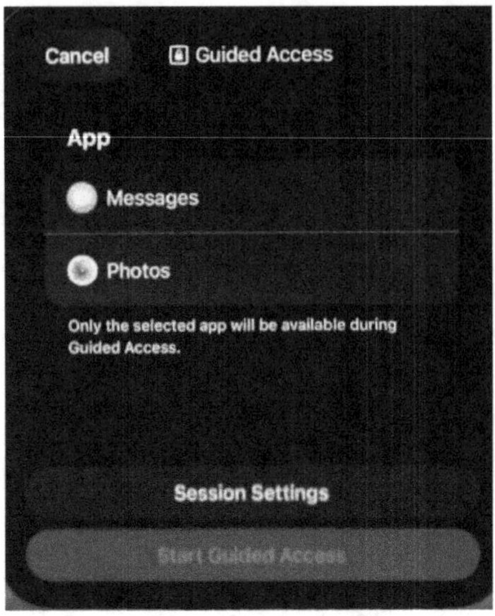

# TYPING

There are a few ways to type on the Vision Pro:

1. With the virtual keyboard - this works one of two ways: one, you look at a letter and pinch to select it; or two, you one handed type by pressing the letter. This works pretty well, but it's definitely the slower of the two methods.
2. Speak to text – This is going to be the fastest way for most people. When the keyboard comes up, just select the microphone and say what you want the text to say.
3. Use a Bluetooth keyboard – this is by far the best and fastest method, but that means you also have to bring a keyboard along if you are traveling.

# MOVING, RESIZING, AND CLOSING WINDOWS

There's one final thing to cover before we jump into an overview of the OS: Resize, Move, and Close apps.

## RESIZE WINDOWS

If you look in the corner of any window, you'll see a curved line on the edge of the window. You can pinch your fingers and move them in or out ot resize the window.

## MOVE AND CLOSE APPS

To move an app use the line on the bottom edge of any window. To close the app, tap on the circle next to that line (which will turn to an X when you hover over it.

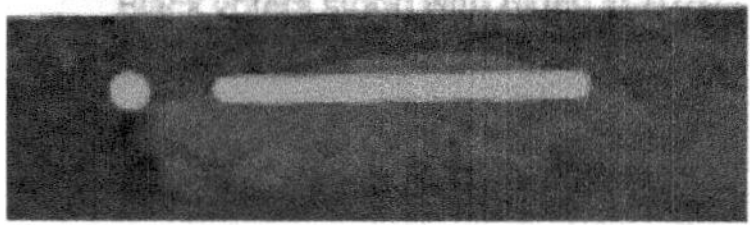

If you are in an immersive environment, look for back buttons—typically in the upper left corner. If all else fails, use the Force Close shortcut (Press and Hold the Top button and Digital Crown at the same time)

# MAIN HOME SCREEN AND NAVIGATION

Let's start learning about the OS behind the headset. I'll do my best to take screenshots that are clean and even, but because of the nature of the device, things aren't always as clear as screenshots on iOS and iPadOS. That's because the way Vision Pro works is it focus on what you're looking at—you don't notice it because of how our eyes work, but you'll see it when you take screenshots. So don't let the images fool you—it's much sharper when it's on your eyes.

The first time you finish setup, you'll see three rows of apps. This is your Home screen. It's very iPad / iPhone like isn't it? You'll find many similarities between visionOS and iOS, iPadOS, and even macOS and watchOS.

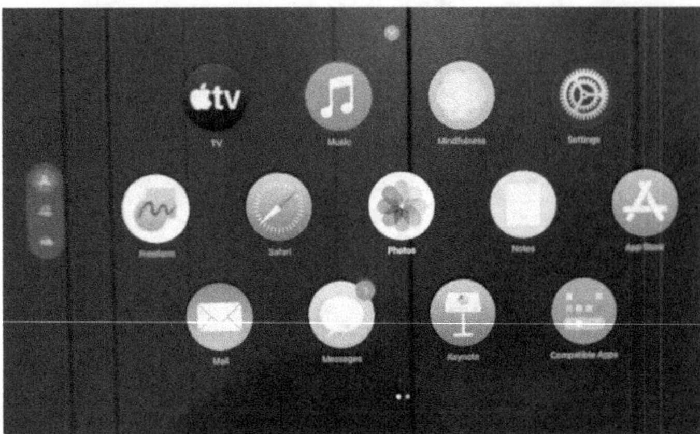

A few things you should know about the Home screen:
- The first group of apps are the ones created by Apple.
- Apps are arranged alphabetically (Except for the Apple built ones, which are always the first to show up).
- Apps cannot be arranged or grouped (except for the folder for "compatible apps" which are apps that came over from iOS or iPadOS.

These constraints are not a deal-breaker, but they are annoying, and it won't take you long for you to complain to yourself about wanting it to work differently. Most likely a future update will address this.

Here's the other thing you should know about the Home menu: pressing the digital crown will recenter the Home screen. So if you turn and want the home screen in the new place, just press the digital crown.

Over on the left side is the Home menu. There's three things there: Apps, People, and Environments.

Apps is the menu that was show above. People is your favorite contacts. You can use the + to add or find someone—this is also how you would make a FaceTime call. Just open the contact and tap FaceTime.

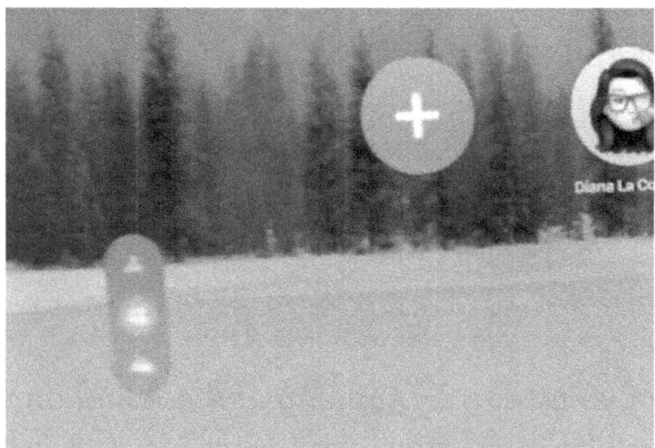

Environments is one of the coolest features of the headset, in my opinion. It lets you change your surroundings into an immersive environment. So you can feel like you are working at the beach or in the mountains. It really does feel life like.

### AVAILABLE ENVIRONMENTS

Below is a list of all available environments with more coming soon:

- Haleakalā
- Yosemite
- Joshua Tree
- Mount Hood
- The Moon
- Beach
- White Sands

- Winter Light

- Fall Light

- Summer Light

- Spring Light

### REMOVING APPS

You can remove an app by tapping and holding on the app you want to remove. It will delete it from the Vision Pro, but it can still be downloaded again from the app store at no cost.

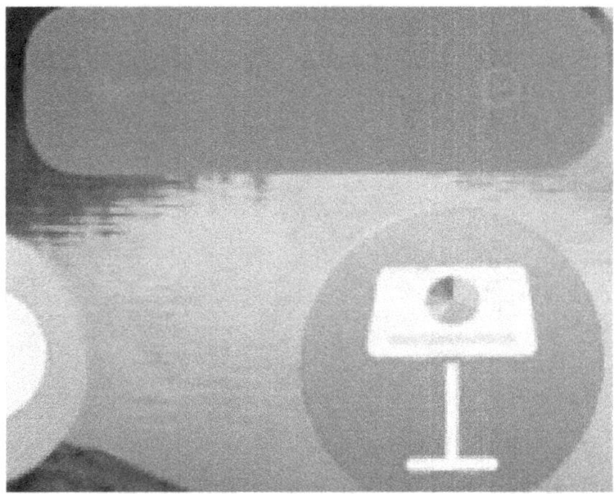

### USING THE DIGITAL CROWN

When you select an environment, you can use the Digital Crown to adjust how immersive it is. The more you turn the more immersive it is. Turning it all the way back will turn it off. Turning it all the way on will make the environment fill everything—look up, down, left and right and you'll see it. Even cooler, if you turn it all the way on, you even hear what it sounds like.

Depending on the time of day, your environment will also be light or dark; you can adjust that in Control Center, which I'll cover next.

What's really crazy about being in these immersive environments is when someone talks to you, it will automatically begin to fade out so you can see them! (that's a setting you can turn off) You can remove them by turning the dial again.

## CONTROL CENTER

Control Center can be accessed at anytime by looking up. You'll see a very small box—so small you might even miss it! Just tap on it to get started.

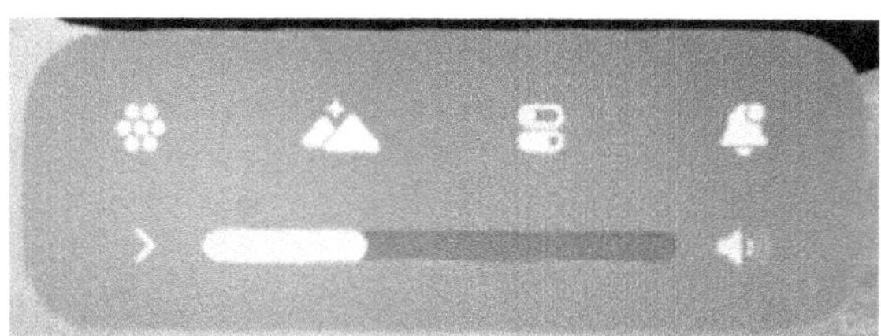

This will bring up a box with four icons and a volume slider. The first icon takes you back to the Home screen. The second icon is for environments. This will bring up the menu to change your environments—if you want Dark or Automatic mode, for example.

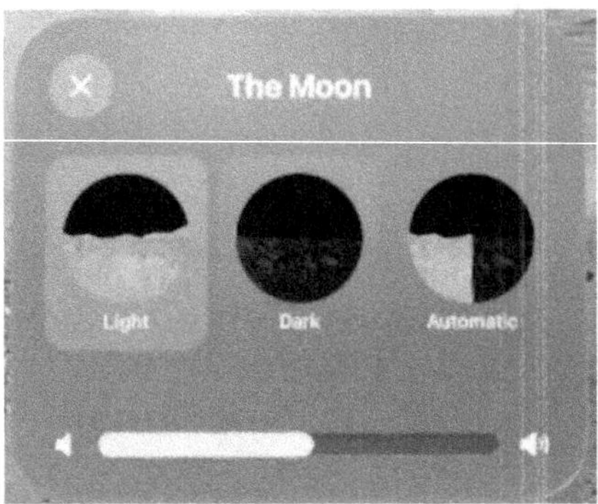


The last option (we'll come back to the third momentarily) is the Notification Center; mine is empty, but if I had any, then they'd show up here.

And finally, the third icon brings up Control Center. Control Center, just like on the iPhone or iPad, is where all your control shortcuts live.

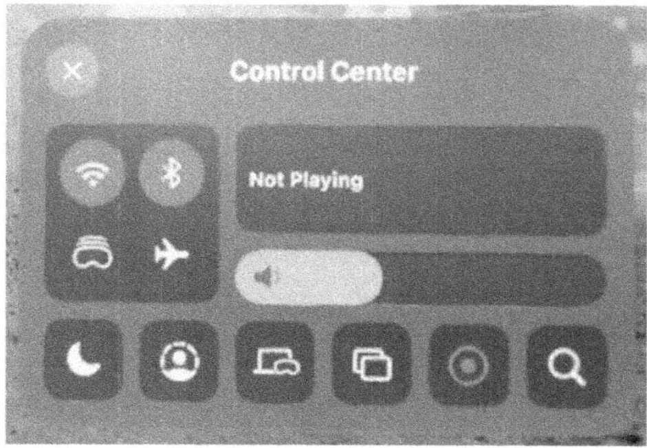

The first four icons will toggle things on and off. You probably know that first is to turn off Wi-Fi and the one next to it turns off Bluetooth; and your probably familiar with the plane, which represents Airplane mode. But what's going on with that icon that looks like the Vision Pro? That's travel mode. It's made for when you are *flying*. It emphasize flying because this is not for when your driving or anything else—Apple specifies that it's only for when you're flying; they also say to stop using it during turbulence. When in travel mode, the Vision Pro works to stabilize your experience.

Now playing shows you what (if anything) is currently playing on your Vision Pro; the volume slider under it will control how loud or soft it is.

Next, let's look at those bottom six icons. The first one puts it into different focus mode. This will pause notifications for a set amount of time.

The second icon is Guest Mode. You'll probably have a lot of requests for this one. This is for when a person says, "Hey! Is that a Vision Pro?! Can I try it?!"

When you press Guest Mode, you'll be asked what the person can see. Guest Mode isn't like handing over an iPad with all your features enabled. Guest Mode lets you decide what a user can and can't see.

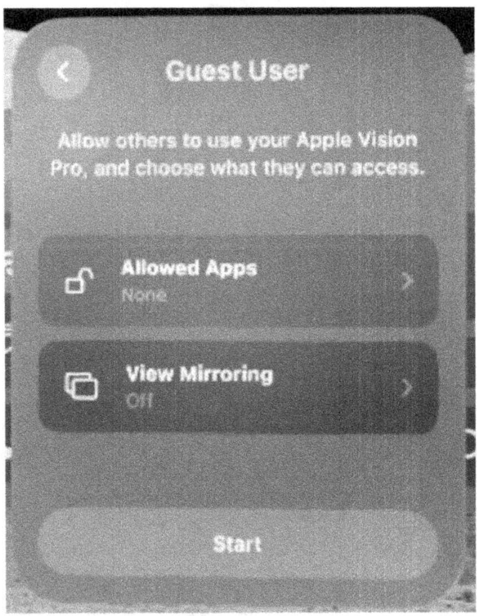


From Allowed Apps, you can decide if the user will see everything or only the apps that you've opened up for them.

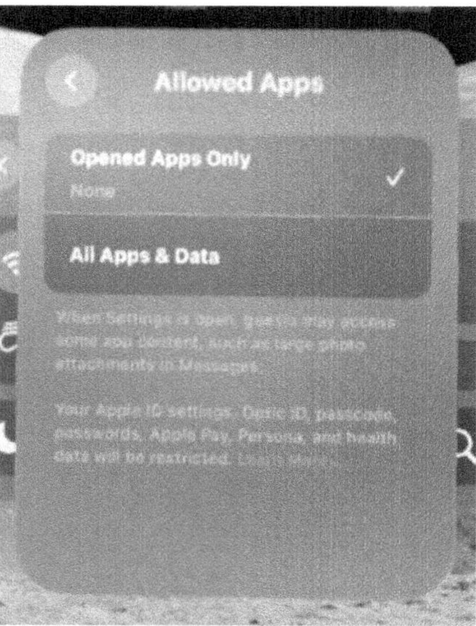

Once you press the start button, the person will have five minutes to start there session; they'll have to go through a setup process that will take a couple minutes (and no, unfortunately, this cannot be saved.

There's one other cool feature to consider before handing it over: View Mirroring. When you select this, you can mirror the Vision Pro to either a compatible iPad or Mac, so you can watch what they're doing and help them if they get stuck.

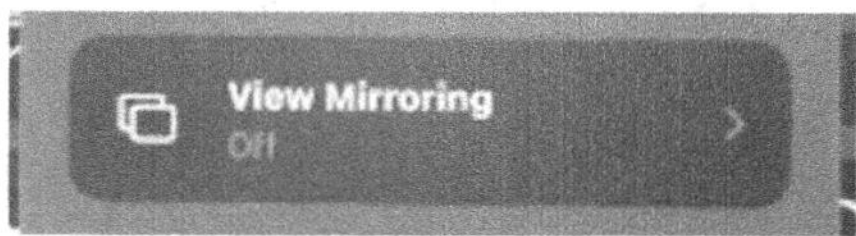

The next icon I'll go a little deeper into later in the book, but this is to bring a Mac to your Vision Pro.

Just make sure it's close and on the same network.

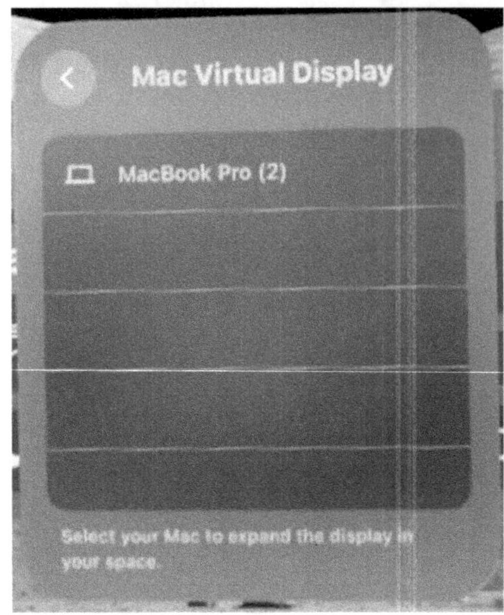


The next icon lets you mirror your Vision Pro to a compatible AirPlay device so others can see what you see.

I mentioned earlier in this chapter how to screenshot a screen. This option takes that up a notch by letting you do a screen recording.

Finally, the last option is the Search, which helps you quickly find apps and documents on your Vision Pro.

So now you know the basics of the Vision Pro. It's really intuitive, so you'll be surprised at how fast much you know without even knowing it. Next, we'll take a look at all the main apps on the Vision Pro.

# [4]

# THE APPS

On day one, the Vision Pro had about 600 apps build just for visionOS; that sounds like a lot, but considering iPad has over a million, that number suddenly seems smaller. But here's the good news: one, and most importantly, most iPad apps are compatible with visionOS, and, as long as the developer didn't disable it, it will be in the store (the reason you don't see apps like Netflix, Spotify, and YouTube isn't because they aren't compatible—it's because they were disabled by the companies).

The other good news is developers seem to be really excited about developing for the Vision Pro and pushing the limits of what it can do.

Finally, the apps that are already on the Vision Pro are good. This book will cover the Apple installed apps, but there are plenty more on the app store to pick from.

## APPLE TV

Apple TV is the first icon you'll see on your Home menu; it's probably going to be one of your favorites because this is where most the 3D movies live. It also has the best movie watching experience. Disney+ let's you change the environment, but Apple TV lets you change the seat position.

The Apple TV menu on the left side is broken up into seven options:

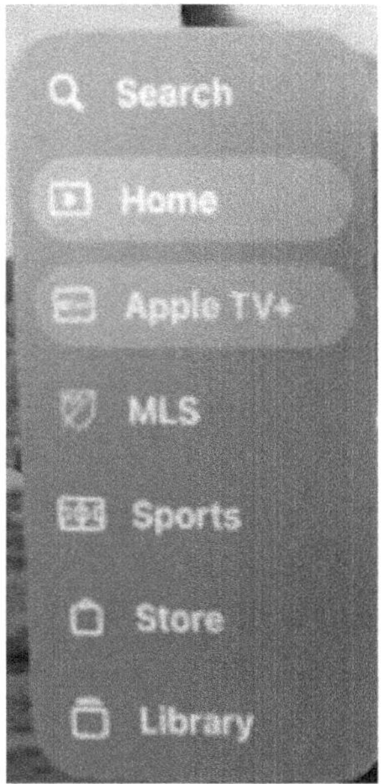

- **Search** – The first option lets you search for all your media content—you can also search for genres or even formats (like 3D)

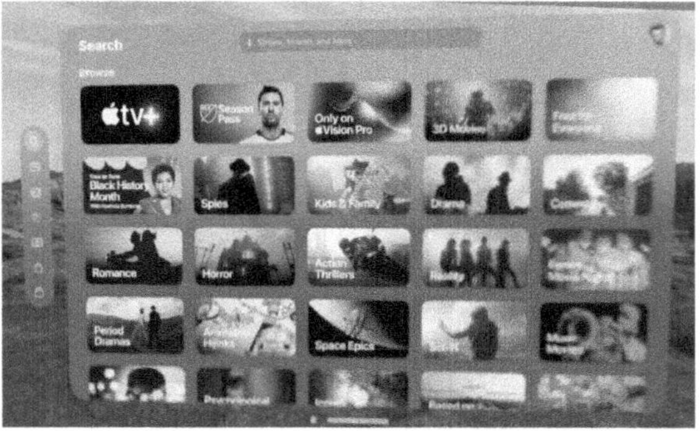

- **Home** – The main Home area of the app is Apple's attempt to make media watching easier; below promos for content, you'll see Up Next which is recommendations for what they think you'll watch next based on what you've watched in the past; so if there's a new TV show that you are known to watch, it will show up here. And not just a TV show on Apple TV—it could be on Peacock, Max or virtually anywhere else.

- **Apple TV+** - This is where Apple has been spending a lot of it's money. It's underappreciated, in my opinion; it may not have as much as Netflix or Disney+, but the content that is here is good—some of the best stuff on TV. If you've never tried shows like *For All Mankind*, then it's the perfect time—and it's a show that's made for this type of viewing..

- **MLS** – Apple has a contract with MLS and the content will show here.

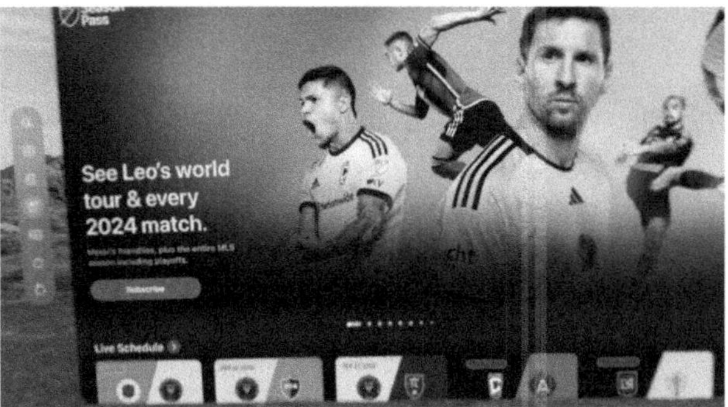

- **Sports** – Apple has been working on several sports licenses that will show up here.

- **Store** – Apple has previously had sold movies and TV shows through the iTunes app; that went away a few months before Vision Pro launched. Now anything you want to buy is in the Apple TV app.

- **Library** – Whenever you buy something (or anything you've bought in the past) will show up here. One of the best things: content you've bought in the past that is available in 3D is free to you; so if you bought Avatar a few years ago in the regular format, it's now upgraded to 3D.

## VIEWING MOVIES

In this section, I'll show you what the Apple TV viewing interface looks like; unfortunately, no movie is showing do to copyright.

On the top portion of the screen is the back icon (to exit a movie) the environment icon, and the volume icon. On the bottom is the forward 10, pause, back 10 seconds, and extra options.

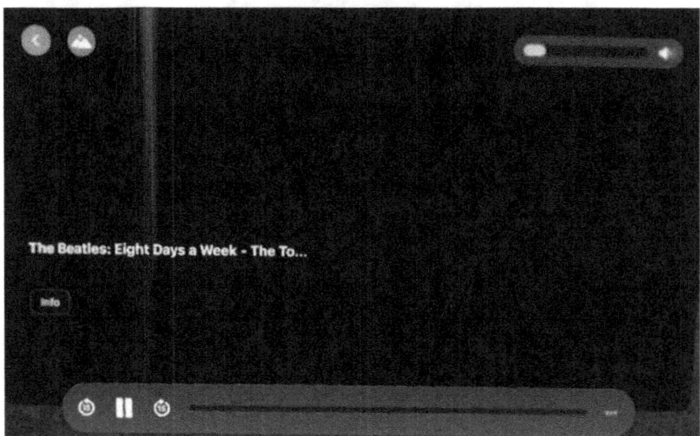

The extra options are for Playback Speed, Languages, Subtitles, and Auto Dimming (if you're watching a movie while working, then you can uncheck this).

When you click on Environments, you can select if you want to stay in your environment or move things into a cinema. The Cinema environment is where things get really cool.

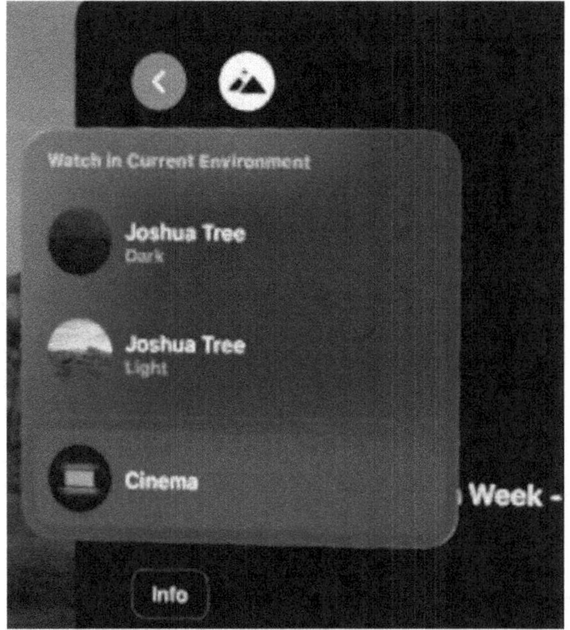


When you select Cinema, you can select the row you want to sit in (front, middle, back) and how high up you are (floor or balcony).

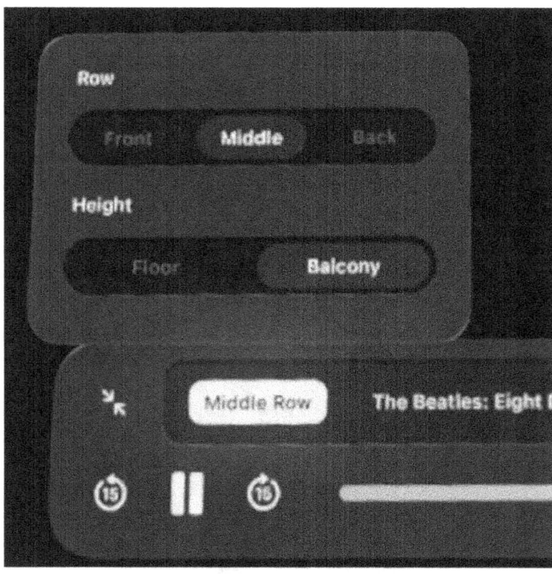


## MUSIC

There may not be a Spotify app on the Vision Pro (yet), but Apple has included their own rival app and if you are already invested in the Apple ecosystem, you definitely should check it out; personally, my house has the Apple One service that includes Apple Music, TV, Arcade, News, and Fitness; it's a great service if you enjoy Apple.

Apple Music currently starts at $10.99 ($5.99 for students); Apple One currently starts at $19.95; each service goes up in price depending on what you get—family or non-family for example, or if you want something like Fitness+ (which, unfortunately, is not included as a Vision Pro app at this time).

Let's take a look at what Apple Music looks like on the Vision Pro.

Vision Pro apps have adopted a pretty standard design pattern where menus go on the left side. So anytime you want to view menus, start by looking on the left.

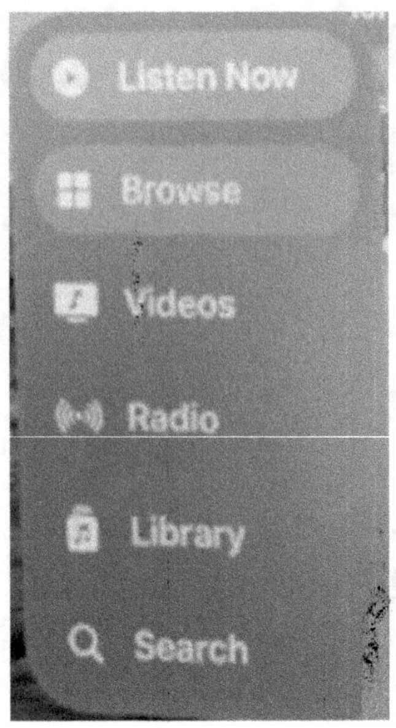

Listen Now
Browse
Videos
Radio
Library
Search

The menu bar on the Vision Pro looks a lot like the options available on iPad and iPhone—this is something you'll hear a lot in this book because Apple has intentionally tried to make the experience as similar as possible, which makes it remarkably easy to pick up if you're already familiar with iOS or iPadOS.

The options on the Menu are:

- **Listen Now** – this is the main area and is like the homepage for recommendations and recently played.

- **Browse** – Let's you see music by different categories / genres and recommendations; if you want to hear music in Spatial audio (a format that takes advantage of the Vision Pro's speakers), you'll find it in here.

- **Videos** – This space is devoted to music videos.

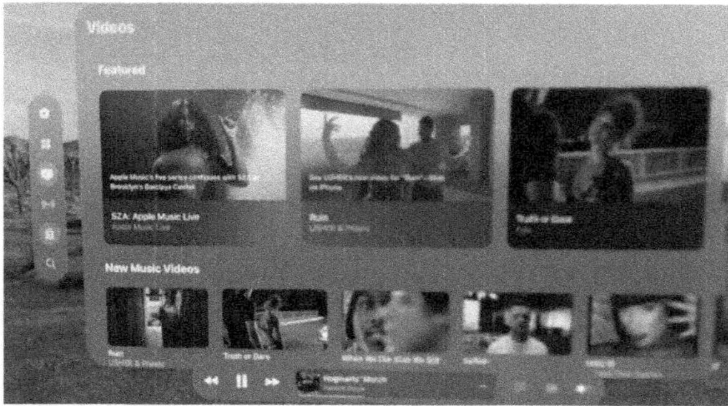

- **Radio** – If you don't know what you are looking for, the Radio area has different commercial free stations in several different genres that is curated by Apple.

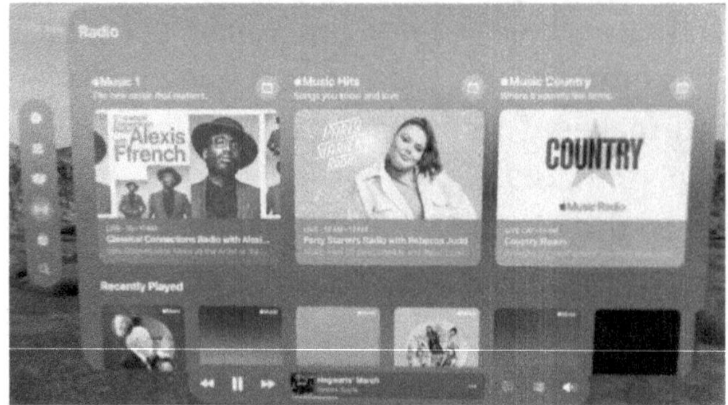

- **Library** – If you own any music, you'll see it here. This is also where you'll find your playlists.

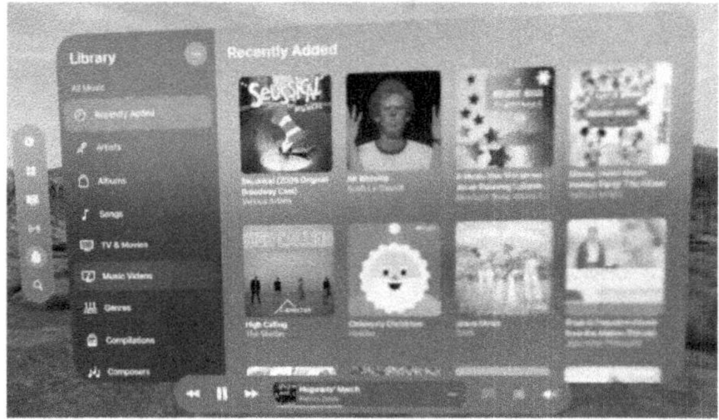

- **Search** – Search lets you search for different artist and gen-res.

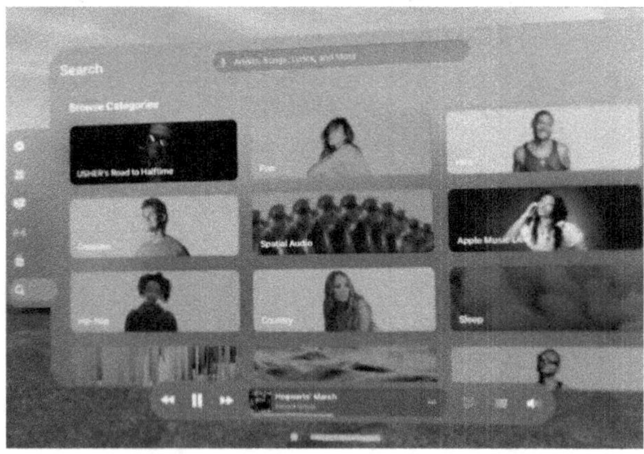

**PLAYING MUSIC**

When you play music, it will show up in the bottom bar; there's a few options as it plays.

Tapping the three dots, for example, will let you add it to your library, create a station, and more.

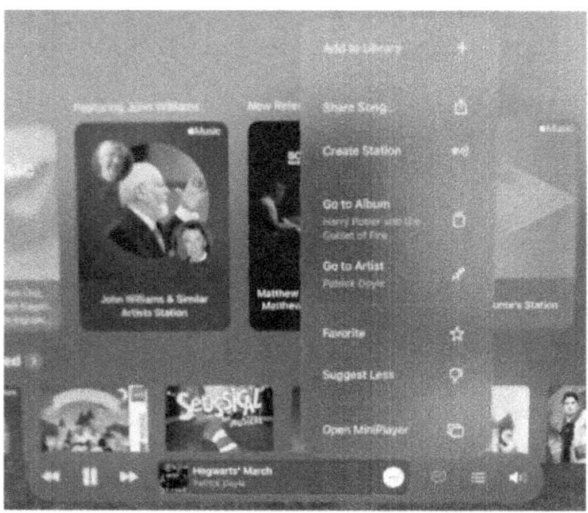

Tapping on the song will let you see the album or artist.

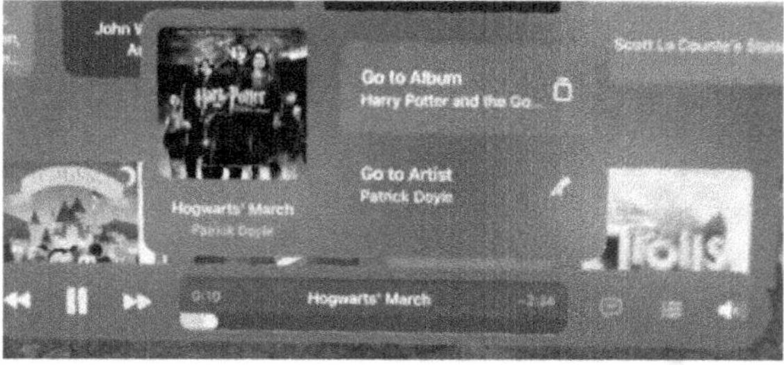

# MINDFULNESS

One of the things that Apple promoted when it showed off the Vision Pro was mediation. In many ways, it's the perfect experience for Vision Pro, because the headset can be so…isolating.

If you feel like you just need to unwind, the Mindfulness is Apple's solution. It's beautiful in its simplicity.

When you open the app, it asks you how long you want to do it, then it says starts. That's it. Like I said: it's very simplistic.

If you tap the number of minutes, it will give you the option to change both the time and the instructor. There's also a self-guided option if you want to do it on your own.

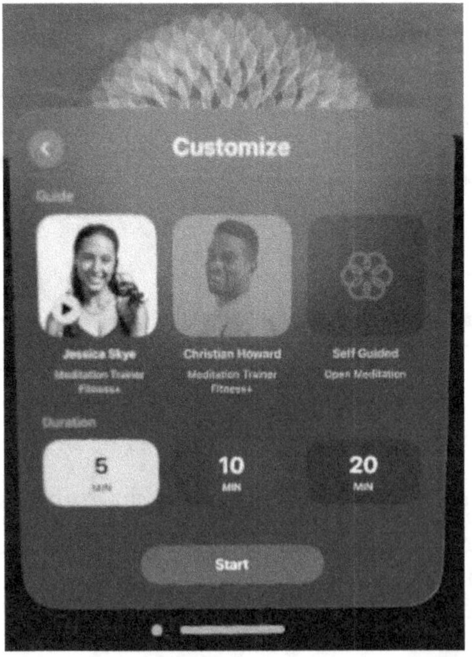

As the meditation goes, you'll see a ball going in and out to help you visualize your breathing.

After the mediation is finished, you can add information to track your session.

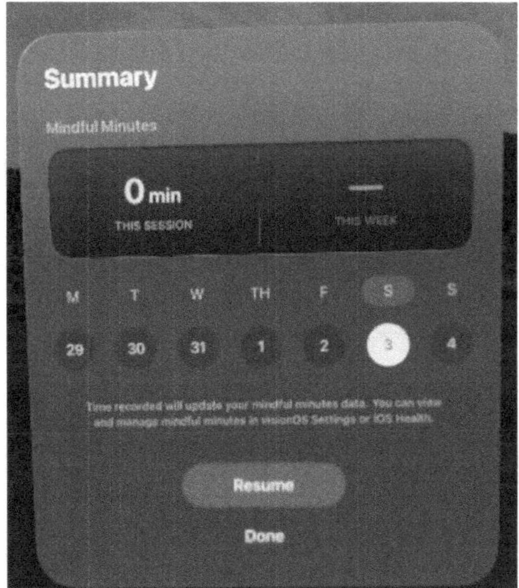

## FREEFORM

Freeform was launched on Mac and iPadOS a few years ago, but Vision Pro might just be where it was ultimately destined to be. Freeform is a digital whiteboard that is ideal for collaboration.

The controls are very simple. On the bottom of the screen are all your options. There are several sets of markets, and each one can have a different color.

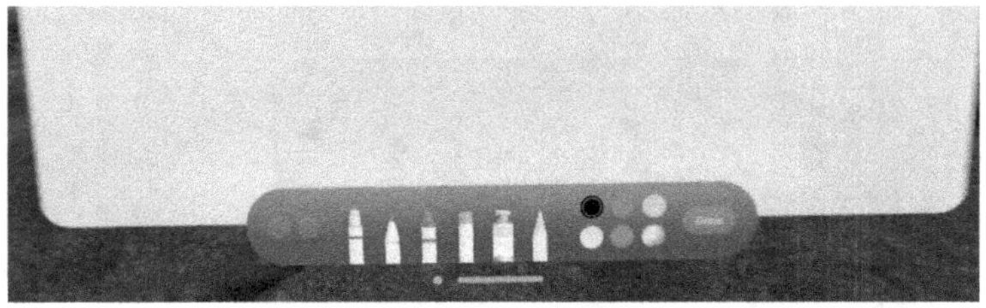

You can pinch and drag your finger across the screen to write (or scribble in my example) with the selected pen.

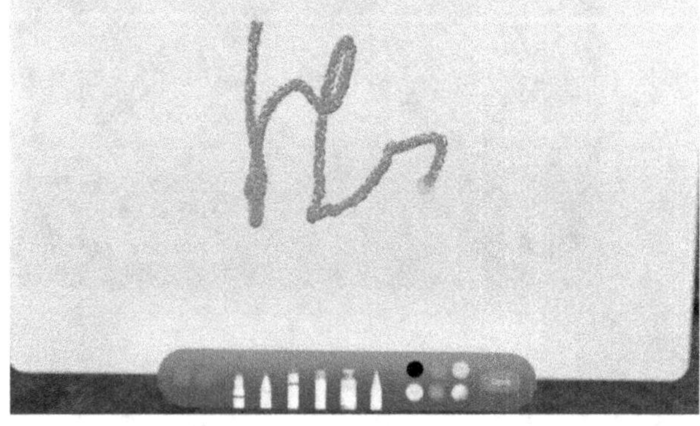

There's also objects that you can add in; you can drag the corners in and out to resize them. You can also add text.

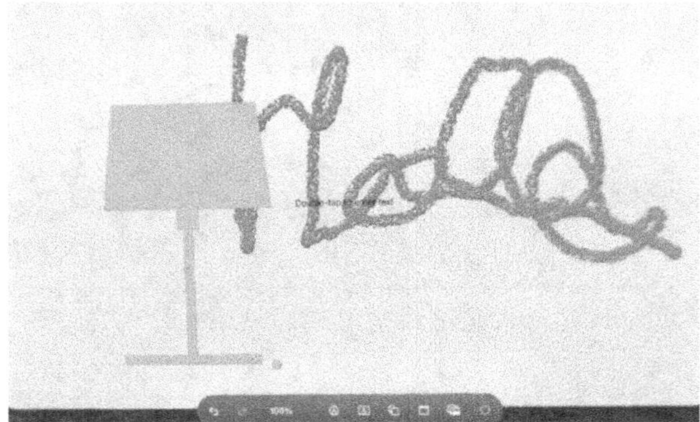

And there's sticky notes you can put everywhere.

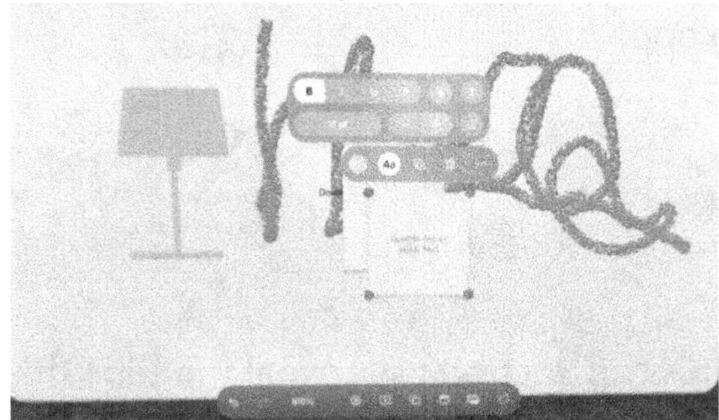

You can, of course, add images too.

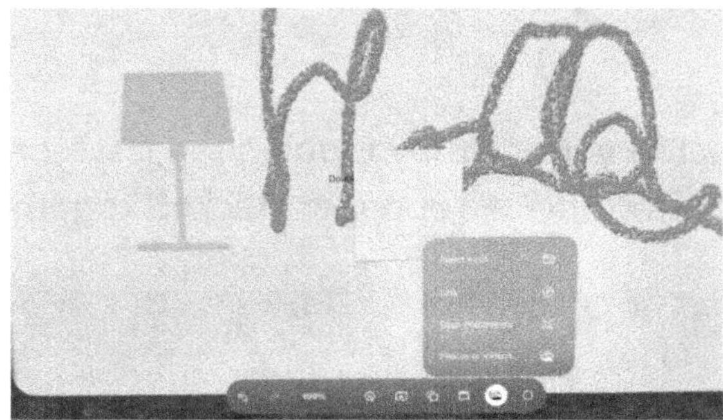

Once you're done, you can tap the name up top to rename it or export it.

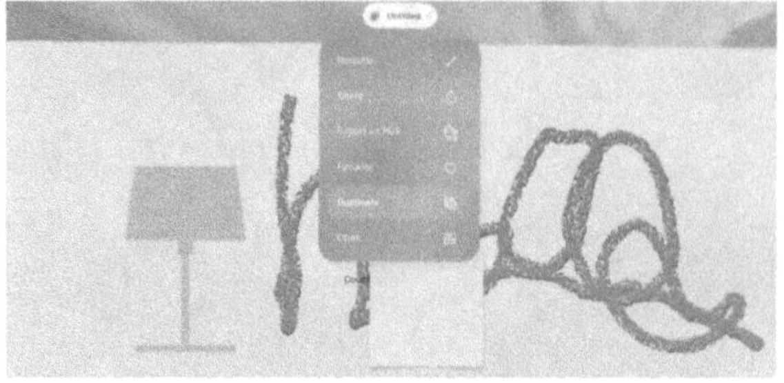

## SAFARI

Safari is the main way you'll browse the Internet. As of this writing, it's your best bet if you want a native Vision Pro app. Firefox is available as a compatible app.

Hovering int his top section will reveal the tabs that you have open. Pressing the + icon will open a new tab.

You can reveal all your tabs by tapping the last icon to the right side—it looks like two pieces of paper stacked together.

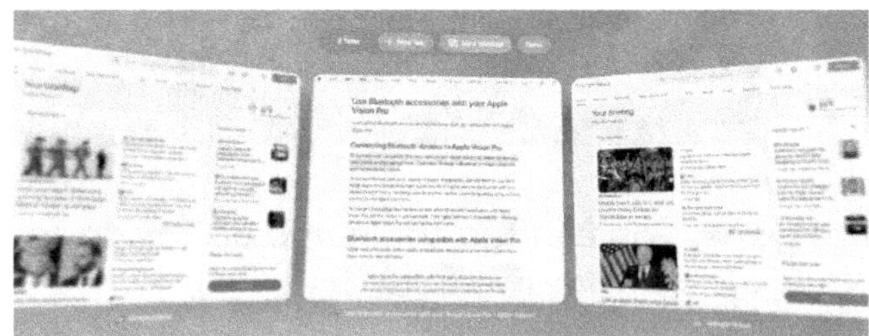

Pressing the AA icon will show you all the page options for what you are looking at.

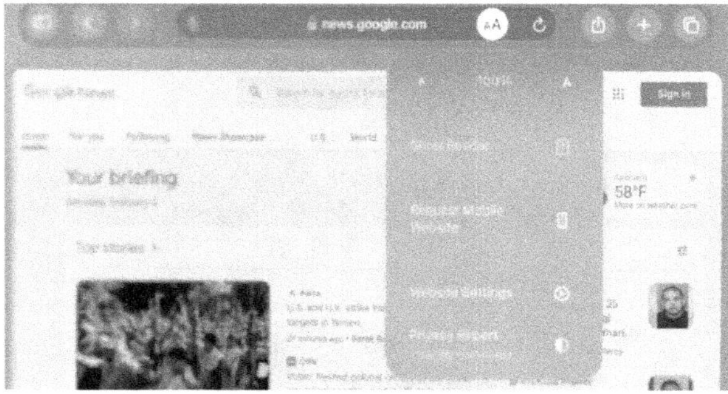

### PRIVATE VIEWING

To view a page privately (meaning your history isn't tracked, tap the icon to the far left to reveal the side bar, then select the Private option. When you open a new tab, it will be in private mode. To get back to regular mode just tap the one above with the Vision Pro icon.

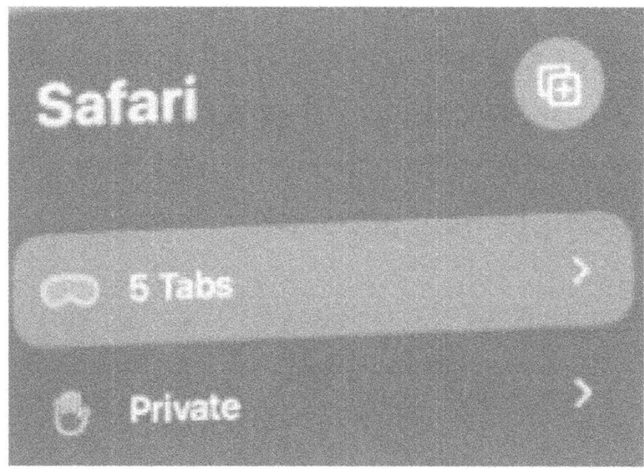


## NOTES

Notes has also been optimized for Vision Pro, but it looks almost exactly the same.

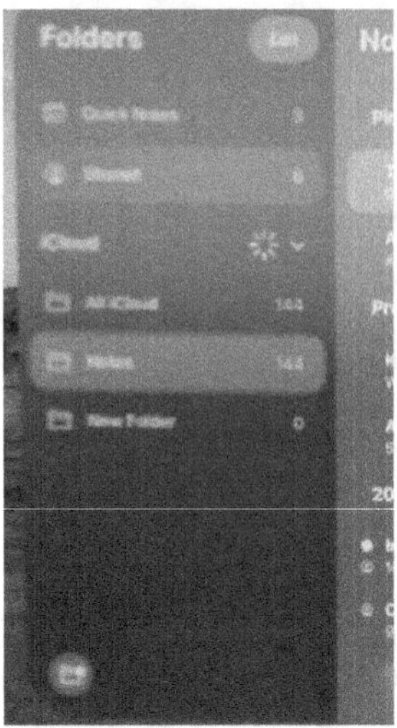

## MAIL

Checking email on the Vision Pro can be done on the Web, but if you want to do it natively, your stuck with either getting a compatible app designed for iPad, or using Apple's Mail app. It looks very familiar to Mail on any other Apple product. When you open it up, you can add your email; you do have the option after you add one account, to add more. So you can have multiple mail accounts.

## MESSAGES

Messages looks almost identical to iPad, but it is optimized for Vision Pro.

# KEYNOTE

Keynote is the only iWork app included on the Vision Pro (though iPad apps of the others are supported.

When you see, I think you'll understand why. Pages and Numbers work just fine as iPad apps; I'm sure at some point they'll be optimized for Vision Pro, and they'll be a little more useful when they are. But Keynote was truly build for the Vision Pro, and, in my opinion, gives one of the best glimpses into the future of this type computing. It shows what might ultimately become one of the greatest use cases of Vision Pro: education.

The app itself is similar to Keynote on Mac or iPad; so if you've used it there, you'll be fine using it here. This isn't a comprehensive guide on how to use the apps, so I won't go into all the features here, but there's one in particular that I want to highlight: doing presentations.

When you select practice a presentation, you are giving the option of rehearsing in either a conference room or the Steve Jobs auditorium!

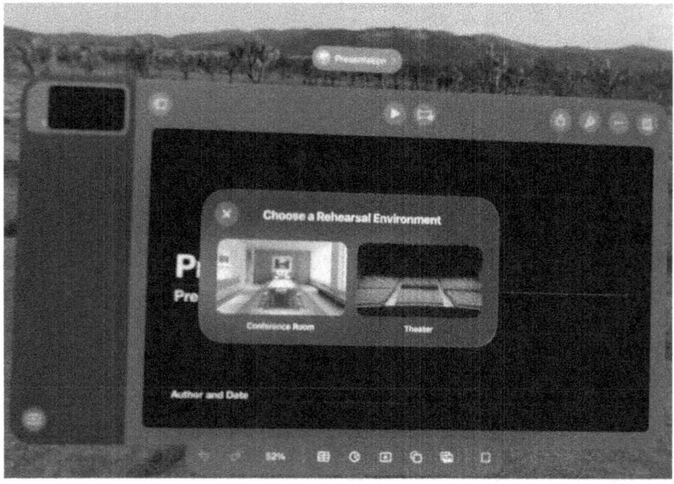


In both setups, you have your slides previewed in front of you, and when you turn behind you, you see your presentation. It really feels like your standing on stage presenting to an empty room, and there behind you is what your empty audience sees.

It's cool, but why is it a glimpse into the future? Vision Pro is at day one; think about the future—think about those kids in elementary school right now who will probably be packing a Vision Pro when they go away for college. Except back up: will they really need to go away to college anymore?

What if what we see here is presenter mode, but in the future there's a "viewer mode"? A mode that lets you step into the auditorium for a college lecture, and you can turn to your right and left and see your peers as you would in the classroom. You can talk to them—even pass notes with them.

We aren't there yet, but this app will make you question how real the possibility will be. It makes you wish your were a kid—to learn about art by virtually visiting museums or learn about the moon by walking on it! The Vision Pro will make you excited for the future and it's apps like Keynote that help you see it.

## FILES

If you download things from the Internet (or mail attachments) you'll be able to find them here. You'll also have access to all your cloud documents. Unfortunately, it's not terrible easy to search.

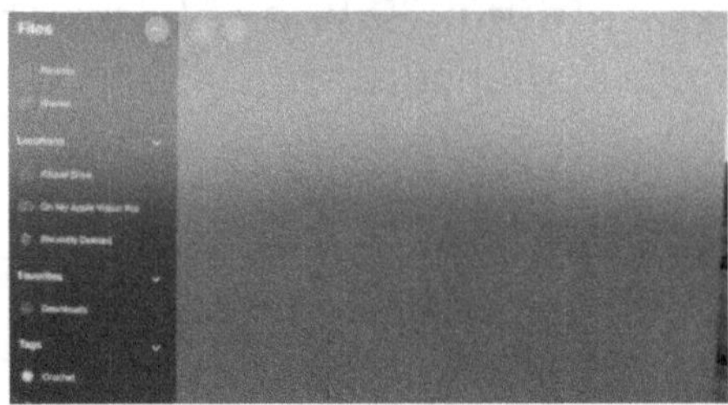

## FACETIME AND PERSONAS

If you look around the Vision Pro OS, one thing you will notice quickly is there's no Facetime app. It's a strange thing, because the app does exists—you just won't find an icon for it. There's also no Phone icon—again, it exists, but there's no shortcut for them.

Instead, to make voice or Facetime calls, you'll go to the People area of the Home menu, then find the person you want to call, then on their contact card, you'll see Facetine as an option.

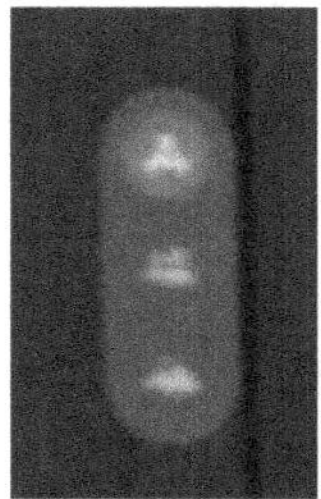

I say all this as a lead-in to Personas; there's no Personas app, but to take advantage of Facetime video calls, you'll need one.

Personas, as of this writing, is in beta. Don't let the beta label fool you, however, because it actually works really well—kind of. If you haven't tried the Vision Pro yet, then you've probably seen the memes of Personas or perhaps heard someone comment on how weird it looks. Chances are, you heard this from someone who hasn't used it on the Vision Pro and has only seen a photo. It's really something you need to experience with the headset on to fully appreciate.

My wife laughed when I called her; she laughed for a little too long! I suppose I could have did my hair. I'm also wearing a pink sweater in my photo, but for some reason it matches my skin and at first glance, makes it look like I'm not wearing a shirt!

Here's one of the biggest things you need to know about Personas: be careful what you wear! If you have a shirt collar that's crooked, that's what people will see until you redo your Persona. Personas is all about your face; that means your hair and clothing will appear stiff.

Make sure you have good lighting when you take your picture for Personas. If you have a webcam light, use it.

Creating a Persona is pretty quick, so experiment and have fun with it. Take a couple of pictures and see which one you like best.

Environments also change how things sound. If your environment is outdoors, you'll notice a very subtle change in how you sound to others. A lot of very fine details went into this experience, and this is one of them.

To anyone you call on the phone, you'll probably look a little—robotic. If you want to see why Personas is better than a meme, then try and find someone else with a Vision Pro to call—that's what Personas was really made for.

### SETTING UP OR EDITING A PERSONA

If you didn't do a Persona at setup or you want to redo it, then you'll need to go into your settings to do it. Settings > Personas. From here you can either edit your Persona, or Recapture it.

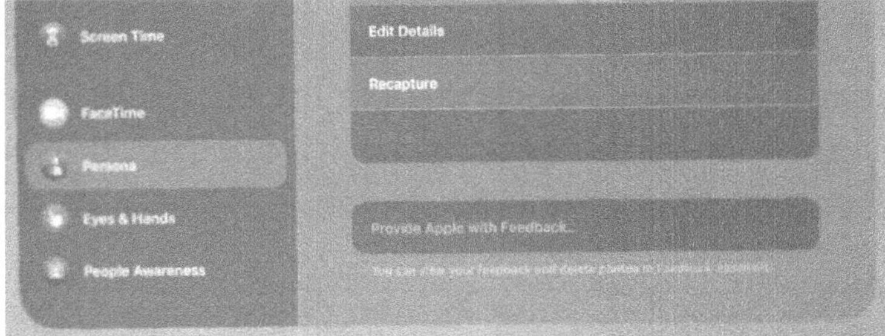

When you edit a Persona (or when you do it for the first time) you are able to pick the lighting of your Persona.

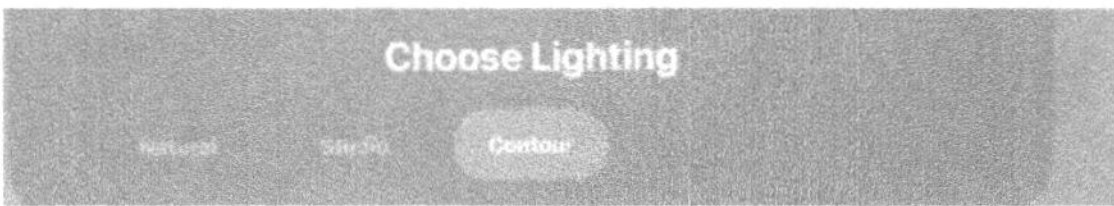

You can also pick the brightness and temperature of your skin tone.

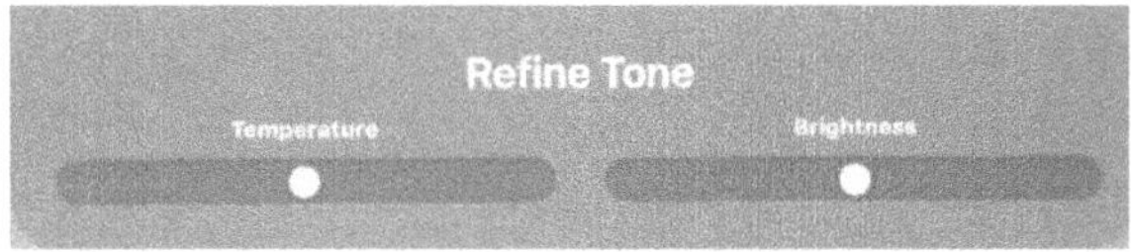

Finally, you can pick if you have glasses.

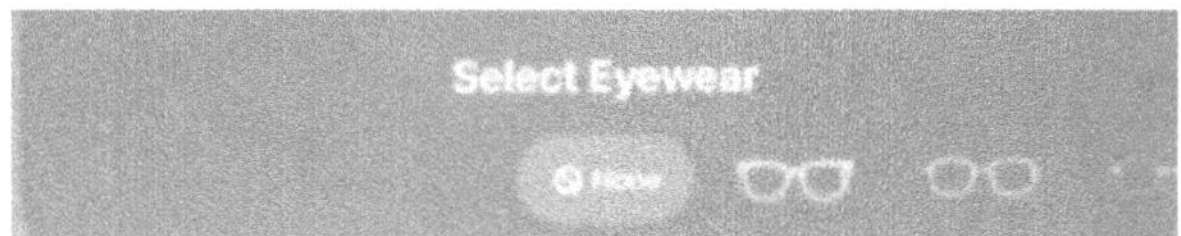

## APP STORE

The App Store is not too different that the iPad app store. Here's the biggest thing to know: when you search for an app, it will automatically show you natively built apps; when the results come in, you can tap the compatible apps to see all apps. So if you are looking for something like Slack or Outlook (both are not currently available natively on Vision Pro) you would need to toggle over to compatible apps to find it.

To buy an app, you can use your password, or enable Optic ID—which means to buy something, you just stare at the screen and it confirms your identity with an eye scan.

## COMPATIBLE APPS

Apps that are compatible with Vision Pro, but not built for Vision Pro (i.e. iPad apps) will show up in this section—that includes both Apple Apps and Apps you download from the App Store.

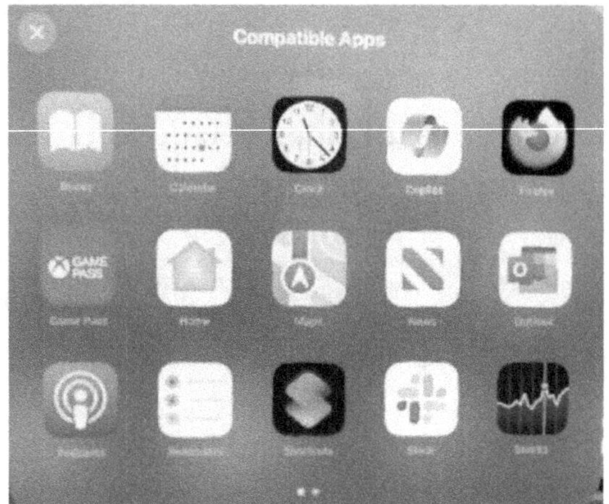

# [5]
# TAKING AND VIEWING PICTURES AND VIDEOS

## TAKING SPACIAL VIDEOS AND PHOTOS WITH VISION PRO

Taking videos with your Vision Pro isn't bad, but, in my opinion, it's not as good as what you'll get on the iPhone 15 Pro. Vision Pro is better at viewing content than capturing it. But if you don't have an iPhone 15 Pro, then, for now, the Vision Pro is your only option—but don't be surprised if you start seeing Spacial capture appear on iPad and even the cheaper iPhone's in the future.

Capturing photos and videos is simple; there's no Camera app to open like you would on any other device. All you do is press down once on the top button.

Once you press down on the top button, it will ask if you want to capture a spacial photo or video.

Press the top button again to take the photo or video; if you are recording a video, you can can either press the top button to stop it, or press the red stop square.

You'll be able to share these photos and videos with anyone—even people without a Vision Pro. But to everyone else, they will appear in 2D.

## TAKING SPACIAL VIDEOS AND PHOTOS WITH IPHONE 15 PRO

If you have an iPhone 15 Pro, then you may have already been capturing memories enhanced for the Vision Pro and not even known it! If you haven't then section will show you how (sorry, but this is only for the iPhone 15 Pro and Pro Max–regular iPhone 15 won't do it…nor will iPhone Pro's earlier than the 15).

### SETTING UP YOUR IPHONE 15 PRO FOR SPATIAL VIDEO MAGIC

First things first, let's get your iPhone 15 Pro or Pro Max ready for this 3D journey. Head over to `Settings > Camera > Formats` and switch on the "Spatial video for Apple Vision Pro" option. This setting is your golden ticket to the 3D world, and is available for iPhone 15 Pro models running iOS 17.2 or later (it wasn't available when the phones first came out, so make sure and do that update if you haven't already).

### RECORDING YOUR FIRST SPATIAL VIDEO

Ready to roll? Grab your iPhone 15 Pro, and let's get filming:

1. **Launch the Camera App**: Open up Camera and switch to Video mode. Landscape orientation is your friend here—portrait orientation isn't an option.
2. **Activate Spatial Video**: Look for the Spatial Video Off button and give it a tap. Now you're set to record in 3D!
3. **Capture the Moment:** Press the Record button or hit either volume button to start. Here are some pro tips for that perfect shot:
    a. Keep your iPhone stable and level.
    b. Position your subjects about 3 to 8 feet away.
    c. Ensure your lighting is bright and even.
4. **Wrap it Up:** Tap the Record button again or press a volume button to stop. To exit spatial video mode, just tap the Spatial Video On button.

### VIEWING AND SHARING YOUR 3D CREATIONS

Make sure you're logged in with your Apple ID and have iCloud Photos on for seamless syncing across devices.

### A QUICK NOTE ON SPECS

Remember, spatial videos on the iPhone 15 Pro and Pro Max are shot in 1080p at 30 fps. Each minute of this 3D goodness takes up about 130 MB of space, so plan your storage accordingly. That choir recital might end up taking over 4GB on your phone!

# VIEWING PHOTOS

The Photos app is optimized for Vision Pro, but in a way, it's also an inferior app to what you get on iPhone and iPad; the Photos app is for viewing photos—not for editing them. It's organized in a very familiar way, but also feels like a reminder that the Vision Pro is a device to see content—not always edit content.

There's three main areas of the app. One the right is the main viewing area where all the thumbnails appear; next to that is the submenu that's based on what ever menu you select.

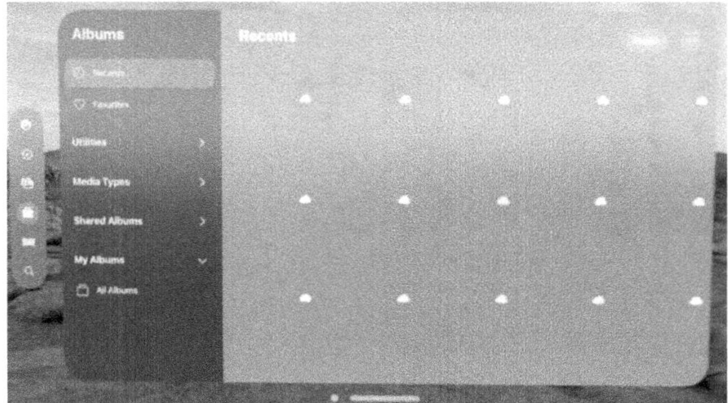

Finally, over on your right is the main menu, which shows: Spacial (where any spacial view shot on your iPhone or on the Vision Pro will show up, Memories (which you can create or Apple will create for you), Library (all photos), Albums, Panoramas, and Search.

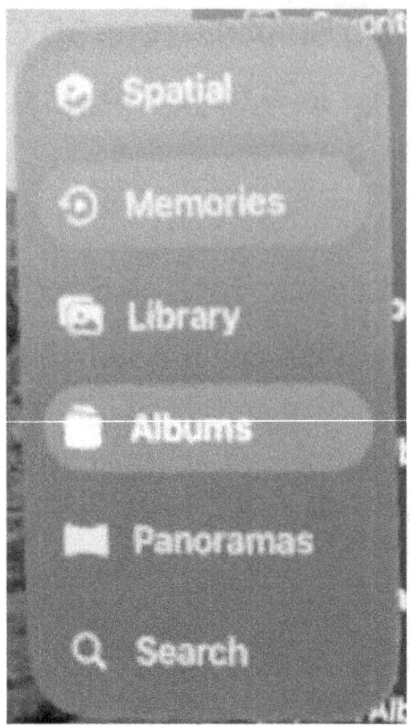


If you haven't tried the Search in a while, it's worth checking out. Don't think of it like searching for the titles of files; that's so yesterday! Search today lets you search for what's in the photos. So you can say "white dog" and it's able to understand what you just said and scan your photos for anything that resembles a white dog.

When you view your photo, you can share it and see it, but that's about it. Pinching and swiping will let you see the photos to the left and right, but, again, at this time there is not an option to edit a photo.

Next to Spacial videos (which, if you don't have a iPhone 15 Pro, it will probably be empty), the best thing about the app is Panoramas; and the great thing about Panoramas is you can take it with any phone—so you might have a few in your library.

When you view a Panorama on the Vision Pro, it will look like just a long photo. But take a look at that icon in the upper right corner—looks like a rectangle box that's being squeezed.

That turns your photo into an immersive 180 degree photo; you can't see it below, but in the headset, I'd be able to turn left and right to view the photo in very crisp HD.

Viewing Spacial photos and videos is a similar process; the normal view is 3D, but not immersive; pressing on that corner icon will turn your Spacial photos and videos into an immersive experience. But be warned! Spacial videos can cause motion sickness! If you are watching this type of content, make sure there's not a lot of movement in the scene. I filmed my dogs playing and nearly fell over when I turned on the immersive mode!

my dogs playing and nearly fell over when I turned on the immersive mode!

# [7]

## CONNECTING TO A MAC

**Getting your Mac connected is super easy!** You've got two simple ways to do it. First up, the Control Center – yup, that handy tool we talked about earlier. Or, if you're feeling a bit more futuristic, just give your Mac a look. Seriously, just a glance and Vision Pro gets the hint. You'll see the connect option pop right up above your Mac's display.

Most of the time, it's smooth sailing. But hey, tech can be quirky sometimes, right? If the option doesn't show up, no sweat. Just hop over to the Control Center, hit Screen Mirroring, and boom – your Vision Pro should be on the list. Easy peasy!

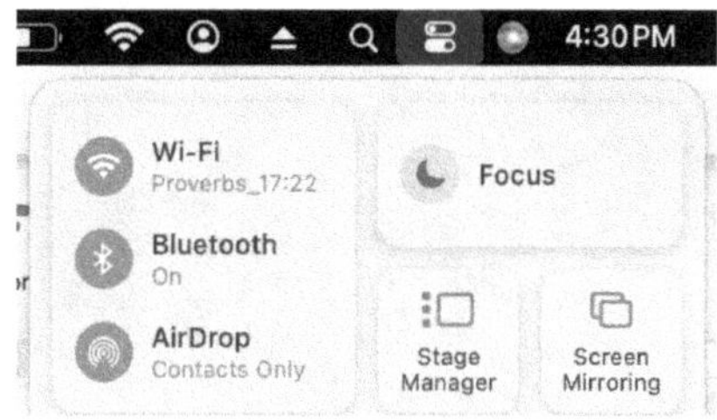

Once I clicked that, it showed up on my display in seconds. So it wasn't always perfect; but once it was there, it worked exactly as I hoped—in beautiful 4K.

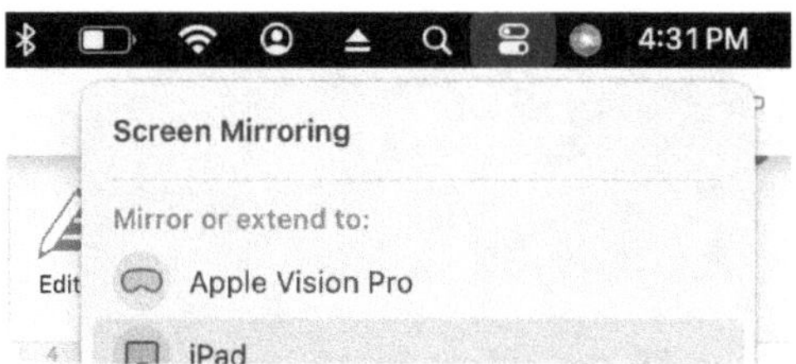

Vision Pro is awesome sauce, but it's not quite ready to kick our computers and offices to the curb just yet. Here's the lowdown on what to watch out for, and fingers crossed, these quirks get ironed out soon:

- **One Mac at a time, please!** I've got a Mac for the grind and one for the home vibes. It'd be awesome to juggle them in the same space, right?
- **Single screen life.** Sure, you can split your mega screen into a bunch of windows, but sometimes you just wanna spread your digital stuff into your real-world space.
- **Go old school with keyboard and mouse.** If you're like me and tuck your dock away, you might play hide-and-seek with it unless you've got a trackpad handy.
- **Remember the setup? Vision Pro doesn't.** I had my digital desk all neat – clock here, Teams there, Slack chilling on the side. But when I shut down Vision Pro for the night and fired it up again, poof! Back to square one. Standby mode, though, keeps it all in check.
- **Scrolling can be a drag.** Literally. Sometimes it's like scrolling through molasses when you connect it to your Mac.

Remember, Vision Pro is just starting out. It's bound to get even better with time. Personally, I've noticed it boosts my productivity for certain tasks. But when it comes to writing, I'm still old school and prefer to skip it.

On the flip side, I've definitely noticed less neck strain. I'm all about that laptop-on-lap life, which usually means looking down a lot. But with Vision Pro, my neck stays in line, even when I'm kicking back. Some folks might talk about its weight, but for me, it's like it's not even there. I can wear it for ages without any trouble.

And yeah, I've given Meta Quest 3 a whirl for work too. Can't say I'm a fan. Pairing it with my Mac was a pain, the display was fuzzy, and it felt like I was getting less done. So, Vision Pro? You're doing alright by me.

## WORKING IN VISION PRO

Once you connect the Vision Pro, then what? How do you take advantage of this massive monitor that's suddenly in front of you?

First—remember that these screenshots just do not give it justice at all; you have to experience Vision Pro to really know what I'm talking about.

I typically work in full screen with my apps. That's not really the best practice for Vision Pro because you have so much extra screen real estate.

Instead, you want to have your windows sectioned off. It's great when you have to compare documents as you work.

You also want to use apps whenever possible; sense you can't break windows out of your virtual space have things like Slack, Zoom and Teams downloaded as apps, so you can arrange it around your virtual space. I also have a clock widget that I put up on top because the one on my Mac is really small.

# WORK APPS TO CHECK OUT

Sure thing! Let's expand on each app with a bit more detail:

## CARROT Weather

Imagine a weather app that doesn't just tell you about the rain or shine but does it with a cheeky grin. That's CARROT Weather for you! It's not your average forecast app; it's like your quirky friend who always has a funny take on everything, especially the weather. And those 3D weather maps? They're not just cool to look at; they make you feel like you're right there in the middle of the action.

## Lungy: Spaces

In the hustle and bustle of life, finding a moment of peace can be a challenge. Enter Lungy: Spaces, your personal zen master in an app. It's not just about deep breaths; it's about transforming your space into a sanctuary of calm with interactive exercises and immersive soundscapes. It's your pocket-sized peace corner for whenever life gets too loud.

## Focus – Productivity Timer

Ever feel like you're juggling a million things and your focus is just... gone? The Focus timer is here to rescue your attention span. It's the nudge you need to keep your head in the game and your productivity on point. Think of it as your personal coach, cheering you on to the finish line of every task.

## Microsoft 365

When it's crunch time at work, and you're knee-deep in Vision Pro, you'll want the big guns by your side. Microsoft 365 is like the Swiss Army knife of office tools. Whether it's crunching numbers on Excel, crafting words on Word, or collaborating on Teams, these native apps are your trusty allies in the digital workspace.

## Things 3

To-do lists are the unsung heroes of productivity, and Things 3 is the leader of the pack. It's the app that turns the mundane task of listing chores into something you'll look forward to. With its arrival on Vision

Pro, you'll have the slickest, most intuitive to-do experience at your fingertips.

### Fantastical

For the chronically busy, a great calendar app is like a lifeline. Fantastical is that and more. It's been the go-to calendar for Apple users who want to keep their lives in sync, and now it's bringing its top-notch organization skills to Vision Pro. It's not just a calendar; it's your personal time wizard.

### Shortcut Buttons

Vision Pro isn't just about seeing; it's about feeling grounded in your digital world. The Shortcut Buttons feature is like having an invisible butler, keeping all your apps and windows exactly where you left them. It's the kind of consistency we all need in a world that's always changing.

### Juno for YouTube

Christian Selig, the genius behind Apollo, is back with a bang with Juno for YouTube. It's the app that fills the void left by YouTube's absence on Vision Pro, and it does it with style. It's the seamless, native VisionOS experience for all your video cravings.

### Zoom

Zoom is redefining virtual meetings on Vision Pro with its early adoption and innovative features. With 3D avatars that mirror your every expression and hand gesture, Zoom's VisionOS app is all about making virtual interactions feel real. And with upcoming features like 3D object sharing and spatial team chats, it's setting the bar high for virtual collaboration.

### Box

Box is taking cloud storage to another dimension with its Vision Pro app. It's not just about storing files; it's about bringing them to life in 3D. Whether you're a retailer planning a window display, a manufacturer inspecting a prototype, or a student exploring complex concepts, Box's app is your gateway to collaborative, immersive experiences.

## Flowwriter

Flowwriter is the ultimate creative companion, blending AI magic with your writing process. It's not just about blocking out distractions; it's about creating the perfect backdrop for your thoughts to flow. With custom cutouts and easy export options, Flowwriter is the bridge between your Vision Pro creativity and your Mac productivity.

## School Assistant

School Assistant is the planner app that's about to revolutionize the way students organize their lives. It's more than just a digital planner; it's a smart, translucent window into your academic world, designed to keep you on top of everything from homework to class schedules, all within the sleek and intuitive VisionOS environment.

There you have it—a more detailed look at each app to spice up your tech writing. Enjoy crafting your friendly and casual piece! 😊 📱

# [7]
# SETTINGS

Now that you know your way around the Vision Pro, we're going to take a look at the settings, where you can see how to configure things.

The Settings app looks almost identical to the iPad; a left panel navigation with the settings for each category on the right. But don't let looks deceive you, because there's a lot of settings that you'll only find on Vision OS. I'll go over each area next.

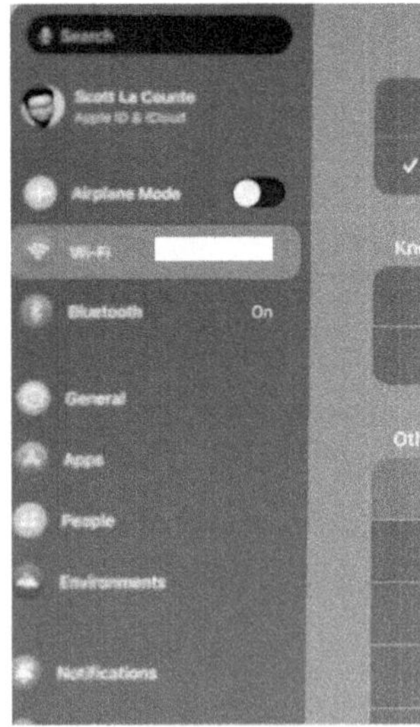

## WI-FI

Anytime you want to change the wireless network that your Vision Pro is on, then you'll go here. It remembers passwords, so if you go into a location you've been before, it will automatically connect if the wi-fi is the same.

## BLUETOOTH

What if you want to use a controller? Keyboard? Trackpad? Or another supported Bluetooth device? You do that in Bluetooth. Most controllers and keyboards are supported, but your best bet for a trackpad is the Apple one. When you use a trackpad, a small transparent circle will appear on your screen.

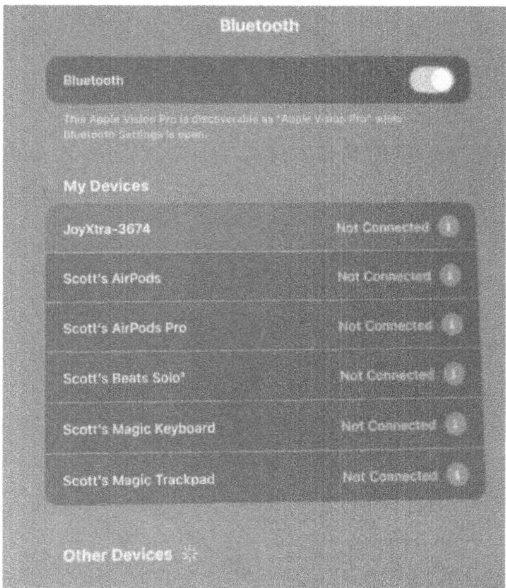

## GENERAL

Some of the most important settings are found in General. Under about, you can get your devices serial number; you can also do software updates, change the keyboard look, adjust the time, change the language, add a VPN, reset your Vision Pro, and also shut it down.

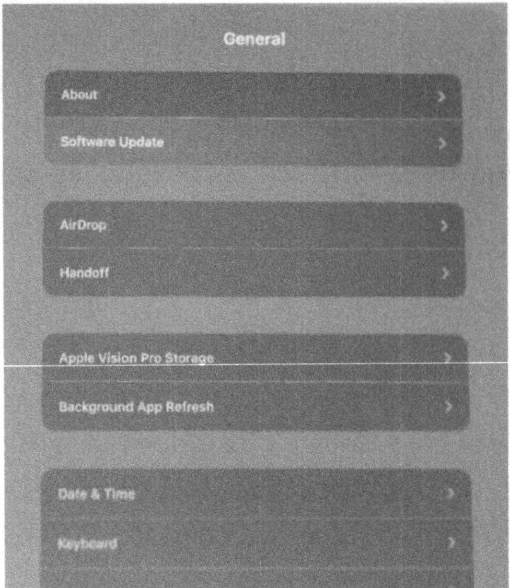

## APPS

As the name implies, Apps is where you'll find a list of all your apps, but it's also where you go to change your app settings. When you tap on any app, you'll see additional things you can add or change.

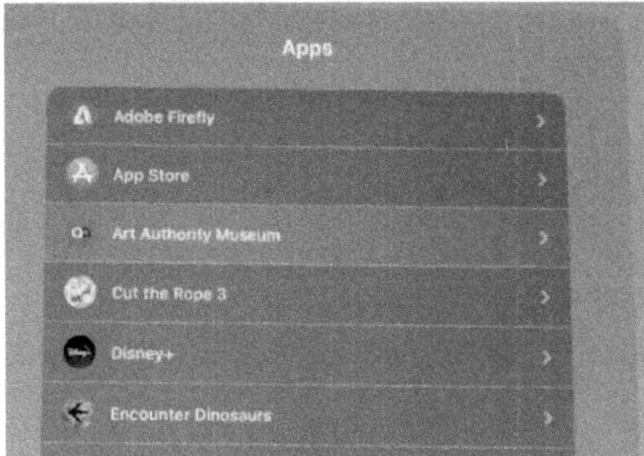

## PEOPLE

People lets you adjust how names appear; it also lets you add people to your blocked list, so they can't contact you.

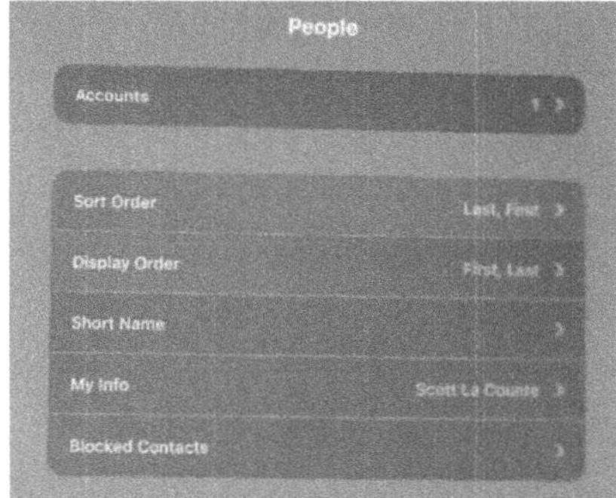

### ENVIRONMENTS

Environments lets you pick if an environment is light, dark, or automatically changed based on here you are. The volume both below isn't for normal sound; it's for the ambient sound that plays in the environment—so if you're out the beach, you'll hear waves in the background, but you can adjust how loud they are.

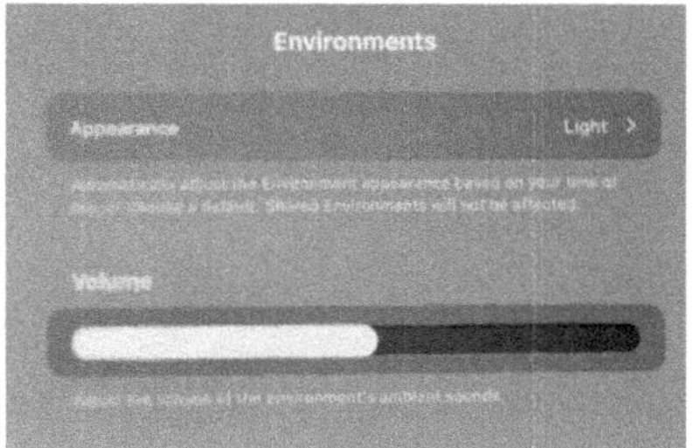

### NOTIFICATIONS

Notifications lets you adjust the types of notifications you get from apps. So lets say you download the NBA app, but don't want notifications from them; you can toggle them off or, if you want them on, select how they appear.

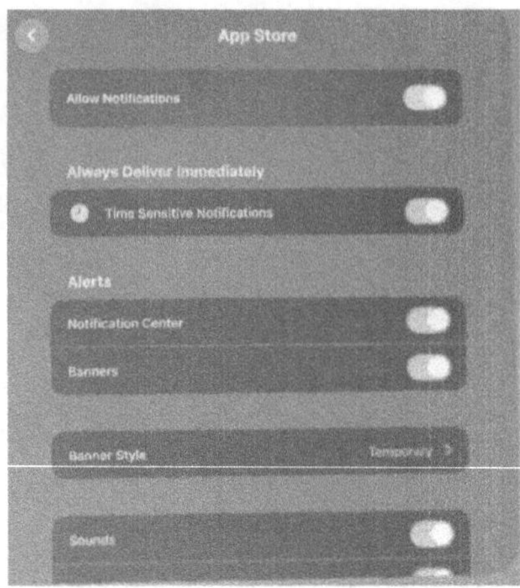

## SOUNDS

Sounds lets you adjust the sound playing on your device.

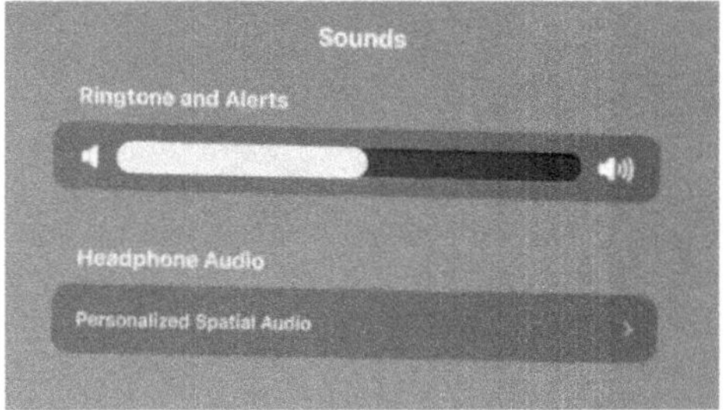

## FOCUS

Focus lets you change what alerts appear; for example, you can set a mode where you won't get email or text notifications, but you still get phone calls from family members; or you can silence everything.

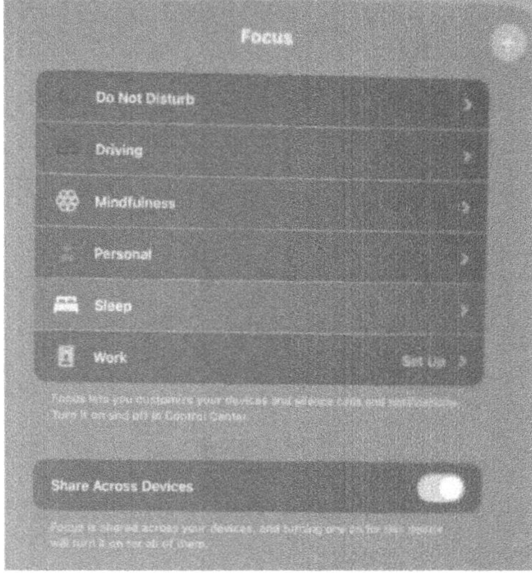

## SCREEN TIME

If you got a Vision Pro, you probably love to consume entertainment, and you'll skip right over this one! But basically what it's for is to set different restrictions—so you can only play games a certain number of hours or you can only watch PG-13 movies.

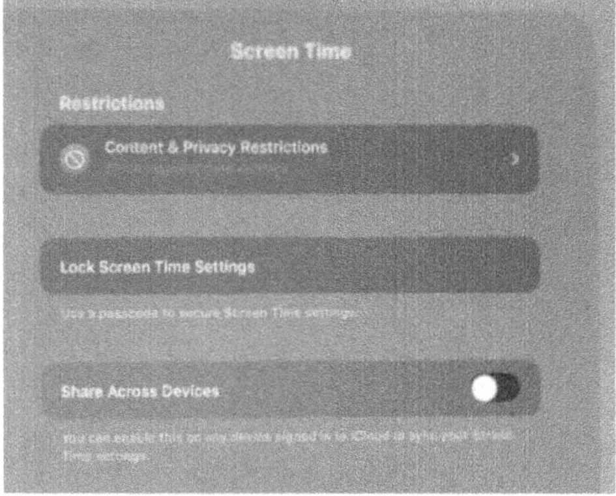

## FACETIME

FaceTime is pretty basic in terms of settings; you can turn Siri and search on and turn FaceTime on and off; one thing you might want to do is add different emails and phone numbers, which is done in the bottom boxes (not shown in the illustration below).

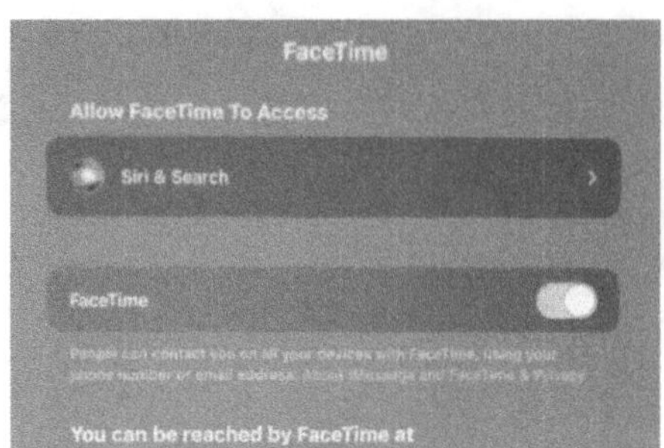

## PERSONA

Persona is where you can make edits or recapture your Persona; it was covered in an earlier chapter.

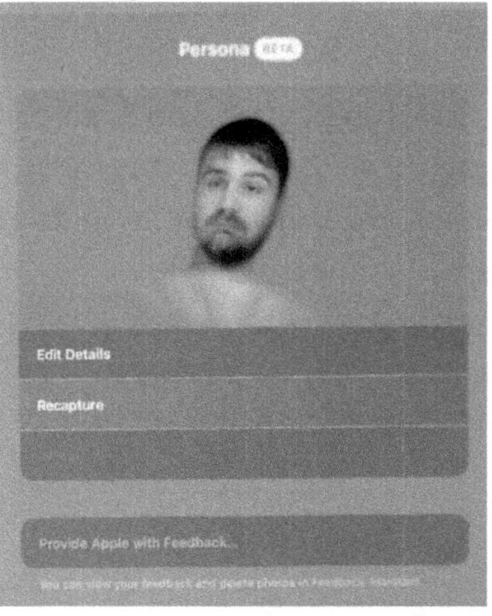

## EYES & HAND

If hand and eye tracking don't seem to work, the first thing you should try is cleaning your lenes with the fabric that Apple included with your Vision Pro.  You can also adjust the light. If that doesn't work, then you can go into this setting and redo the tracking. You might also want to try restarting your device. The tracking on the Vision Pro is incredible, but sometimes it does get a little…buggy—like you can't select corners or smaller buttons.

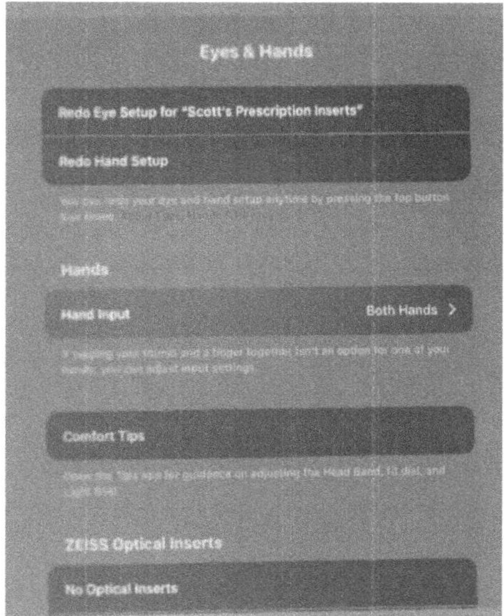

## PEOPLE AWARENESS

When people walk up to you while you're wearing the headset, your environment will disappear, and you can see them. I think it's pretty cool and helps me not completely disappear from the world; but if you'd rather not see anyone, then you can toggle off people awareness in this setting. You can also pick if you want to see people when you are watching something immersive or only if you have up an environment.

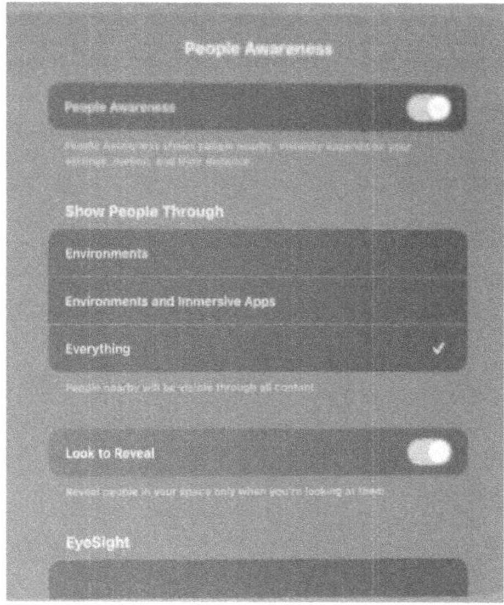

## ACCESSIBILITY

Next to the General setting, Accessibility is the most comprehensive. You can go in here to reduce motion, add a hearing aide, make text bigger, and more much more.

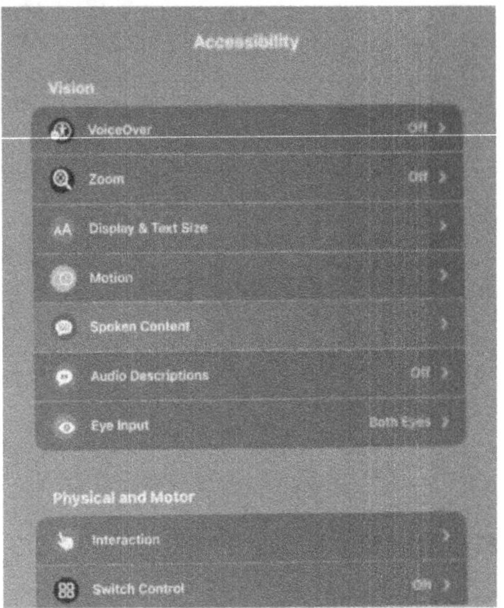

## CONTROL CENTER

If you've never customized your support center, you should consider it. When you go into the Control Center settings, you can add and remove shortcuts that appear but pressing the + or − icon next to the shortcut. In VisionOS, you can also adjust the position of where it appears; if you want the icon to appear higher or lower, you can move the slider to find the best position.

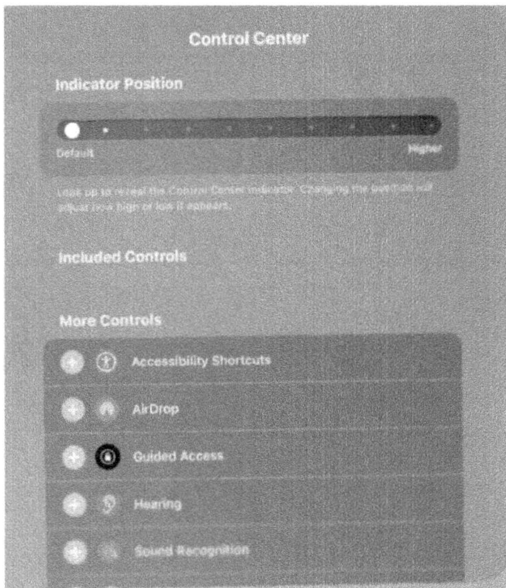

## SIRI & SEARCH

If you want to change how Siri is activated, what the voice sounds like, and more, you can do so in this setting.

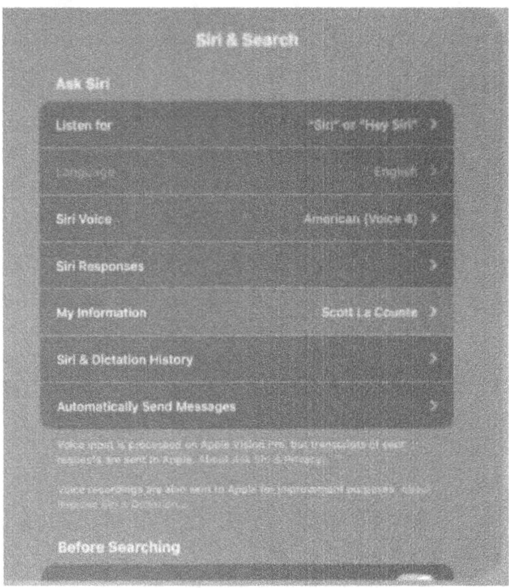

## PRIVACY & SECURITY

Your apps track different things; it may track your location, for example; you can toggle that on and off here. But be careful—turning off tracking might change the behavior of the app; a weather app, for example, needs to know where you are to show you the weather of your location.

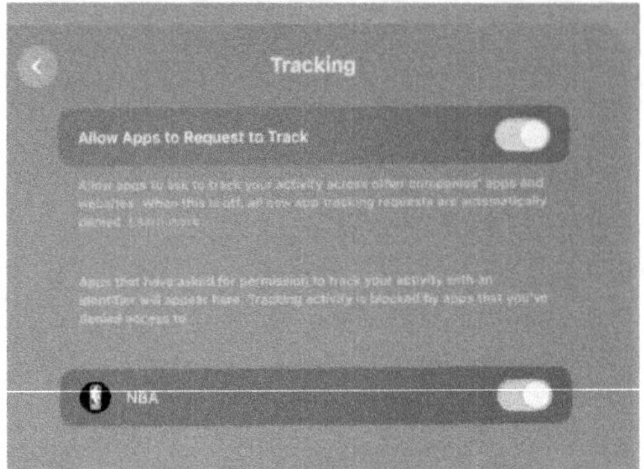

### DISPLAY

If things appear to large or small, or to bright or dim, then you can go in here to adjust it.

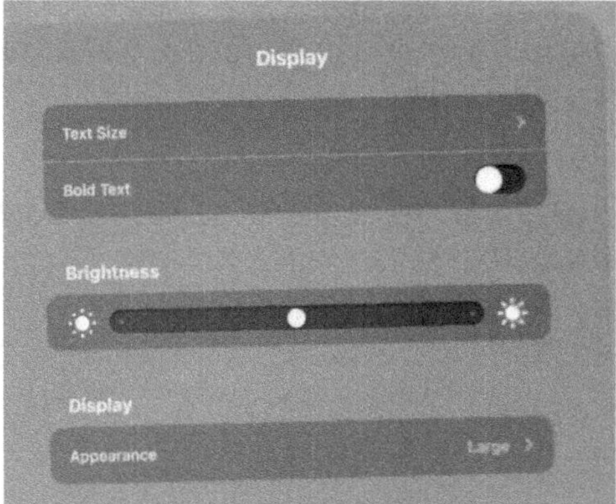

### BATTERY

The battery section is very basic, as of this writing; it is just a toggle that lets you turn on and off the battery percent.

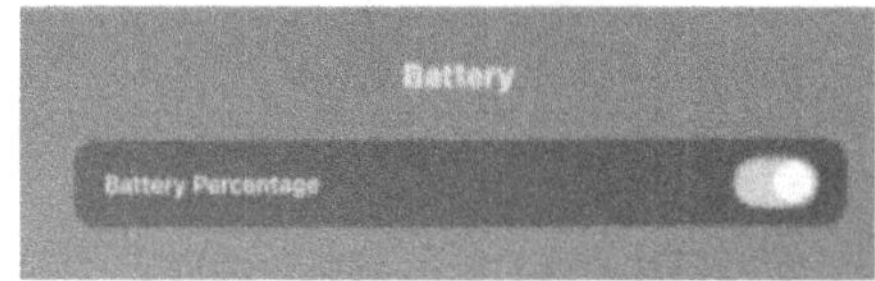

### STORAGE

Storage will visualize where all your space is being used. Some things you can't do a lot about; for example, visionOS and System Data can't be reduced. Other things can either be offloaded or deleted to save on space.

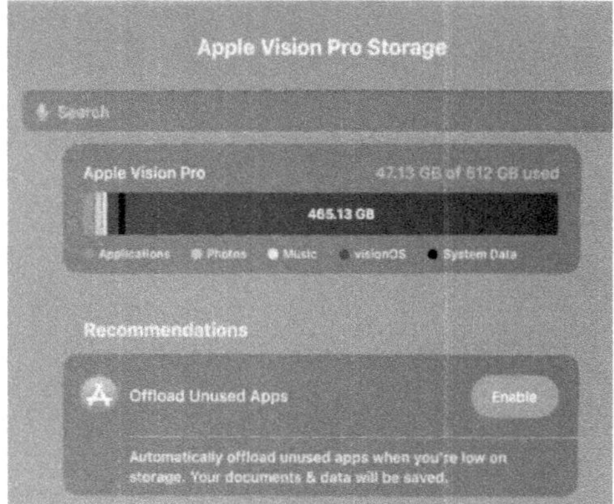

Scrolling down, you can see the amount of space each app in particular uses; some apps take several GB.

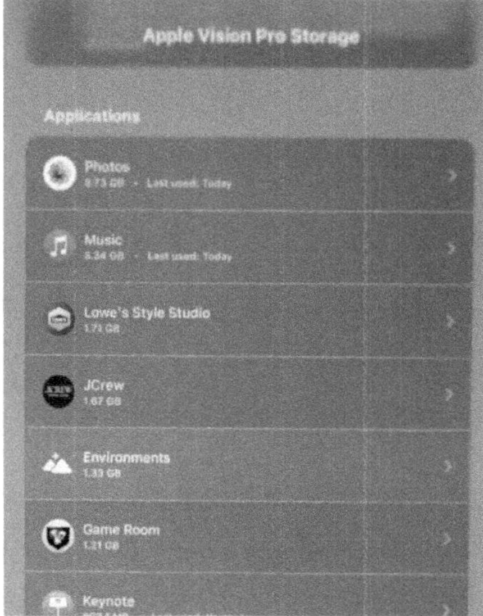

## OPTIC ID & PASSCODE

Paying for things and using your password is a little different on Vision Pro; unlike other devices where you might use your fingerprint or face, Vision Pro uses your eyes. If you'd prefer to do somethings the old fashion way by typing in your password, you can toggle where it is used here.

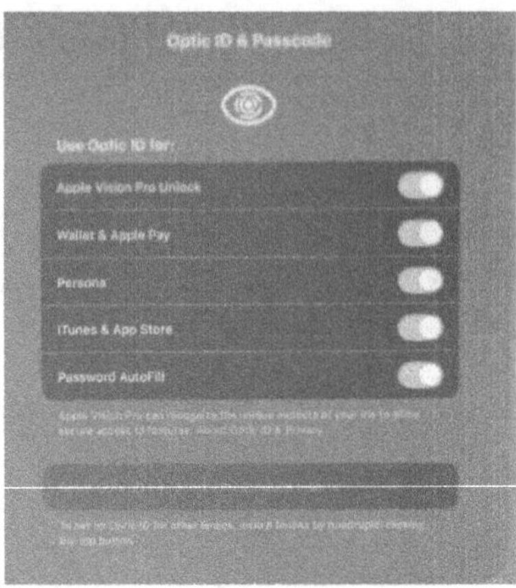

## PASSWORDS

In the password section, you'll see both recommendations and what passwords were used; so if you can't remember what password you used for a specific website, you can go in here and see it.

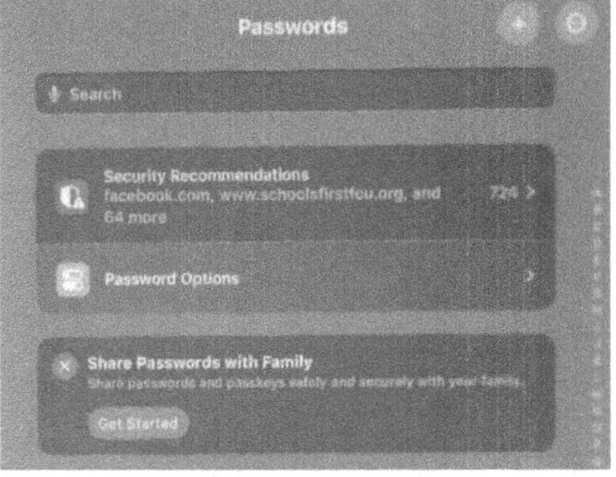

## GAME CENTER

Game Center is what is used if you want to play games against friends or other users; it also lets you track game achievements. This section lets you turn it on, see your user name, and invite others to see you.

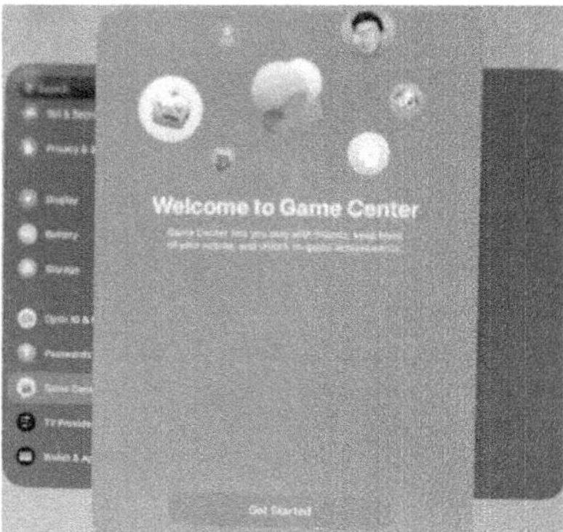

## TV PROVIDER

If you subscribe to cable for TV, you can login to your provider in this section; this lets you watch certain apps without a subscription.

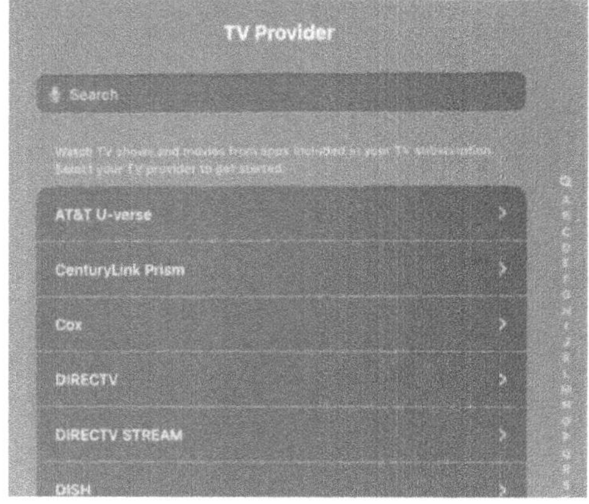

## WALLET & APPLE PAY

Wallet is where all your payments are stored, and where you would go if you wanted to add a new credit card; you can also turn on and off Apple Cash here.

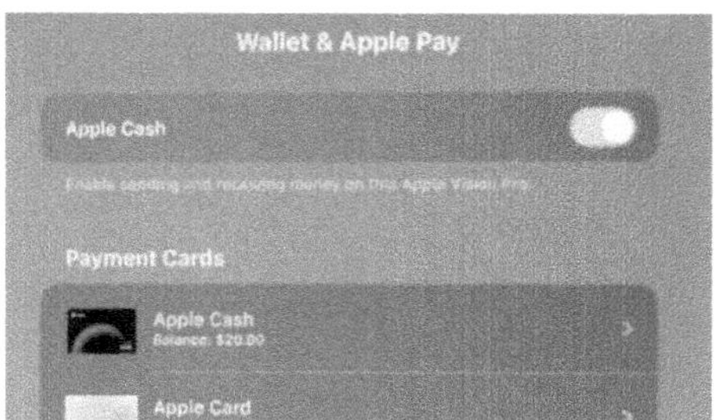

# APPENDIX A: PROTECTING THE VISION PRO

Let's talk about keeping your cool new Vision Pro safe and sound. You've probably heard of AppleCare+, and for the Vision Pro, it's an option you might want to seriously consider. Here's the lowdown on what it offers and why it might just be a lifesaver for your device.

## THE VISION PRO WARRANTY

Right off the bat, your Apple Vision Pro comes with a one-year hardware warranty and up to 90 days of complimentary tech support. That's pretty neat, but if you're looking for more comprehensive coverage, AppleCare+ is where it's at.

## APPLECARE+

You can opt for a two-year coverage at $499 or go for a monthly plan at $24.99, which continues until you decide to cancel it.

Here's what you get with AppleCare+:

- **Accidental Damage Coverage**: We've all been there - accidents happen. With AppleCare+, you get unlimited incidents of accidental damage protection, though each incident carries a service fee. Think of it as a safety net for those oops moments.
- **Express Replacement Service**: Nobody likes being without their tech. With this service, you get a replacement device shipped to you, so you're not left in the lurch while yours is being fixed.
- **24/7 Expert Access**: Got a question at 2 AM? No problem. AppleCare+ gives you round-the-clock access to Apple experts.
- **Comprehensive Hardware Coverage**: This includes your Vision Pro, the battery, and even the included cable.

### Why Consider AppleCare+?

I'm sure you've felt a little…scammed…by a warranty. Is AppleC-are+ a scam? Definitely not. It's peace of mind. Hopefully you'll never need it, but without it a simple cracked cover glass could set you back about $799, and other repairs might go as high as $2,399. Yikes! With AppleCare+, these costs are significantly reduced. For instance, other accidental damage is covered for $299 per incident.

### Getting AppleCare+

How exactly do you get AppleCare+? There's two ways:

- **Buy When You Purchase**: The easiest way is to grab it when you're buying your Vision Pro.
- **60-Day Window**: Missed it at checkout? No worries. You've got 60 days from your device purchase to get AppleCare+ through the settings menu or at an Apple Store.

AppleCare+ for your Vision Pro is like having a trusty sidekick, ready to swoop in when things go sideways. So, whether you opt for the two-year deal or go monthly, it's an investment in peace of mind.

# APPENDIX B: ACCESSORIES

The Vision Pro isn't Apple's most expensive device ever; that honor goes to the original Gold Apple Watches–remember those? Not many people do! But they maxed out at $17,000. Still, after spending over $3,500 on the headset, there's even more you'll have to consider buying from Apple (not including the $499 for Apple Care+).

I'm not including the ZEISS Optical Inserts here, because I wouldn't really call these optional accessories–if you wear prescription glasses, you'll need them.

## APPLE VISION PRO TRAVEL CASE

The first thing you'll want to consider is a case. There will be plenty of third-party companies who make cases (Spigen was one of the first; they have a pretty nice one for just under $100) for the Vision Pro over the next few months and years, but if you want the official one from Apple, it will cost you $199.

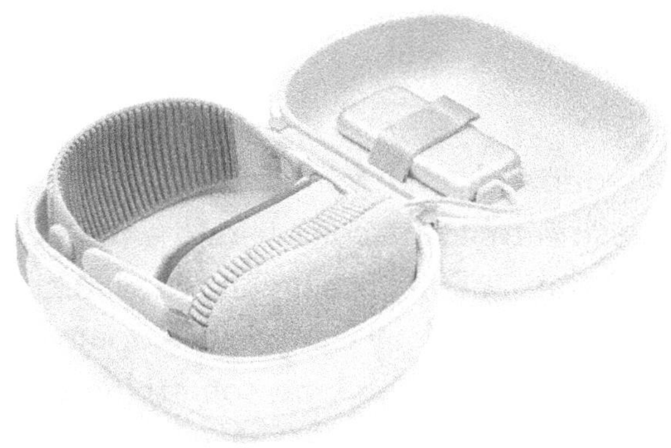

They call it a "travel case" but realistically, you'll probably want this for everyday use. It's a pretty durable headset, but most people will probably not feel comfortable tossing it on their couch or desk and walking away.

## BELKIN BATTERY HOLDER FOR APPLE VISION PRO

There is currently only one third party company (aside from ZEISS) that Apple has partnered with on accessories: Belkin. The Vision Pro battery pack is something that is conveniently missing from a lot of the Vision Pro photos; it's not that Apple is hiding the fact that you need one–they probably just know it looks a lot more interesting when you don't have something dangling from the side of you. You can obviously put it in your pocket, or set it next to you, but for $49, Belkin has created a holder for the Battery pack, so you can also clip it to you.

Do you need it? It really depends on how you will use the Vision Pro. If you are sitting at your desk with it, the cord is long enough to set it down with no trouble at all; the same is true if you are watching a movie. Where things can get a little dicey is if you are doing a workout or moving around–especially if you are wearing something that doesn't have pockets. If you don't want to spend $49, this is one thing you'll probably find a lot of very cheap solutions for by other third party companies.

## APPLE VISION PRO BATTERY

You can buy extras of almost every single part on the Vision Pro. Do you need to? If you are sharing the device with family members, and their head size is bigger, then that might be a good investment. But for most people, the answer is no. One thing, however, some people might want to pick up is an extra battery for $199.

The Vision Pro will last about 2 hours in normal use. If you're on a flight, that's probably not enough time. But, and this is an important but, you can charge the battery pack while you are using it. You could also charge the battery pack with a USB-C battery pack while you are using it. An extra battery pack might be more convenient for some people, but there's plenty of ways to keep using your Vision Pro without it.

## MAGIC KEYBOARD

The Vision Pro has a built-in on-screen keyboard. It also has very easy to use dictation. The keyboard takes a little getting used to, but it's pretty intuitive once you get the hang of it. Still, if you plan on using your Vision Pro alongside your Mac to get work done, a keyboard will be a nice to have. Apple's official solution is the Magic Keyboard for $99. You can technically use most bluetooth keyboards, however.

You also can pair the Vision Pro with trackpads and mouses. Should you? Again, it really comes down to comfort and how you use the Vision Pro. If your heavy on productivity and graphic design, then perhaps. Apple's official trackpad is $129, but you can use pretty much any bluetooth mouse you may have at your desk. That said, eye tracking is far superior to on-screen typing, so you might want to try it out before you spend the extra money on a mouse.

Personally, I have an Apple mouse and keyboard, and I picked up a fitted acrylic tray (it was about $30 on Amazon) to put them in; so when I'm using my Vision Pro for work, I have the keyboard and mouse in my lap (see below image).

# AIRPODS PRO (2ND GENERATION)

The Vision Pro's sound will probably blow you away–and also annoy the person sitting next to you, who can't see what you see! If you are around others and need sound, then the AirPods Pro is a good investment (2nd generation also has USB-C charging). You can technically use any bluetooth headset, but only the AirPods Pro has spacial audio.

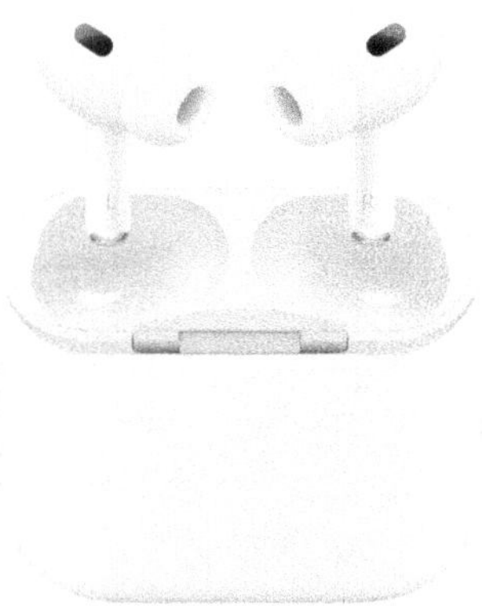

# SONY PLAYSTATION® DUALSENSE™ WIRELESS CONTROLLER

The last thing you may want to pick up is a game controller. Apple is promoting the Sony controller ($69.95) on the Apple Store app, but most gaming controllers will work just fine.

Anything on the Vision Pro will work without a controller, but some games will work better if you have one.

# GETTING STARTED WITH MACOS

# MAC FOR WINDOWS USERS

Let me preface this chapter by saying: it's not for everyone! Because many readers are Windows users switching to Mac, I think it's important to include a chapter to help you out. Not a Windows user? Just skip ahead.

So exactly how is Mac different from Windows? Throughout the book, I'll be making comparisons to help you, but first I want to give a rundown of some of the major differences.

## RIGHT CLICK

Right-clicking is probably second nature to you if you are a Windows user; on the Mac, it's all about gestures—touching the Trackpad (Mac's mouse) a certain way (or on new Macs, using more or less pressure) will bring up different options and menus.

As weird as it sounds, the first time I used a Mac, the right-click (or lack thereof) drove me crazy…until I figured out that right-clicking was actually there. To right-click on a Mac, click with two fingers instead of one. Alternatively, you can press Control and click with one finger.

If you have an old Windows USB mouse, you don't have to toss it—you can plug it into your Mac and it will work with no installation. The right-click will even work.

I'll explain how to customize your Trackpad later in the book, but if you'd like to jump ahead, you can go to System Preferences > Trackpad.

And don't worry about messing something up; it's very hard to harm a Mac!

## KEYBOARD SHORTCUTS

This section will give you a very quick rundown of the more popular keyboard shortcuts; for a more detailed list, see Appendix A at the end of this book.

On a Windows computer, you might be used to using Control (CTRL) frequently; Control is on the Mac keyboard, but don't get confused—on a Mac, the Control button equivalent is the Command (⌘) Key (to the right of the keyboard). The good news is the letter combination for the most frequently used Windows shortcuts is almost always the same on a Mac—Control-C to copy is Command-C on the Mac; Control-X to Cut is Command-X; Control-V to Paste is Command-V.

On a Windows computer, you can hold Alt and Tab to cycle through programs...on a Mac you use Command and Tab.

The two most frequently used function keys (the buttons above the numbers) are F3 and F4; F3 will show a list of the programs you have open, and F4 brings up your Launchpad (all of your available programs...kind of like the Start menu on Windows).

Just keep reminding yourself that while it looks different, it's really not...Windows has File Explorer, Mac has Finder; Windows has the Start Menu, Mac has Launchpad; Windows has the Ribbon menu, Mac has the Top Navigation menu.

Below is a quick overview of what things are called on Windows and what they are called on a Mac:

| Windows | Mac |
| --- | --- |
| Windows Explorer / My Computer / Computer | Finder |
| Control Panel | System Preferences |

| Programs | Applications (often shortened to apps) |
|---|---|
| Task Bar and Start Menu | Dock |
| Tray | Menulets |
| Recycle Bin | Trash |
| Task Manager | Activity Monitor |
| Media Center | iTunes |

## TRANSFERRING DOCUMENTS

The thing a lot of people worry about when updating any computer is how to get all of your information from your old computer to your new computer. With Macs, it's a pretty simple task—you can even take it into your local Apple Store for free help (appointments are needed, so don't just walk in).

If you don't want to wait for an appointment or you just like doing things on your own, there's already a tool on your computer to help: it's called Migration Assistant. Be advised, you do need an Internet connection.

To start, go to your Windows computer and either search any search engine for "Windows Migration Assistant" or go directly to https://support.apple.com/kb/DL1557?locale=en_US. Once you are there, download and install the program on your Windows computer.

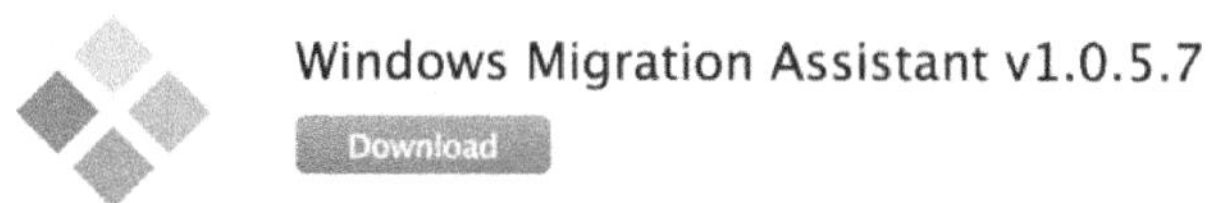


This software will help you migrate data from a Windows PC running Windows XP, Windows Vista, Windows 7 or Windows 8. The Migration Assistant will launch automatically after it has been installed.

For more information, please see http://support.apple.com/kb/HT4796.

From your Mac, click the Launchpad icon (i.e. the rocket on your taskbar).

Next, click on Other and then click Migration Assistant.

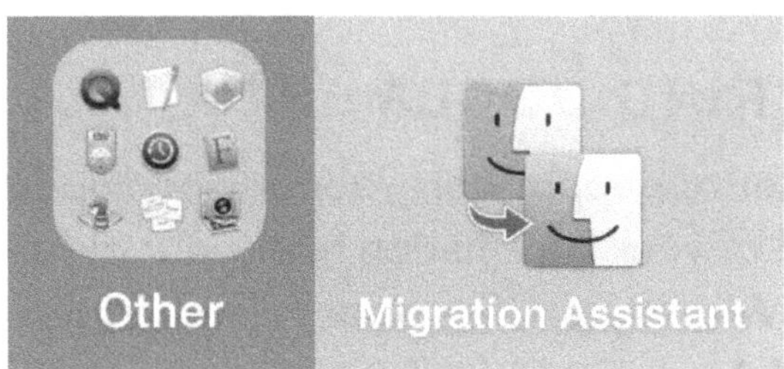



To use Migration Assistant, everything that is open on your Mac will be closed, so make sure and save your work, and don't start until you are ready.

From the setup, click Continue, and then select "From another Mac, PC, Time Machine backup, or other disk," then select Continue and then "From another Mac or PC." The next window should show the Windows computer that you want to transfer files from. Click Continue, verify on the Windows computer that the passcodes match and click Continue again. Lastly, the assistant will ask you to select the types of files you want to transfer.

If you don't do the assistant right away, you can always use it later. There's no timeline for using it, so if you dig up an older Windows computer in the garage and want to transfer everything from it, the option will always be there.

## COMPATIBILITY

Now that you have everything copied over, let's talk briefly about compatibility. While many files will open on a Mac, the software will not. That means if you have Word on Windows, you can't just move it over; most popular software (like Word) is available on the Mac, but you will have to purchase it.

Don't stress too much; most the files that you have just transferred will actually still open even if you don't buy software to open them. Word files (Doc, Docx) for example, will open in Pages (which is free on new Macs).

If your file does not open, then you will probably be able to find free software online that will open it.

## SETUP ASSISTANT

If you are starting up the Mac for the first time (and you are the first owner), then the first thing that will happen is an automated setup assistant will guide you through creating an account and getting everything set up.

The first thing you'll do is select your country; if you don't see yours, then click See All. Click Continue after you finish each section. Next, you'll choose your keyboard layout; if you are an English speaker, then the United States is probably your first bet, but if you are going to be typing primarily in another language (like Chinese) then you may want to pick that country instead—this can be changed later.

Picking the wireless network is the next thing you will see after clicking Continue—you don't have to set up wireless at this point, but if you do, it will also trigger the Migration Assistant (which will help you transfer files); this is all optional so you can skip it (you can also come back to it later).

The next screen is one of the most important: entering your Apple ID. If you have any other Apple devices (iPad, iPod, iPhone, etc.) or if you have an ID that you use with Windows, then you'll want to use it because all of the apps, music and other media you've paid for are tied to your account. If you don't have one, you'll have the option of getting one—it's free and includes iCloud (also free), which I'll be talking about later.

The next part of the setup is Find My Mac (which you need iCloud for); this is a great feature that lets you see where your Mac is from your Internet browser; if it's been stolen it also lets you wipe away all of your content.

After agreeing to the terms, you'll be taken to the Time Zone selection. After that, you are asked if you want to enable the iCloud Keychain. What's the iCloud Keychain? Basically, this stores passwords in the Cloud so you can use them on any device.

Next, decide if you want to send diagnostics and usage data to Apple; this is all for statistical purposes to help Apple make their software and hardware better, but it's entirely up to you. It won't slow your computer down if you do decide to do it—it's all done in the background. After this step, you decide if you want to register your installation with Apple.

Finally, you are ready to start using your Mac!

# [3]

# WHAT'S SONOMA?

One of the best things about macOS is there's a fresh new update every year–it's kind of like getting a new computer Fall.

The time has come again. macOS Sonoma has landed, offering an enriched experience for Mac users seeking the perfect balance between powerful utilities and delightful features. Some features aren't as obvious as others, so let's take a moment to explore what's different in the latest macOS. And don't worry if you are a little confused with some of the features–they'll make more sense when I cover them in more detail later in the book.

## SCREEN SAVERS

With breathtaking slow-motion screen savers featuring locations worldwide, your Mac display just got a visual upgrade. Seamlessly transform these screen savers into your desktop wallpaper upon login. If you have an Apple TV, these screensavers will probably be something your already familiar with.

### WIDGETS ON DESKTOP:

Enhance your desktop with widgets from the new gallery, enabling functionalities like playing podcasts and managing lights directly from a widget. Additionally, via Continuity, iPhone widgets can be integrated without installing corresponding Mac apps.

### VIDEO CONFERENCING REVOLUTIONIZED

The Presenter Overlay ensures you remain the focal point during screen sharing, offering both large and small overlays. React dynamically with hand gestures and augmented reality effects for more engaging conversations.

With the new Screen Sharing picker, share multiple apps effortlessly. Maintain video composition using zoom, pan controls, and Re-center features.

### SAFARI, PASSWORDS, AND PRIVACY

Profiles & Enhanced Search: Separate browsing activities with Safari profiles and experience a faster, more relevant search.

Web Apps & Password Sharing: Turn websites into apps and share passwords securely with trusted contacts.

Enhanced Private Browsing: Experience more secure browsing with locked private windows and eliminated tracking.

### MESSAGES AND SHARING

Search Filters & Catch-up Feature: Find messages swiftly with combined search filters and never miss a conversation with the catch-up arrow.

Location Sharing & Sticker Drawer: Share locations seamlessly and access Live Stickers and Memoji in one place.

### PDFs

Fill out documents quickly with enhanced AutoFill and view PDFs directly in Notes.

### GAME MODE

Experience more games on Mac and level up with Game Mode, ensuring top priority for gaming applications and reduced latency with wireless accessories.

## UPGRADING TO SONOMA OS

Upgrading to Sonoma is not all that different from updating OS on your phone. To start, you'll want to go to the little apple in the upper left corner.

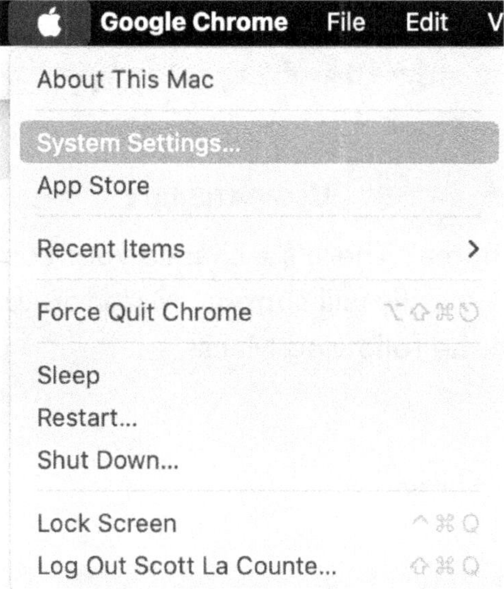


Next, select system settings. From here, go to software update. It will tell you if you have the most recent version of macOS.

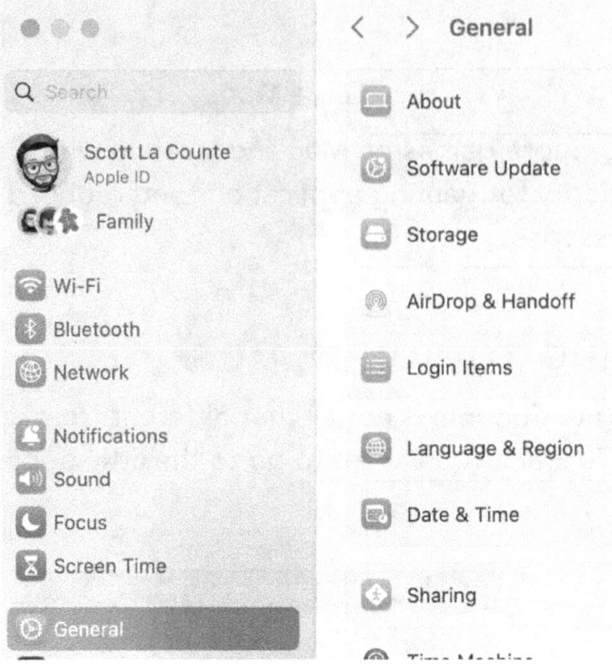

### COMPATIBILITY

Not seeing Sonoma? There's a chance your computer might not support it. Apple typically will support Macs for about 5 years. Sonoma is compatible with the following Macs:

- iMac
  2019 and later
- Mac Pro
  2019 and later
- iMac Pro
  2017
- Mac Studio
  2022 and later
- MacBook Air
  2018 and later
- Mac mini
  2018 and later
- MacBook Pro
  2018 and later

How do you know what you have? Click the Apple up in the upper left corner of your screen, then select About This Mac.

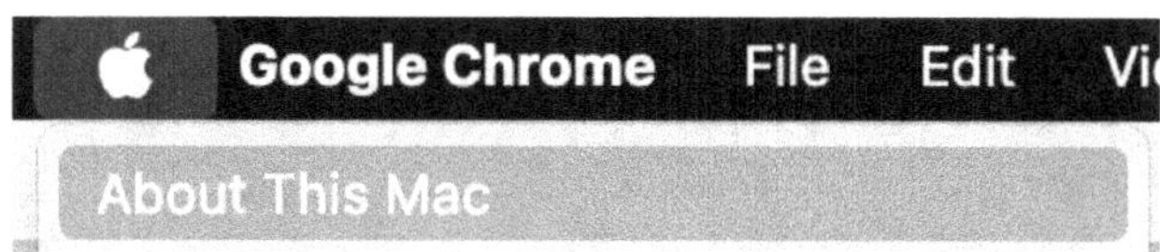


This will bring up a window that shows the make and model of your Mac.

# [3]

# LET'S LEARN THE BASICS

The best way to learn is by doing, so I'm sure you're eager to get your hands wet and start using the Mac! If you are new to Mac, however, that can be a little intimating—it's not hard to use, but you have to, at the very least, know what you are looking at. In this chapter, I'll give you a crash course in the MacOS interface. By the end of the chapter, you won't be an expert, but you'll know where things are and how to start opening and using things.

## KEYBOARD

The keyboard?! I know what you're thinking: a keyboard is a keyboard! Well, sort of. While it is true that you could use a Windows keyboard on a Mac, there are keyboards (including the one that's free with your Mac or built into your MacBook) that are specifically designed for Mac.

There are not a lot of differences; below are the four main ones.

### Apple Key

On a Windows keyboard, there is a button that looks like a Windows flag called the Windows Button. There's no sense putting a Windows button on a Mac keyboard, so where the Windows button normally is, you'll find the Apple button, which doesn't look at all like an apple! It actually looks like this (⌘); it's more commonly known as the Command Button—though some people also call it the Clover Key and Pretzel Key.

*Delete (Backspace)*

On a Windows keyboard, the backspace button is a 'Backwards Delete' key and the delete button is a 'Forward Delete' key (removing the space immediately after the cursor). On a Mac keyboard, the backspace key is labeled 'Delete' and is in exactly the same location as the Windows backspace key. Most Mac keyboards don't have a Forward Delete key anymore, though larger ones do—it's called "Del->". If you don't see it, you still can use forward delete by hitting the FN button (button left corner of your keyboard) and Delete button.

## THE DESKTOP

Hopefully, by now, your files are transferred, you've completed the initial startup, and you have a pretty picture on your desktop. At last, you are ready to use your computer!

The desktop is where you'll be spending much of your time, so let's take some time getting to know it.

The first thing you should notice is that it's really not that much different from Windows—it's a vast space that you can either leave empty or fill with icons or documents.

## APPLE HAS A DARK SECRET

Deep in the halls of Apple, developers have been working on something very...dark. It's called Dark Mode. Does anyone want to guess what happens when you switch it on? If you said "Disney emoji's dance happily on your screen" then go back and reread the question. So, what is dark mode and why would you want to use it?

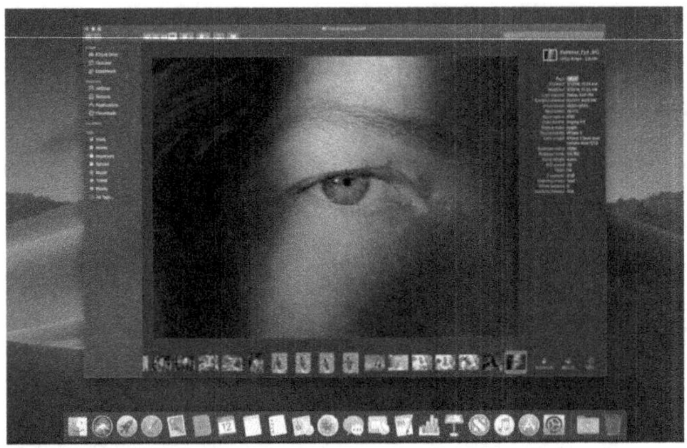

The point of dark mode is to put an emphasis on what you are working on or what you need to find. Let's say you're editing a photo. What's important? The photo. All those things in the background are just noise. Sometimes you need the noise for what you're working on, but you'll work more effectively by having them darkened. It's not like things in the background are harder to see—the contrast just helps you be more creative. At least that's what Apple thinks. If you think otherwise, you have the option to turn it off.

In the image above, you can see the difference between dark mode (left) and light mode (right). In dark mode, those thumbnails should pop a little more than in light mode.

Not all apps will look different. It's up to the company that makes the app to redesign an app that takes advantage of it. Apple has obviously updated many of its apps (like Calendar, iTunes, Mail).

If you've updated to MacOS Catalina then you'll be asked if you want it on. If you want to turn it on, or if you turned it off but now want it on, it's easy to do:

Go to System Preferences (you'll find that in the app launch area of your Dock).

Select General and select the option.

When you're in System Preferences > General, you'll also notice you have the option to change the accent color that goes along with light / dark mode; this changes all the arrows, toggles, etc. throughout the OS. You can always go back to default settings, so don't be afraid to play around: you won't break anything!

## IT'S DYNAMIC!

Apple always likes to put emphasis on making things more aesthetically pleasing when they update the OS. Dark mode is one way they do that; Dynamic Desktop is another.

When I heard the name, I imagined it would let your wallpaper come alive by having something more...dynamic—like the wallpaper could be a looped video or something. It's a little less dynamic than that, unfortunately, but still a cool feature.

So what is it? Well, the wallpaper on your desktop will change, but it's a little slower. Basically, the wallpaper changes appearance depending on what time of day it is. So in Apple's example, there's an image of the Mojave desert; in the morning it's bright and throughout the day it gets darker.

To use it, make sure you have Location Series on—the OS has to know what time it is in your time zone.


## THIS OS IS STACKED

Mac excels in many ways; one of the biggest ways is in how it keeps you organized. Apple is always working hard thinking about how to help you stay organized and keep all your content structured in a way that makes it easy to find.

Apple is a bit like a library; other OSes are a bit like used bookstores. Both places have the same thing: books. But one is organized in a way to help you find what you need quickly; the other is organized in a way where you really need to browse for things.

If your desktop looks a little like the below image, then Stacks can help.

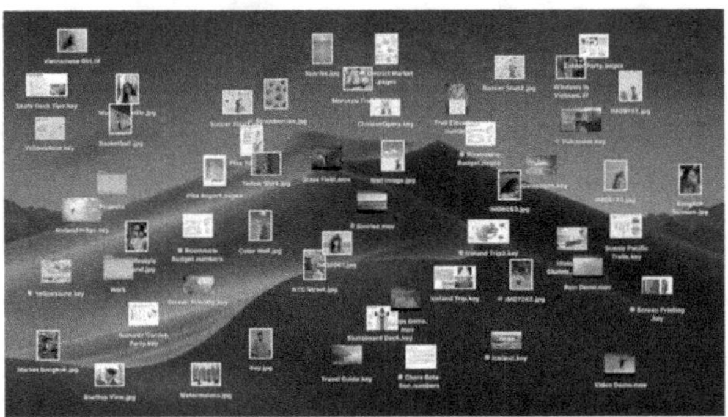

How does Stacks clean this mess up? When it's enabled, the above screenshot would look a bit like the below one.

Everything is still there, but it's grouped together. All the images, documents, and movies are in one group. If you want to see anything within that group, then just click the thumbnail and it will expand. If you add a new file to your desktop, it's automatically put in the appropriate group.

If you're on your desktop, you can turn it on by clicking and selecting Use Stacks. You can also do this by going into Finder and then choosing Use Stacks. You can also pick how you want things stacked. By default, it's by kind, but you can also stack by date or tag.

If you want to turn it off, repeat the process above but uncheck Use Stacks.

## MENU BAR

One of the most noticeable differences between Windows and Mac on the desktop is the top menu bar. I'll be referring back to this menu bar throughout the book, but right now what you need to know is this bar changes with each program that you open, but some of the features remain the same. The little apple, for instances, never changes—clicking on this will always bring up options to restart, shut down, or log out of your computer. The little magnifying glass at the far right is also always there. Any time you click on that, you can search for files, emails, contacts, etc., that are on your computer.

Finder   File   Edit   View   Go   Window   Help

## MENULETS

At the top right, you'll see several "menulets," which include Bluetooth, wireless connectivity, volume, battery, time and date, the name of the account currently logged in, Spotlight, and Notifications, as well as other assorted third-party icons (if installed).

As this book continues, we'll refer back to this part of the menu.

## SPOTLIGHT

Spotlight used to be the way you found files. It still is. But it's evolved too more than that. Type in a word or phrase (I use dog photos in the example below) and it begins searching for not only files, but web matches, documents where the phase is used within it, Siri suggestions, and more.

You can find Spotlight in the top right corner of your Mac—it's the little magnifying glass.

# CONTROL CENTER

If you have other Apple devices, then you might notice that things on the Mac look a little familiar. That's on purpose. Each update, Macs add new features that resemble what you find on iPhones and iPads. It helps make the experience more friction-free, which makes it easier to get things up and running.

This is especially true with the Control Center, which is on the top menu right next to the Siri icon. Clicking on it will bring up a series of options. This is where you can change the Wi-Fi, mirror your screen, and more.

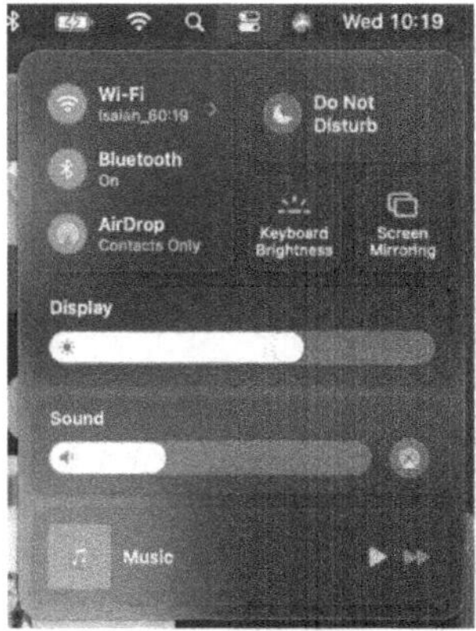

It may not look like a lot of options, but each control has subcontrols. Just click on the arrow next to it.

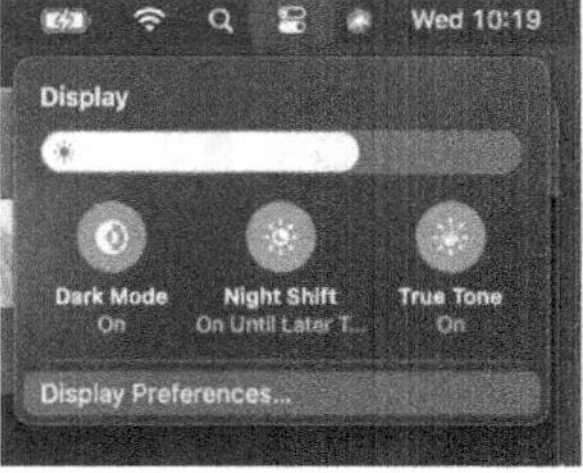

# DOCK

Windows has a taskbar on the bottom of the screen, and Mac has a Dock; the Dock is where all your commonly used applications are.

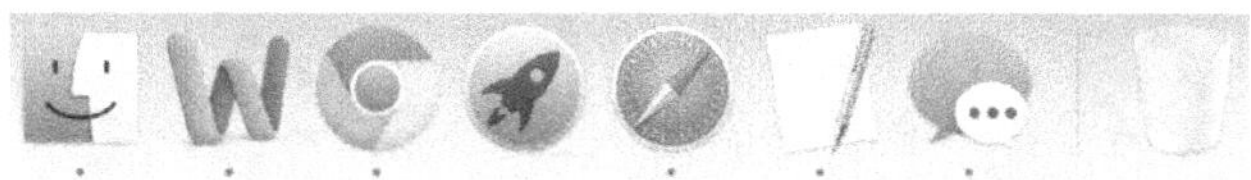

If you see a little dot under the icon, then the program is currently open. If you want to close it, then click the icon with two fingers to bring up the options, and then click Quit.

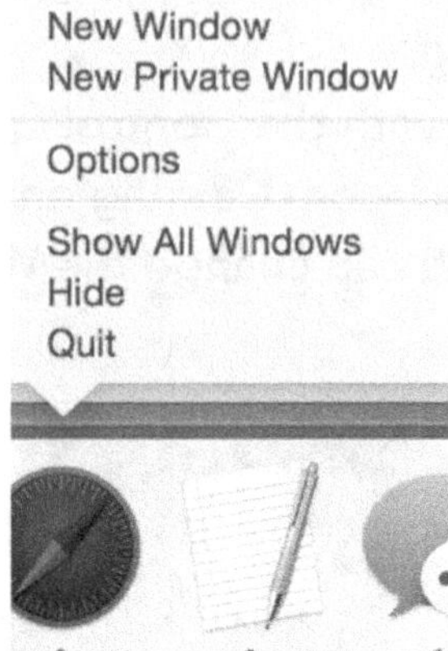


Removing a program from the Dock is pretty simple—just drag the icon to the Trash and let go. This will not remove the program—it only removes the shortcut. Finder, Trash, and Launchpad are the only programs that you cannot remove.

If you want to add a program to the Dock, then open it; when the icon appears on the Dock, click with two fingers, then go to Options and select Keep in Dock.

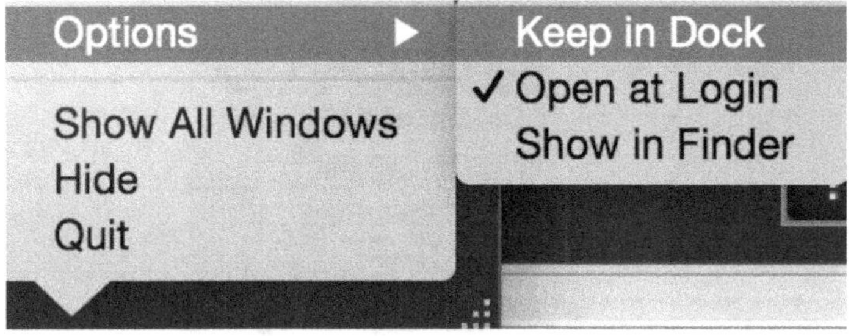

# TRASH

At the right end of the Dock is the Trash. To delete a folder, file or application, drag the item to the Trash, or right-click (two-finger click) the item and select Move to Trash from the pop-up menu. If you want to eject a disk or drive, such as an iPod or USB flash drive, drag the volume into the Trash. As the volume hovers over the Trash, the icon morphs from a trash can to a large eject button. Release the mouse, and your volume will be safely ejected and can be removed from the computer. To empty the Trash, right-click (click with two fingers) on the Trash icon in the Dock, and select Empty Trash.

You can manage the Trash yourself, but I also highly recommend an app called "Clean My Mac" (https://macpaw.com/cleanmymac); it's a little expensive, but when I use it, it normally helps me free up 1GB of storage just by deleting installation files and extensions that I don't need.

# APP BUTTONS

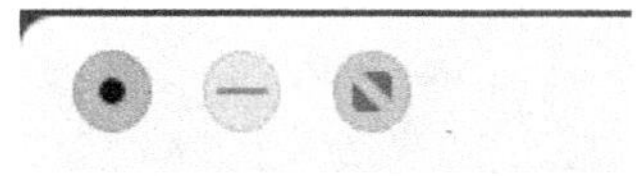

The little lights in the image above have no name. Some people call them traffic lights. You'll start seeing a lot of them because nearly all Mac programs use them. On a Windows, you've seen them as an X and a minus in the upper right of your screen. On a Mac, they appear in the upper left of the running program. The red light means close, the yellow light means minimize, and the green makes the app full screen.

Full screen means the program takes up the entire screen and even the Dock disappears. You can see the Dock and other programs quickly by swiping the Trackpad to the right with four fingers. To get back to the app, swipe with four fingers to your left.

## LAUNCHPAD

Launchpad is essentially the Start menu on a Windows computer. It shows your programs.

When you click it, you'll see rows of programs; you can immediately start typing to search for an app, or you can just look for it. If you have a lot of apps, then you probably have more than one screen. Swipe with two fingers to the left to see the next screen.

Launchpad takes a lot of cues from iPhone and iPad. If you want to remove a program, for example, you do it the same way you remove an iPhone or iPad app. Just click and hold until an X appears above it, then click the X to remove it. Similarly, to rearrange icons, use the same method for rearranging iPhone / iPad apps—click and hold over the icon until it begins to shake, and then move it wherever you want it to go. You can even put programs into groups the same way as an iPhone / iPad—click and hold over the icon, then drag it on top of the app you want to group it with; finally, when the folder appears, you can let go.

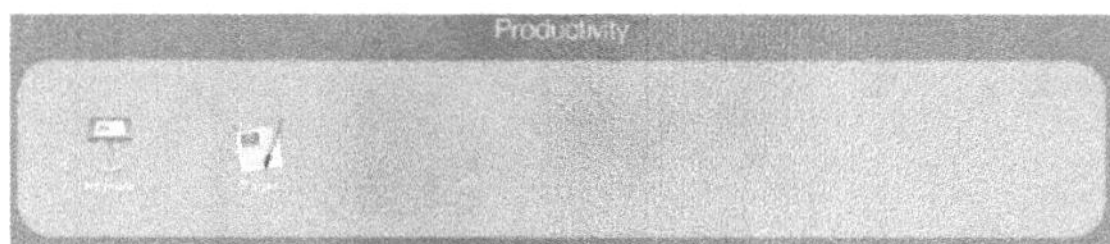

After you delete a program, you can re-download it anytime, by going into the App Store (as long as you downloaded it from the App Store and not from a website).

## NOTIFICATIONS

For the past few updates, Apple has attempted to replicate iOS (iPad / iPhone) features; the move is meant to make using a Mac much like using a mobile device. This attempt at replicating features is especially true with Catalina OS.

Notification was a new feature to OS X Yosemite. You can find it on the top menu button at all times; it's to the far right-hand corner and looks like this:

Click it any time you want to see alerts. You can also access it by swiping with two fingers to the left from the edge of your Trackpad.

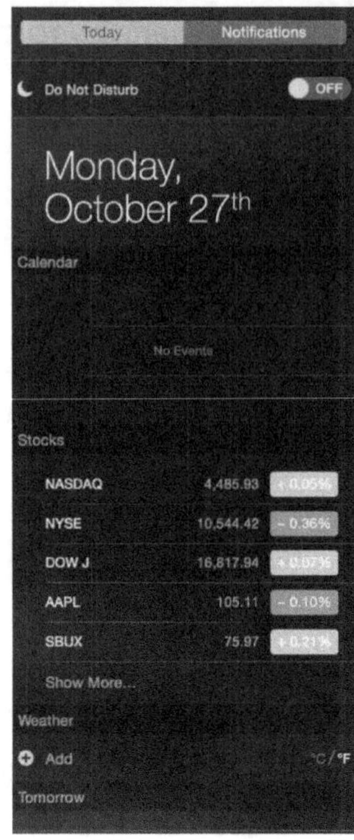

When you swipe down from the top of an iPad or iPhone you will get a similar screen. There are two parts of the Notifications menu: Today and Notifications.

The Today tab is where you'll see things happening more in the moment—what's the weather, what's in your calendar, what's going on with your stocks, etc. The Notifications tab is where you'll see things like Facebook messages or emails. Later in this book, I'll show you how to customize it.

## STAGE MANAGER

Stage manager is a way to multitask between apps. Look at the example below. Notice how there's several windows open in the background? Makes it hard to navigate around doesn't it?

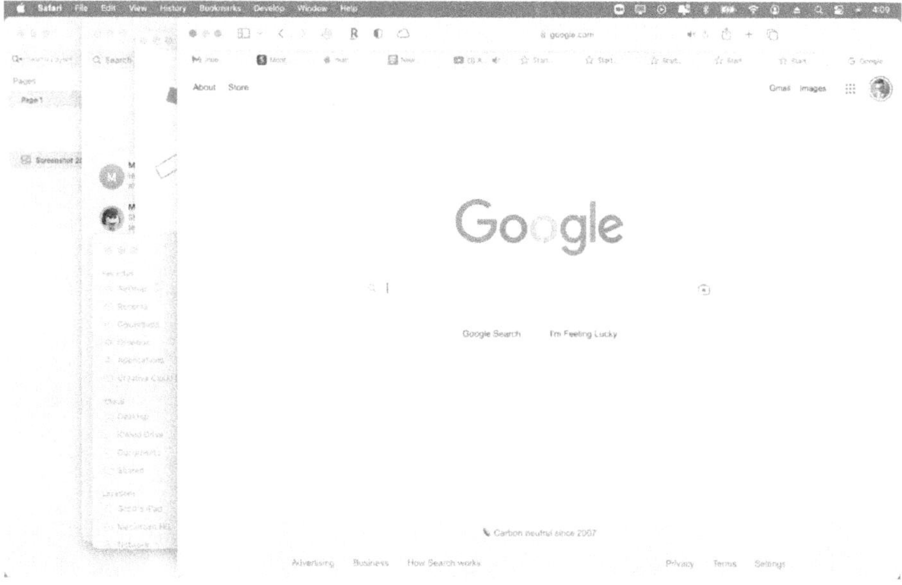

With Stage Manager turned on, it looks like the image below.

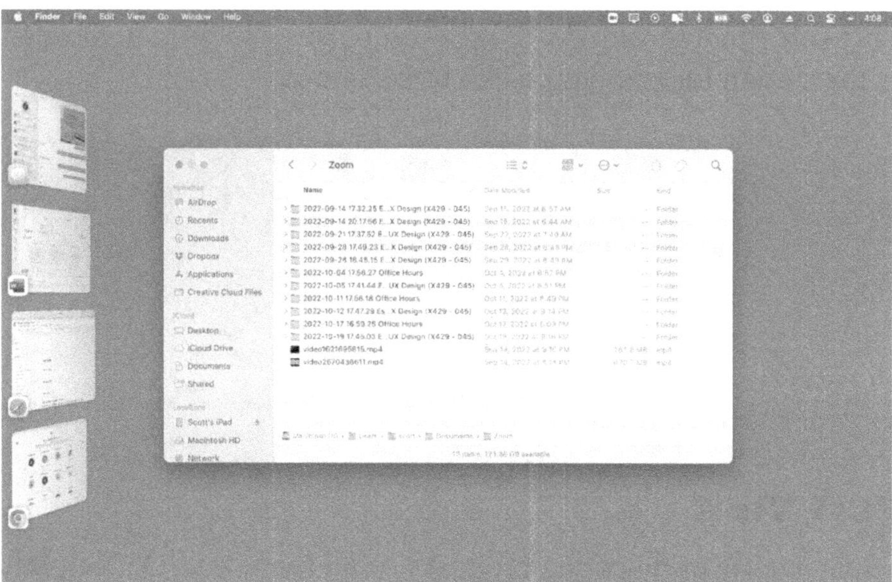

The thumbnails let you quickly toggle between the apps that you have open.

Go to the control center in the upper right corner of your screen to turn it on.

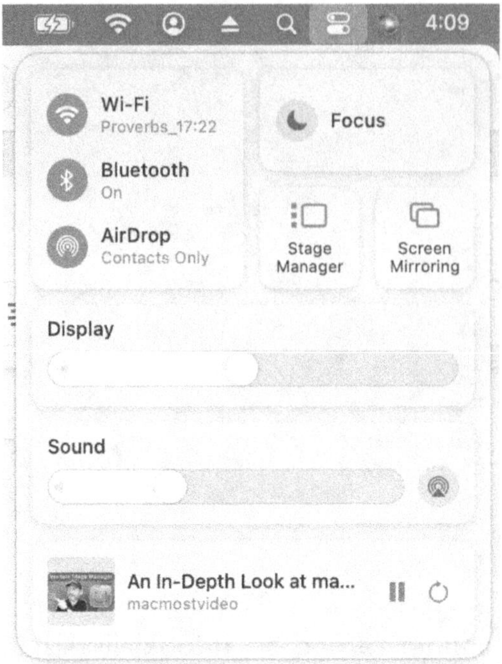

Press it again to turn it off. When you press it again, it will also give you the option for how you'd like to sort apps.

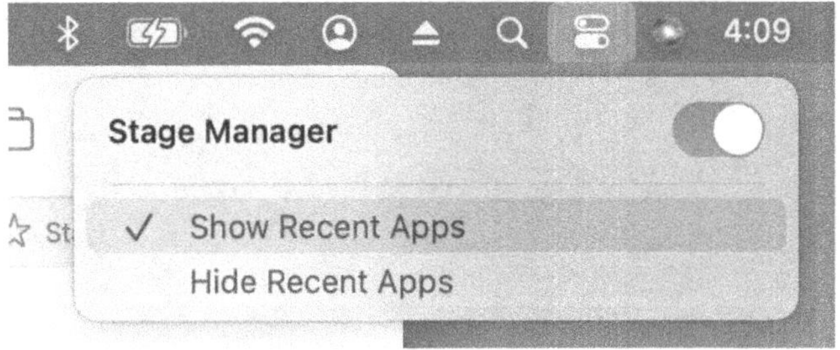

## SPLIT VIEW

Split view is perhaps the biggest added feature to OS X. It lets you run two apps side-by-side—but there's a catch: not all apps are compatible. So if you're scratching your head because this feature won't work for you, then chances are it's not that you are doing it wrong—it's that the app doesn't support the feature.

There are two ways to get the split view to work. Let's look at both of them. First, make sure the two apps that you want to run side-by-side are not running in full screen mode.

Method 1

Click and hold the green button in the upper left corner of your app.

A transparent blue box will appear; drag and drop the app into it (by default, the blue is on the left side, but if you drag to the right side, it will also turn blue and you can drop it in).

Next, click the program you want to use side-by-side.

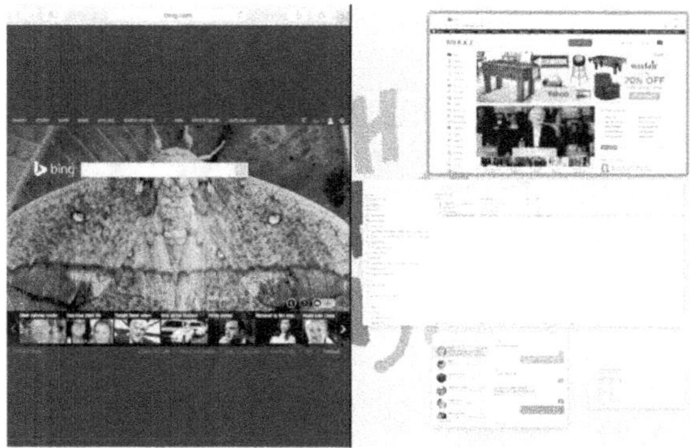

A side-by-side window now appears; you can use the middle black line to make one bigger or smaller, by dragging left or right.

To return to the normal view, click the green button in the upper left corner of the app once more (you can also hit the ESC key on your keyboard).

Method 2

As you are probably noticing, most things in OS X can happen by several different methods; side-by-side view has two. The second way to get apps is to open your Mission Control, and drag the app to the top menu.

You'll notice, a grey box appears and the box appears to split.

Once you drop the app into that box, you'll see a side-by-side preview. Once you click the preview, it will maximize.

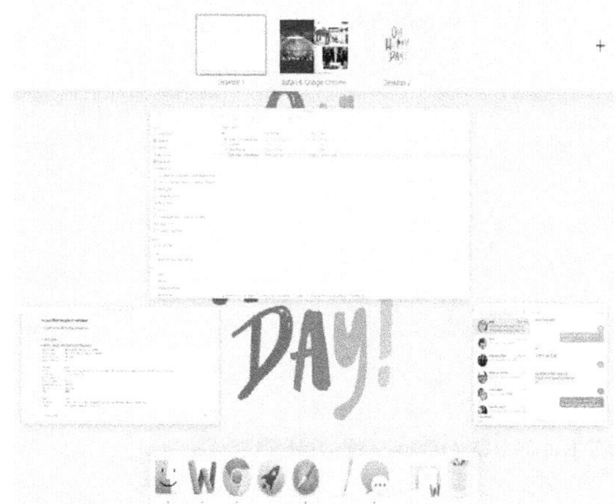

Returning to the non-split screen is done the same way as Method 1 (click the green box in the upper left corner or hit the ESC key on the keyboard).

## TABBED SOFTWARE

If you've ever used Tabs on Internet Explorer or Chrome, then this next feature might interest you. It allows you to open documents (such as Maps and Pages) with tab viewing. Note: not all Mac apps support this feature.

To use it, open two windows of the same app. I'll use Maps in the example below.

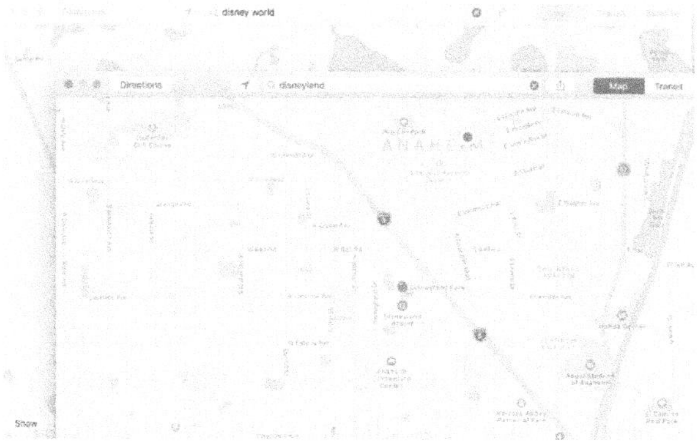

Next, go to Window and Merge All Windows.

Your windows should now be merged.

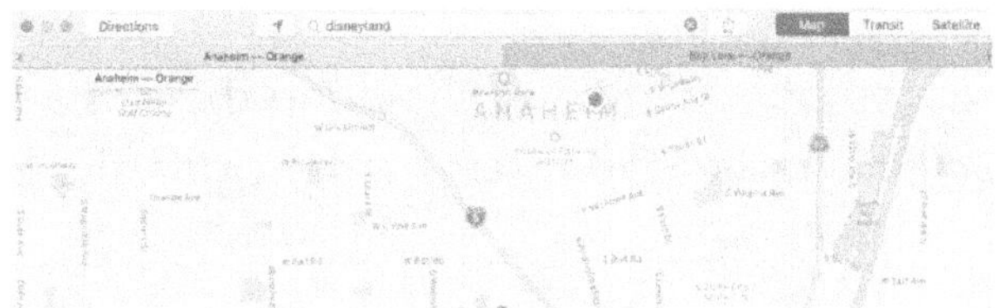

## PICTURE-IN-PICTURE VIDEO

If you'd like to watch a video while you work, then you're in luck! If you already own the video (a video you purchased on iTunes, for example), then just start playing the video and go to View and Float on Top.

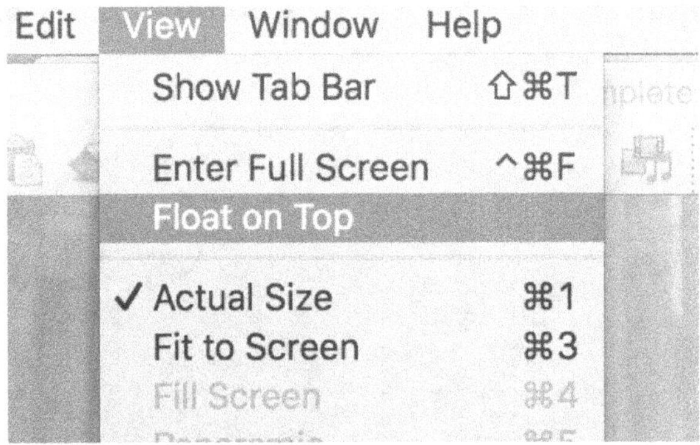

But what about Web videos? Such as Vimeo and YouTube? That's easy too. Just double-click the video you are watching, and select Enter Picture-In-Picture.

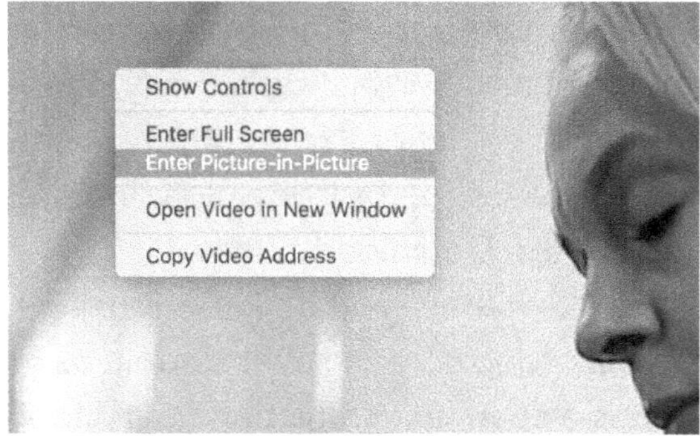


Your video will immediately begin playing above other windows.

## SCREEN SAVERS

If your as old as me, you might remember the old Window's screen savers—floating toasters that went across your screen. Maybe you even loved them so much that you went into CompUSA or Fry's Electronics and bought a floppy disk that had even more screen savers. And if you are not old enough, you are probably reading this saying, "Wait, you actually paid money for screen savers?"

macOS blows those floating toasters off your screen, and over the moon! Gone are the days of photos or 8 bit graphics as screen savers; macOS incorporates something far more visually stunning.

macOS offers a variety of video screen savers, including breathtaking views of landscapes and underwater scenes.

The overall effect is subtle yet impressive, and the best part? Setting it up is a breeze, taking just a few minutes. Here's a step-by-step guide to help you:

Step 1: Open the System Settings app on your Mac and select Screen Saver from the sidebar.

Step 2: Explore four categories of video screen savers: Landscape, Cityscape, Underwater, and Earth. Additionally, there's a Shuffle Aerials group that combines selections from different categories. Click on your preferred screen saver to start downloading. If it doesn't start automatically, simply hit the Download button.

Step 3: After the download, you have options! Switch on 'Show as wallpaper' to let your video screen saver double as your desktop background. This enables a seamless transition from video to static image. If you prefer keeping your existing wallpaper while enjoying the video screen saver, leave this option disabled.

Another feature, 'Show on all Spaces', applies your chosen settings across all your desktop Spaces. Choosing a shuffle option? Decide how frequently you'd like the screen saver to switch between different videos.

Step 4: There's more! Navigate to Wallpaper in the System Settings sidebar. Here, you can set a wallpaper from a video screen saver even without activating the screen saver feature. Choose from the categories mentioned in Step 2 and pair it with a video screen saver if you desire.

Step 5: The vibrant images from video screen savers aren't limited to your desktop; they can adorn your Mac's Lock Screen too! If your wallpaper is selected from a video screen saver category, it animates on your Lock Screen and smoothly transitions to a static image upon logging in. This applies whether both your wallpaper and screen saver are from a video set, or just the wallpaper. If you choose a different image for your wallpaper, the Lock Screen will display your regular desktop background without animation.

## WIDGETS

you're a new Mac user, you might be delighted to discover how you can personalize your desktop with widgets. Widgets are handy little tools that provide quick access to information and functionalities. Here's a straightforward guide on how to add them to your desktop in macOS:

Step 1: Start by right-clicking on any empty space on your desktop. This will open a contextual menu.

Step 2: From the menu, select the option labeled "Edit Widgets." This will lead you to a new interface.

Step 3: Once you've clicked "Edit Widgets," a window will appear at the bottom of your screen, displaying a list of available apps. Here, you can browse through various apps and explore the different widgets they offer.

Step 4: When you select an app, you'll see several boxes to its right, representing different widget types. Each widget serves a unique purpose, offering various functionalities or pieces of information. Feel free to explore and see which ones suit your needs!

Step 5: After browsing, it's time to make your selection. Simply click and drag your chosen widget from the window to your desktop. Place it wherever you like; it will stay there once you release the click.

# [4]

# WHERE IS…

One of the greatest things about Mac is how easy it is to find things. Sure, Windows has a search, but it feels clunky and doesn't always work the way you expect. I'll cover how to find things in this chapter.

## FINDER

The first icon on your Dock—one of three that cannot be deleted or moved—is the Finder icon.

Finder is the Mac equivalent of Explorer on a Windows computer; as the name implies, it finds things. Finder is pretty resourceful and powerful so this section will be a little longer than others because there's a lot you can do with it.

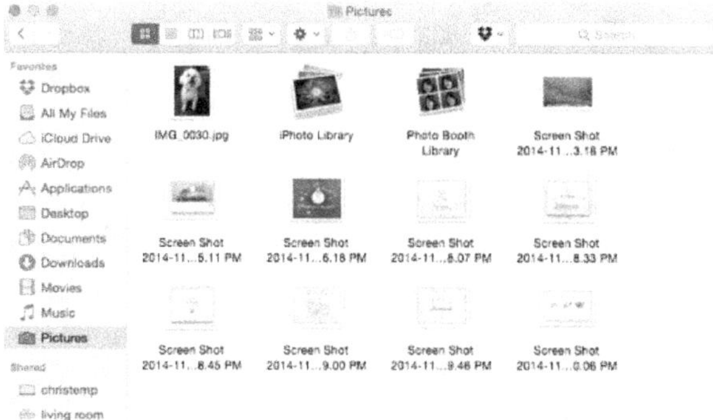

Let's get started by clicking on the Finder icon.

# FINDER REIMAGINED

Finder is how you find things on a Mac—clever name, right? Like a lot of things in MacOS, there are similarities between how it works on Mac and iPhone. Mojave added a few new features still present in Catalina you should know about, however.

*Gallery View*

There are several different types of views in Finder (where you find things—like File Explorer in Windows). Examples of views are: list, columns, and icons. Gallery view was a new view in Mojave that you still see in Catalina.

Gallery view displays a large preview of the file with thumbnails of everything else in the directory below it. And by "preview" this isn't just for images where you can see what the image looks like—this works across all kinds of docs. If it's a PDF, for example, you can see a preview of the PDF.

To the right of the file, there's a side panel that will tell you the more detailed metadata for the file.

*Quick Actions*

Apple is all about efficiency; to be more efficient, it helps to be able to do things a little quicker. That's where Quick Actions help. With Quick Actions, you can, for example, change the orientation of a file or add password protection. The actions available depend on the type of file.

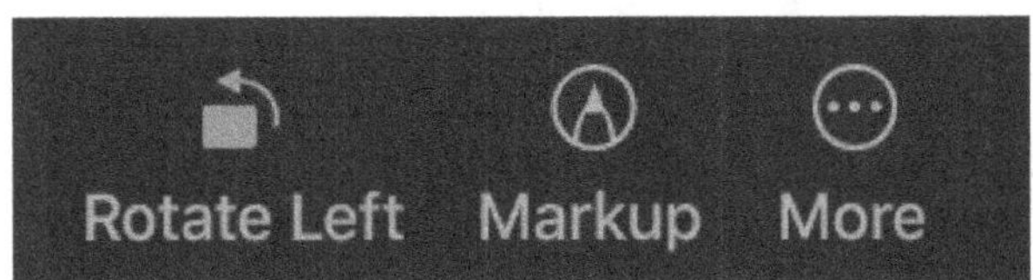


## OTHER VIEWS

There are four other ways to view folders on your Mac—icons, lists, columns, and Cover Flow. Different views make sense for different file types, and you can change the view using the View Options icons (pictured below).

*Cover Flow View*

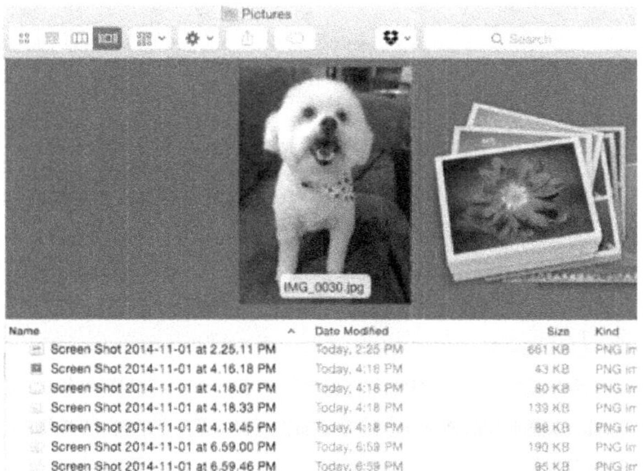

Cover Flow lets you quickly go through thumbnails / previews of photos (it's a little like Film Strip in Windows); you can also sort any of the columns by clicking on the header—so if you are looking for a larger file, then click the Size column, or if you are looking for a recent file, then pick the Date Modified column.

*Icon View*

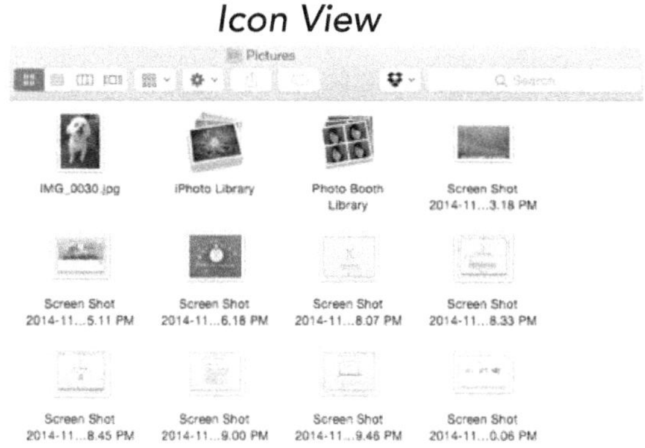

Icon View can help if you need to sort through several image files or applications. It gives you either a thumbnail of each picture or an icon for each file or app.

*List View*

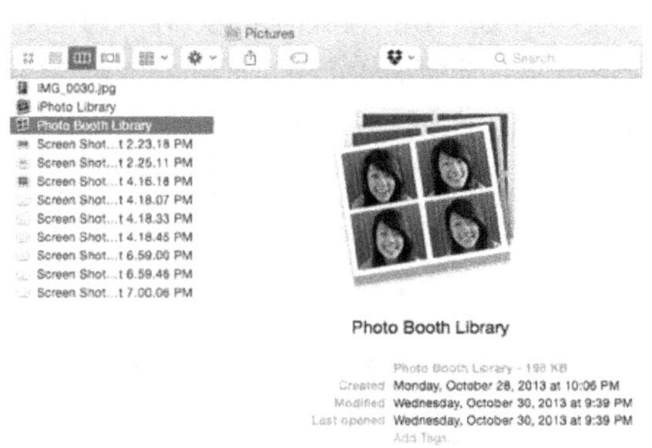

List View, on the other hand, gives you more information about the file, including the date it was last modified. This is the perfect view for sorting.

## Column View

Finally, Column View which is kind of a hybrid of List View and Cover Flow View. It shows the folder hierarchy a file is located in. Notice that Finder doesn't include the Windows "go up one level" button—Column View is a good way to get the same results and navigate easily through your file structure.

## SORTING IN FINDER

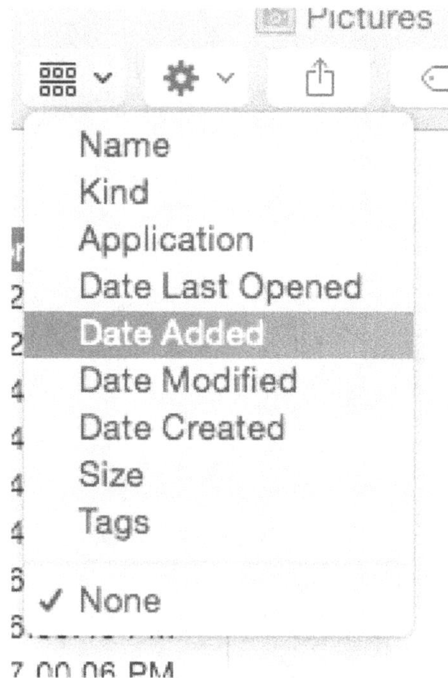

Finder gives you a number of ways to sort your files and folders. You can sort by name, type, the application required for opening the file (like Microsoft Word, for example), the date the file was created, modified, or opened, the file size, and any tags you may have applied.

## FILE MANAGEMENT

Most file management tasks in OS X are similar to Windows. Files can be dragged and dropped, copied, cut and pasted. If you need to create a new folder, use the Gear icon in Finder, which will give you the option you need.

Catalina also allows you to batch rename files (i.e. rename several files at once instead of one at a time), potentially saving you hours of time, depending on your file system. To take advantage of this, select the files you'd like to rename (hint: use Command-click to select multiple files, or use Command-A to select everything). Then right-click (two-finger click) the selected files and choose "Rename X Items."

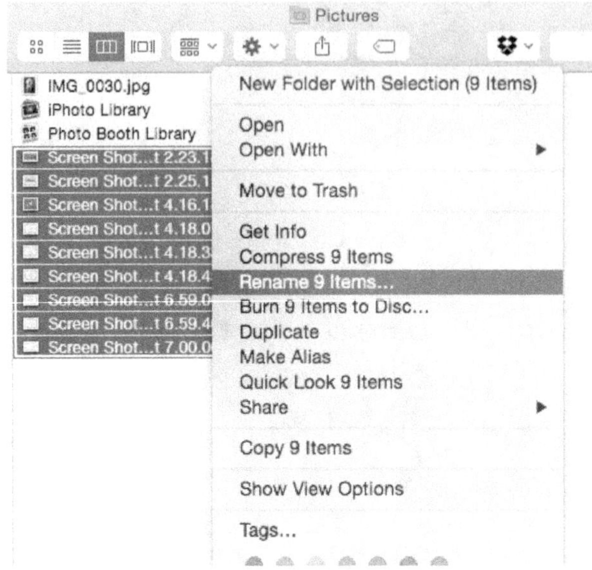

You'll then have the option to replace text or to add text to the file names.

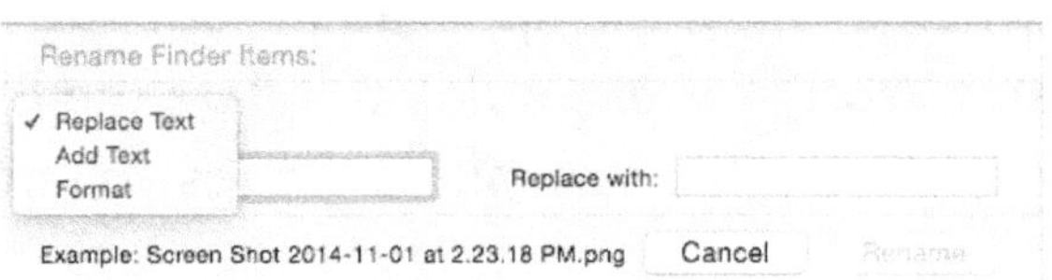

## FAVORITES

If you look on the left side of the Finder Window, you'll see a Favorites sidebar. This section includes high-frequency folders, like Documents, Pictures, Downloads, and more.

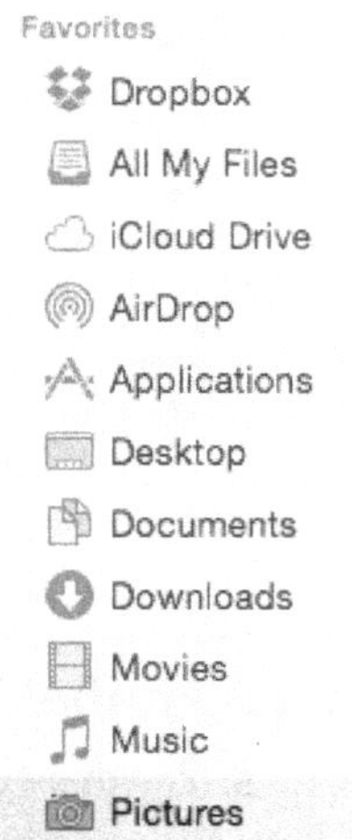

To add an application or file to your Favorites menu, just drag it over to the Favorites area and drop it. To remove an item from Favorites, right-click it (click with two fingers) and select Remove From Sidebar.

## TABBED BROWSING

Apple took a page from Internet browsers by adding something called "Tabbed Browsing" to Finder. Basically, instead of having several Finder boxes open (which is how you had to do it in older OSes) you open tabs. To open an additional Finder tab, press Command-T or click File and New Tab.

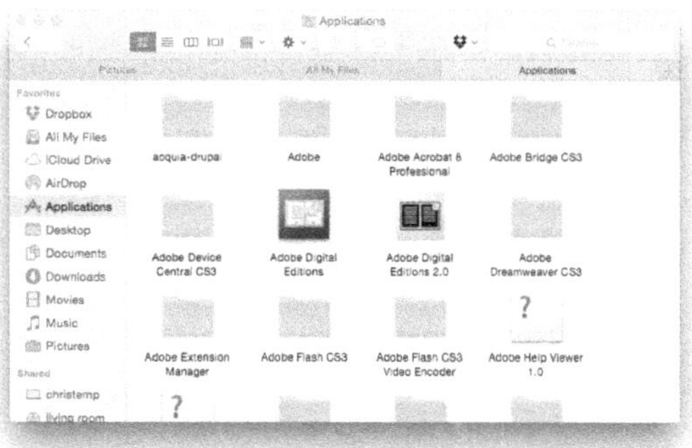

If you want to merge all of your tabbed windows, just click Windows in the file menu on the top of your screen, and then Merge All Windows.

## TAGS

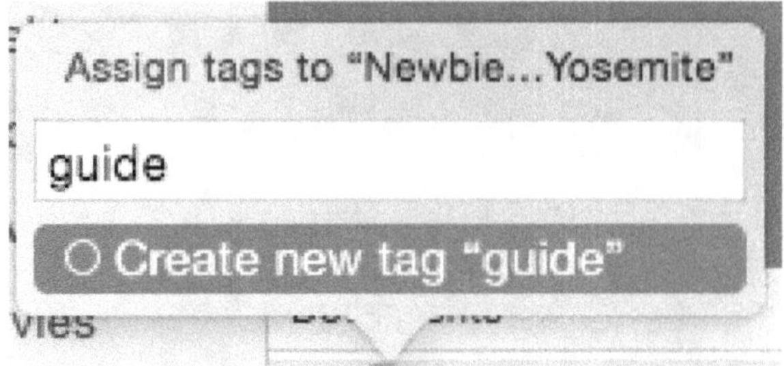


If you use photo apps like Flickr, then you probably know all about tagging; it's essentially adding subjects to your file to make it easier to find. Let's say the file is regarding the 2015 tax year—you can add a tag to the file called "2015 Taxes" or whatever you want it to be. You can also color code it.

To assign a tag to a file (you can also assign it to a folder), click the file / folder with two fingers, and then click tags; if this is your first tag just type it in and hit Enter; if you've already tagged a file and want to use the same name, then click the name of the tag as it appears.

# [5]

# How To Do Things

This chapter will cover:
- Setting up Internet
- Browsing with Safari
- Setting up and sending email

The Mac is a beautiful machine, but you can only admire that desktop for so long; eventually, you'll want to get on the Internet—how else will you get your daily dose of cat memes or keep in touch with the Nigerian prince trying to give you money? I'll show you how in this chapter.

There are two methods: Ethernet (i.e. plugging in a LAN cable to your computer) and Wireless.

## SETTING UP WITH ETHERNET

All new Mac computers are set up with Wi-Fi; iMacs also have Ethernet ports to plug in a network cable. This option isn't available on any of the Mac laptops—though you can buy an adapter if you absolutely must have it.

If you have a basic Internet modem, then set up is pretty easy. Just plug a network cable into your Internet hub, and plug the other end into your Mac. Once it's plugged in, the Internet should work.

Newer Macs come with top of the line wireless radios for Wi-Fi, so you should be perfectly fine without using the Ethernet port.

## SETTING UP WIRELESS NETWORKS

Setting up a wireless connection is also pretty simple. Just click the Wi-Fi menu on the menu bar. It looks like the image below and is near the upper right corner:

As long as there's a wireless network in range, it will show up when you click it (sometimes it does take a few seconds to appear).

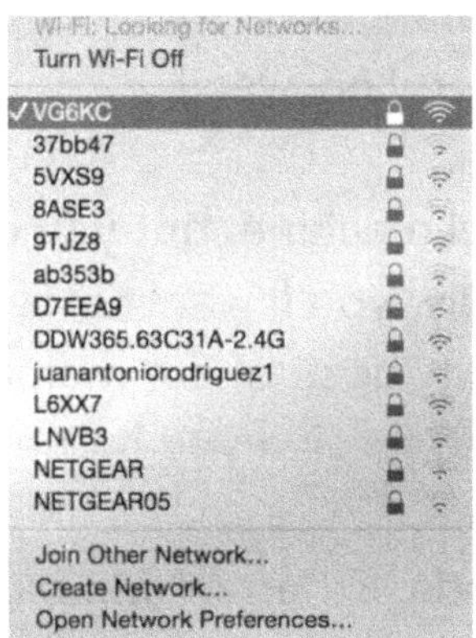

If there's a lock next to the Wi-Fi name, then you'll need to know the passcode (if it's a home Internet connection, then it's usually on the bottom of your Internet modem; if it's at a business, then you'll have to ask for the code. If there's no lock, then it's an open network. You usually see this kind of network at places like Starbucks.

If it's a locked network, then as soon as you click on it, it will ask for the code; once it's entered and you click Connect, then you're connected (assuming you added it right); if it's not locked then once you click on it, it will attempt to connect.

# SAFARI

If you've used Safari before, it's probably going to look a little different for you. In 2021, Apple gave Safari a facelift to make it even more resourceful. It's great on the MacOS, but even better when you have an entire ecosystem of devices (i.e. iPad and iPhone).

Let's dig into the anatomy of the browser, then I'll break down how it works.

The top toolbar looks pretty bare. Looks can be deceiving because there's a lot here. Starting on the far left is the side menu button, which brings up your Saved Tabs (more on that later), private viewing mode, history and more; the middle is where you can either type or search for the website (the microphone lets you say it instead of type it), and finally the Plus button lets you open a new tab.

Tabs don't look like tabs in MacOS. In the example below, there are three opened tabs. The middle one is the opened website, the smaller two (Start Page and Amazon) are the opened, non-active, tabs.



There are a few ways to close a tab. One is to tap the X next to the website name (this is only on the active tab); the other way is right-clicking on the tab, then selecting to close the tab.

When you click and hold over the Plus button, you'll see a list of recently closed tabs that you can open again.

If you need to open a private tab (meaning a tab window that doesn't keep track of your passwords or history—it's great for gift shopping if you share a device), then go to File>New Private Window.

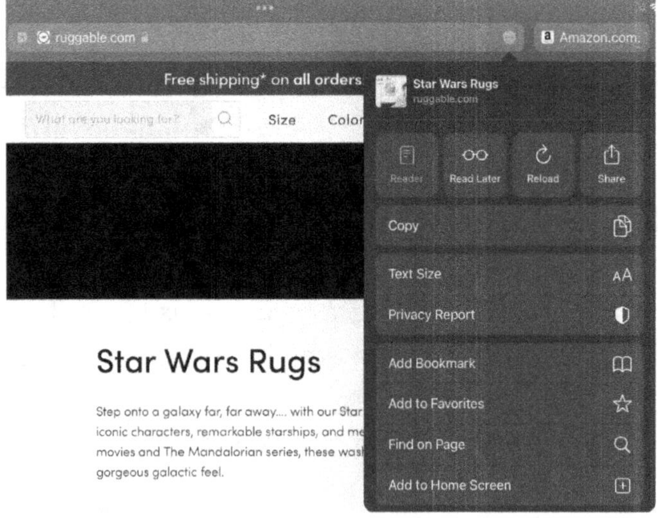


## WEBSITE OPTIONS

When you click the three dots on the page you are currently visiting, you'll get several more options. This is where you'll go if you want to add the page to your Bookmark or add it to your Favorites (Favorites show up whenever you start Safari when it's been closed—it's known as your "Start Page." You can also share the page with someone, change the text size, and see a Privacy Report. Privacy Report shows all the trackers on a page, so you know what information a company is collecting about you.

## MENU OPTIONS

On the far left side is the option to bring up the menu pane. The menu can be shown as you browse, or you can collapse it once you pull up what you are looking for.

There are a few things you can do here. First is Group Tabs; there's a lot to Group Tabs, so I'll go over it in the next section. Start Page is your homepage; Private turns your browser into a private web surfing experiences where your web history and passwords aren't saved.

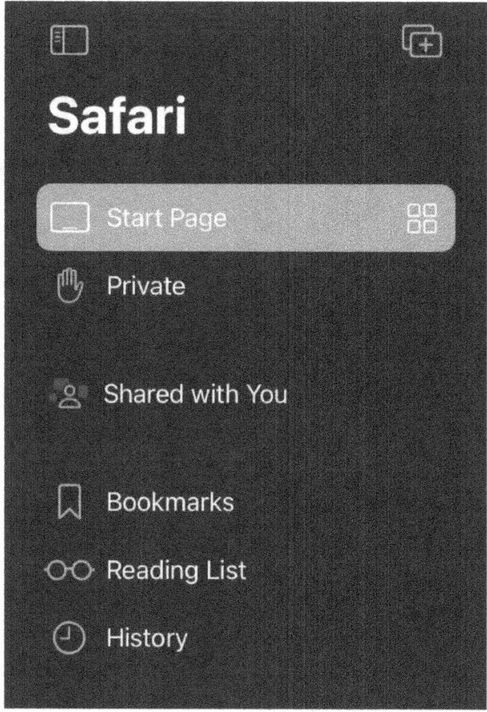

## SHARED WITH YOU

Shared With You is where you'll see things that have been shared recently. As an example: my wife and I share a lot of links through text. When she sends one, they'll automatically show up here. That way, I don't have to search through dozens of texts to find the page she mentioned—it's already been saved.

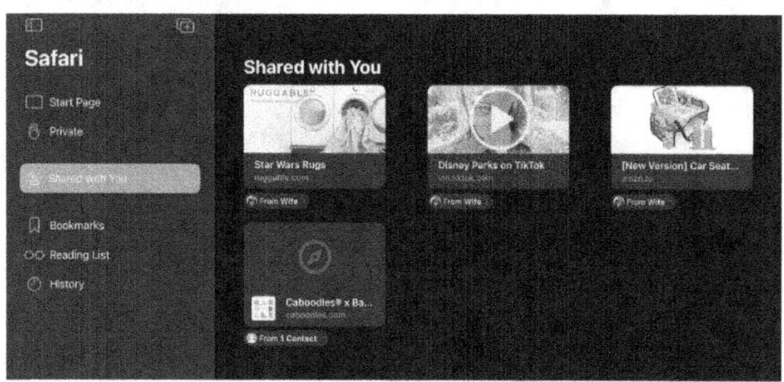

If you want to remove the link, then tap and hold your finger on the page preview. This brings up several options—one is remove. You can also use the options here to reply to the message, open in the background or copy the link.

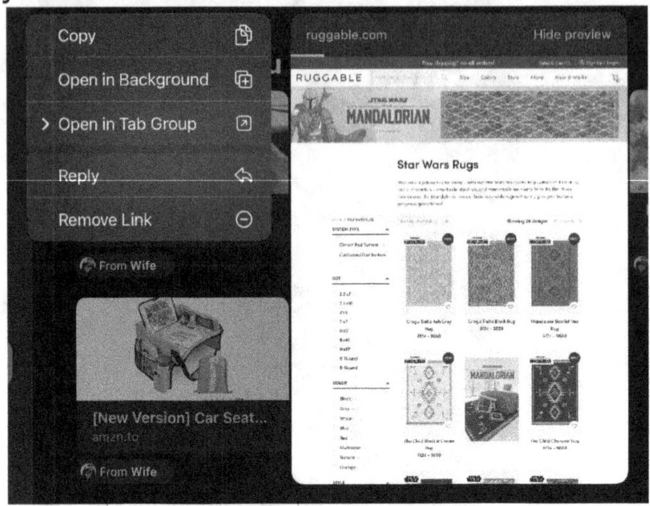

## SAFARI BOOKMARKS

Below Shared With You are the Bookmarks; Bookmarks are pages you save because you regularly go to them. When you start getting a lot of Bookmarks, it's a good idea to put them into organized folders.

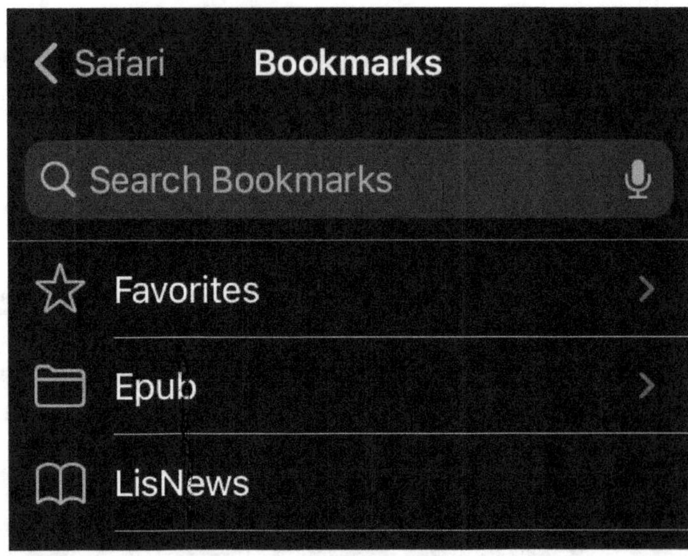

To create a folder, just go to the bottom of the page to Edit, then select New Folder. When you have selected Edit, you can also delete Bookmarks and move them into folders.

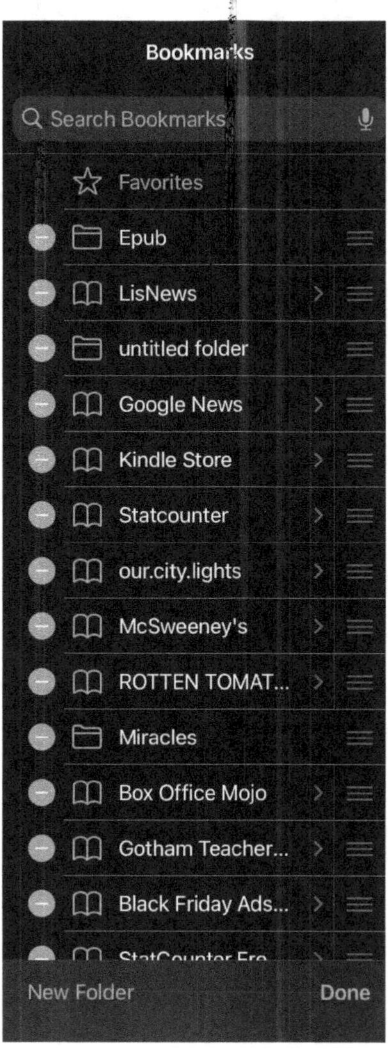



You can put folders into folders when you create them.

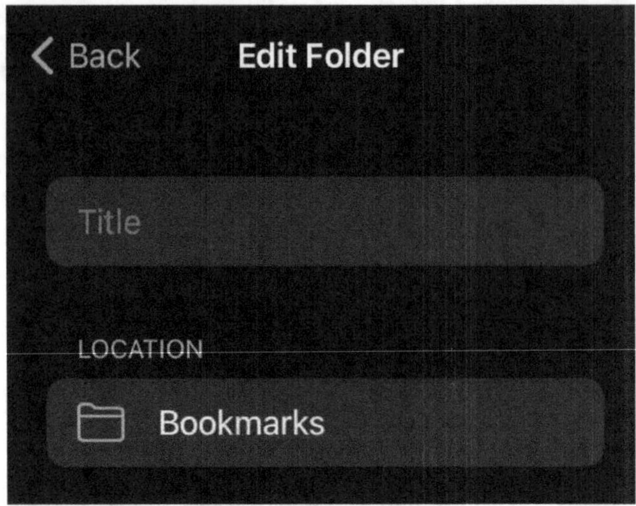


### WEB HISTORY

If you are not using Private mode, then all your history is saved; this is helpful if you ever forget a website you went to, but you know what day you went to it. If you ever want to clear your history, just tap the Clear option at the bottom of the page when you are viewing your history.

## TAB GROUP

Tabs can be your best friend. Tab Group is the evolution of this friend. Tab Groups are kind of a combination of bookmarks and tabs. You basically save all your tabs into a group. So, for example, you can have a group called "Shopping" and when you click it, like magic, all your favorite shopping websites open into tabs.

To get started, open all the tabs that you want to be in your group, then go to the left menu, and click on the + button from the side menu and select New Empty Tab Group.

Type in the name of your group. Remember to be descriptive, so you know what your Tab Group is for.

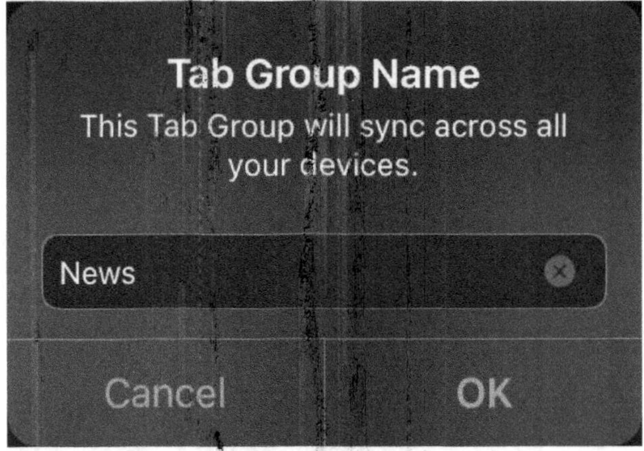


All the tabs are now saved in your group; in the example below, there are two tab groups; when I toggle between them, new tabs will open.

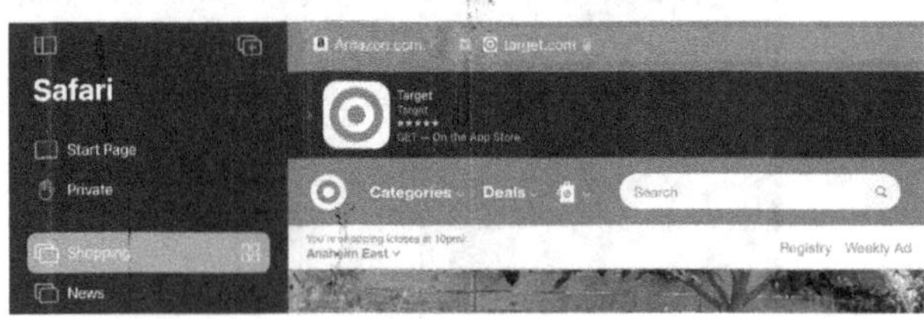


You can make changes to your group by tapping and holding on it.

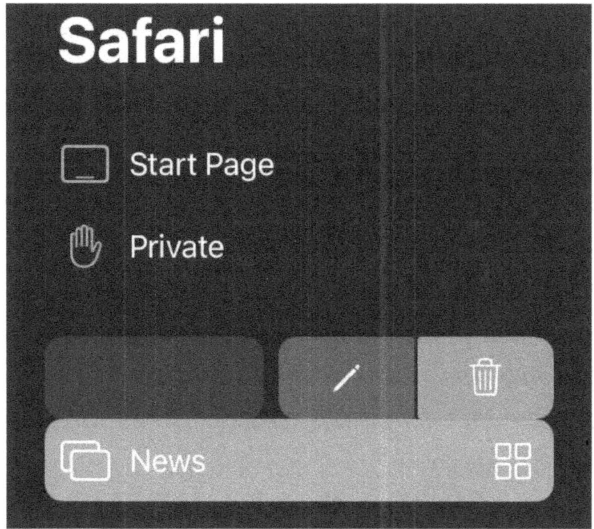



If you want a new tab to show there, just open up the tab while in that group and it will automatically be saved in the group.

## SAFARI PROFILES

Proiles is the evolution of Safari. This handy feature, available from Safari 17 onwards, allows you to have separate browsing experiences for different topics like work, school, or personal stuff. Each profile comes with its own history, cookies, website data, extensions, Tab Groups, and favorites. Here's how you can manage it all:

*Creating a Profile*

1. Open Safari and go to the menu bar, select Safari > Create Profile or Safari > Settings, then click Profiles.

2. Click "Start Using Profiles" and set up your new profile by giving it a name, choosing a symbol, picking a color, and managing your favorites. Then, click "Create Profile".

3. That's it! Safari opens new windows and new tabs to your start page by default.

*Switching Between Profiles*

After creating a profile, a button shows up in the Safari toolbar indicating your current profile. Clicking this button lets you either open a new window in that profile or switch to another profile without open-ing a new window. Neat, right?

### *Customizing & Managing Profiles*

Some Safari features are shared between profiles, while others are not. For example, browsing history and cookies are kept separate, but AutoFill and Passwords are shared.

You can rename a profile anytime by going to Safari > Manage Pro-files, selecting a profile, and typing a new name in the Name field.

Safari extensions are available to all profiles, but you can manage them separately for each.

### *Syncing Profiles Between Devices*

Your profiles will automatically sync across all your devices using the same Apple ID and having Safari turned on in iCloud settings. Handy for those of us with multiple Apple devices!

### *Opening Links with Profiles*

You can set links from specific websites to open in a designated profile. Just visit the website, go to Safari > Settings > Websites, select "Open Links With Profiles", and choose the profile you want from the pop-up menu next to the website.

### *Deleting a Profile*

Decided you no longer need a profile? Go to Safari > Manage Pro-files, select the profile, and hit the Delete button. But remember, you can't delete your default profile!

## WEB APPS

Diving into macOS, you'll find a cool feature that lets you create web apps from your favorite websites using Safari. These web apps can hang out in your Dock just like your other apps. For instance, let's see how we can turn Google.com into a nifty Mac app!

*Turning a Website into a Web App*

1. Open Safari and go to the website you want–so Google in this example.

2. Go to the menu bar, select File -> Add to Dock.

3. Want a different icon or name? You can change them before clicking the blue 'Add' button.

The web app lets you roam around within the host website, but clicking a link to a different host opens it in Safari.

No longer want it? Just drag it to your trash.

*Logins, Notifications, and Privacy*

When you create a web app, Safari ensures you stay logged in by copying the website's cookies. Apple has also integrated Password and Passkey AutoFill for easy logins. If the website has web push notifications, you'll get them in your web app, complete with the website's icon for context. These notifications and their sounds are manageable in System Settings -> Notifications.

Worried about distractions? Web apps respect Focus modes, letting you manage notifications based on your activity. And for the privacy-conscious, macOS lets you control a web app's access to your camera, microphone, and location in System Settings -> Privacy & Security, just like with native apps.

# MAIL

Mail is the Mac equivalent of Outlook; like Safari, it works in a very similar way to iPad and iPhone. Apple will provide you with a free email address that ends @icloud.com, but you can also add normal email into the application (like Hotmail, Yahoo, and Gmail).

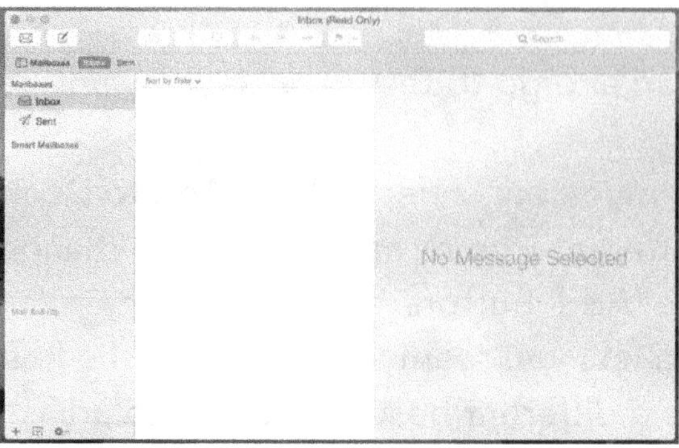

## ADDING ACCOUNTS

To get started, you need to add your email account. Locate the Mail app by clicking on Launchpad, and then clicking the Mail app icon.

Once the app opens, go to the top menu bar and click Mail > Add Account. This will load the Add Account dialogue box.

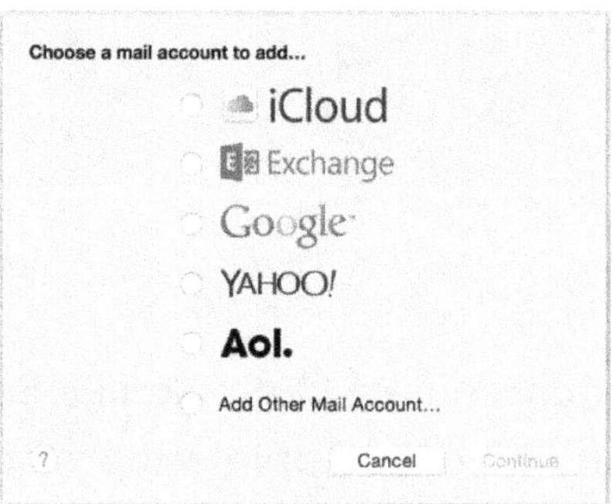


Select the provider that you will be adding in (Note: you can go back and add as many accounts as you want) and click Continue. Next, you'll be asked what your Name, Email Address, and Password are.

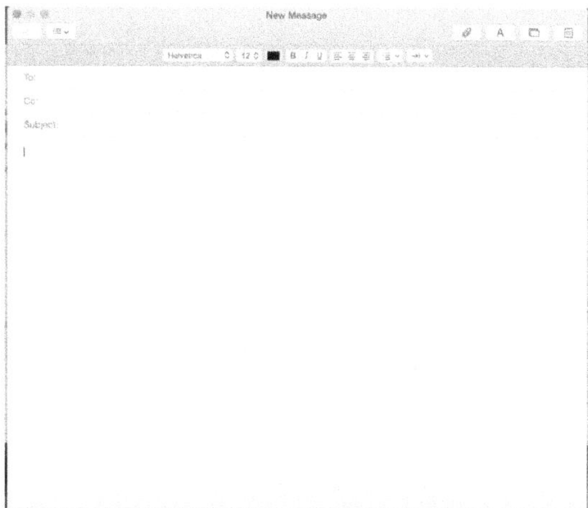

If you are using a popular email provider, set up is pretty self-explanatory. If you are using a business email, then you will probably need to work with your system administrator to get it added in correctly.

Once it's set up, you should start seeing mail show up on your computer.

## SENDING AN EMAIL

Now that you have an account added, you can start sending mail; to send mail you can either press Command-N on your keyboard, go to the top menu and select File and New Message, or click the Compose icon (it looks like a pencil going through a square).

The New Message dialogue box will appear. In the To field, enter the email address or addresses that you'd like to send a message to, add in a subject and message, and then hit the paper airplane in the upper left corner when you are ready to send the message.

You can also add formatting to the message by clicking on the "A" button. Formatting is very basic—you can bold, add italics, underline, and change the coloring.

## FOCUS

Computers can distract us from things we need to be doing. To help you, there is a Focus mode. To access it, click the control panel in the upper right corner of the screen, then click Focus.

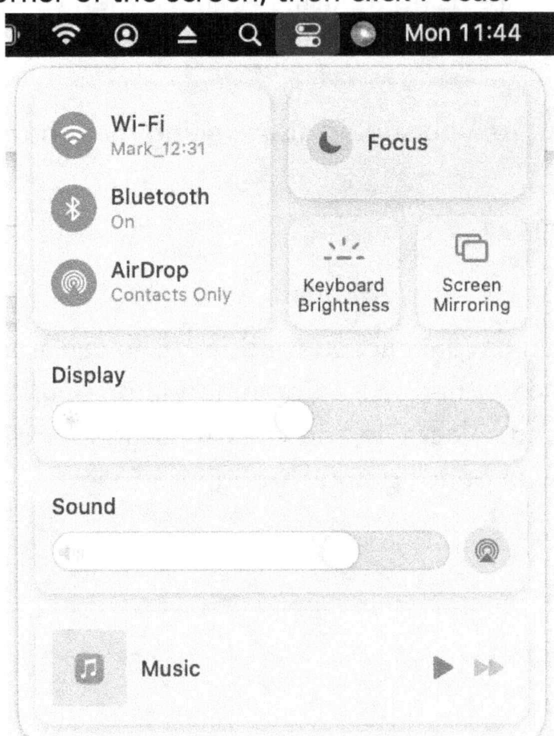

There are several different Focus modes—each with different settings. Some will send you notifications, but not calls, for example.

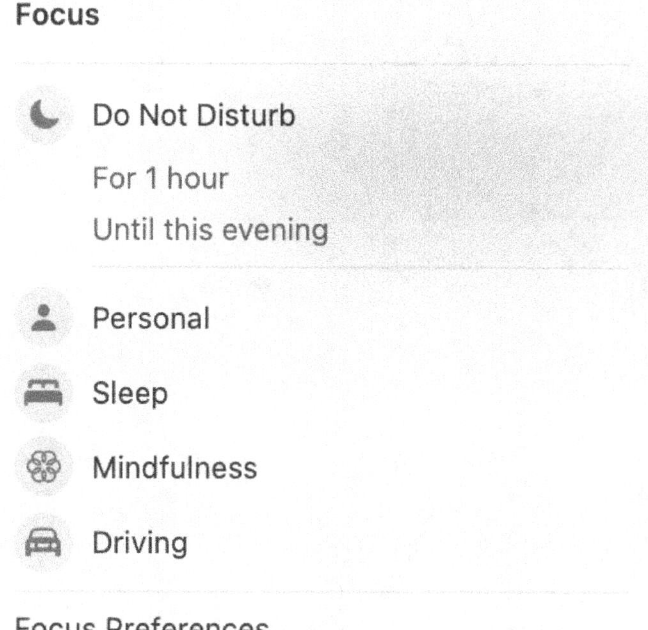

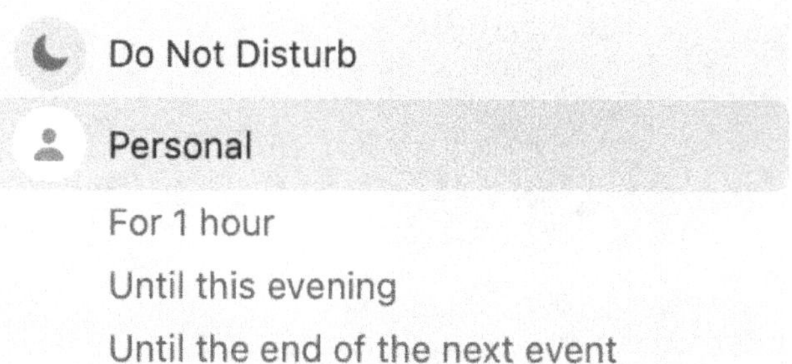

When you click on your Focus, you can select how long you want it on for.

If you click the last option, Focus Preference, you can see information about what each Focus includes—if, for example, it allows messages from certain users. You can make adjustments appropriately—clicking on the + icon will let you add people and times, for example.

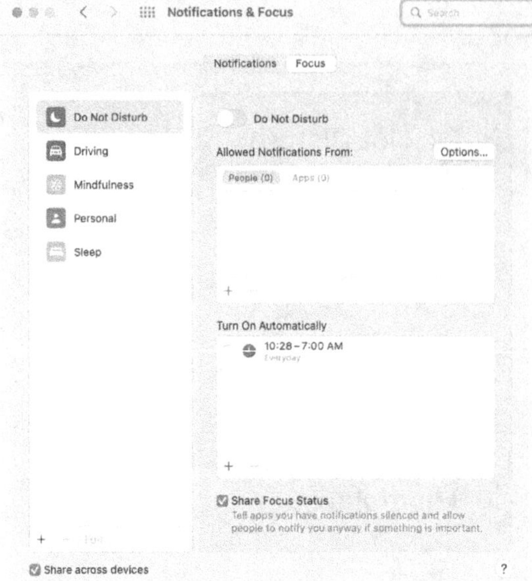

You can add a new Focus by clicking the + icon in the lower left corner of the Focus Preference box.

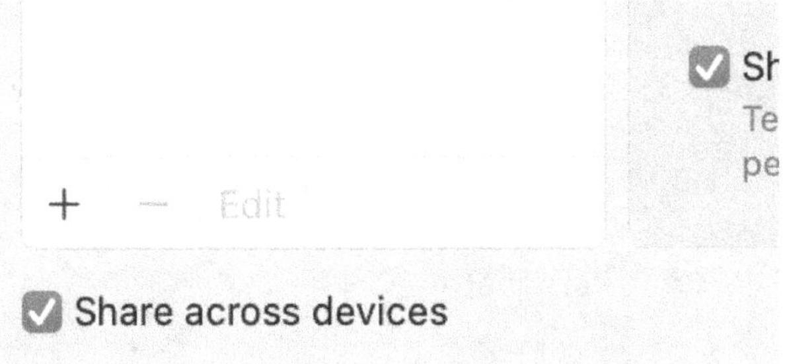


Click the custom option when prompted.

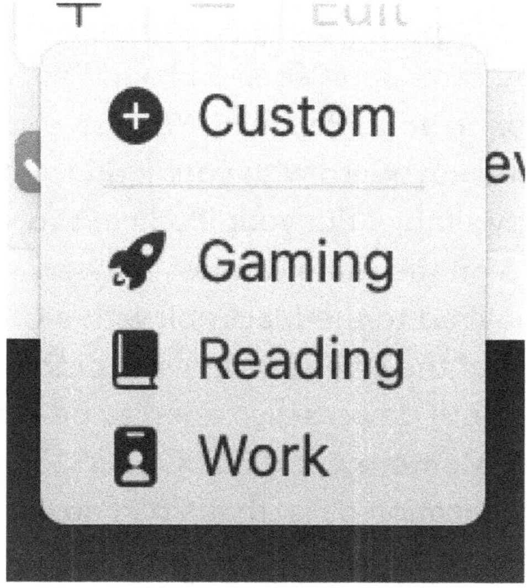


Give your Focus a name, pick the colors, and set an icon, then click the blue Add in the bottom right corner.

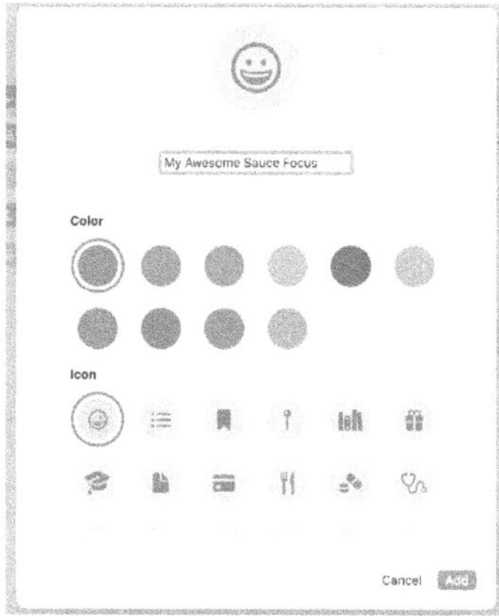


It will now be added and you can go in and make any edits to it. It will also be available on any other device you are signed into with iCloud.

## UNIVERSAL CONTROL

Some people like to really invest in the Apple ecosystem—and who can blame them? They make great products. So they might have an iMac, MacBook, and iPad. Apple understands these users and has created a feature called Universal Control. Universal Control lets you share things (from files and images to keyboards and trackpads) easily. What does that mean? Let's pretend you have a MacBook and iPad mini. When enabled, you can open Pages on your iPad, and drag an image from your MacBook to your iPad mini. You can also share your MacBook's trackpad and keyboard with your iPad.

Using it is pretty simple. Put your iPad next to your MacBook and make sure they are on the same wireless network and have Bluetooth on—or connect the iPad to the MacBook with a USB-C, then drag your mouse to the edge of the screen to move it onto your iPad screen. It's all pretty intuitive. Both devices also need to be running the latest version of MacOS (OS Monterey) and iPadOS (OS15). If you are reading this book at the publication date, that's bad news for you because MacOS Ventura is not quite out as of this writing. It also might not launch with the first OS update. It is expected in the fall.

If you want to prepare for it, then you just need to set up a couple of things. First, on your MacBook or iMac, go to the Apple Menu in the upper left corner, then select System Preference, and finally go to General. In the General menu, check off Allow Handoff between this Mac and your iCloud devices. Next, on your iPad, go to the Settings app, then General; next, turn on AirPlay & Handoff if it is toggled off.

## SHORTCUTS

Shortcuts has been a popular mobile app; it's now available on Mac. It allows you to create automated tasks to help you get more work done. You can find the Shortcut app in the Launchpad.

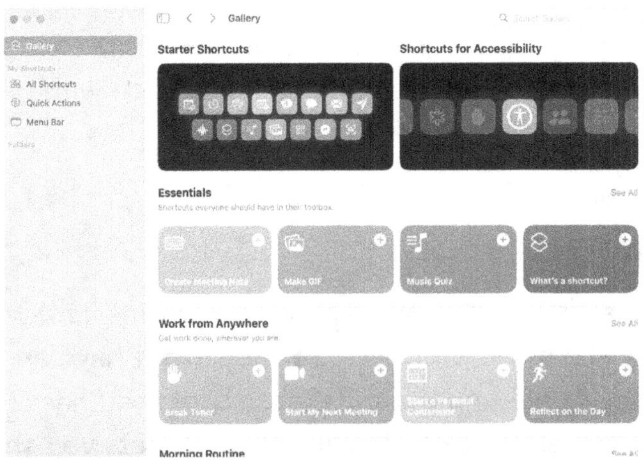

## LIVE TEXT (PHOTOS)

Photos become smarter in Ventura. You can now do more than stare at your gorgeous face! You can pull information from the photo! What do I mean by that? Let's say take a look at a picture of one of my dogs as a puppy. Adorable, right?! But what kind of dog is she?

With Live photos you can find out! Go to the top bar, then click the "i" icon with the stars on it.

If there's something in that photo that Live photo picks up on, then you'll see a small icon hovering over the photo. In this case there's a little paw print. That should tell you that it thinks this is some sort of animal.

When I click on the icon, it brings up a popup that tells me, that's not only a dog—that's a Jack Russell Terrier; it then has information about the breed.

It's not just dogs this kind of look up works on. It works on land-marks, and other things as well.

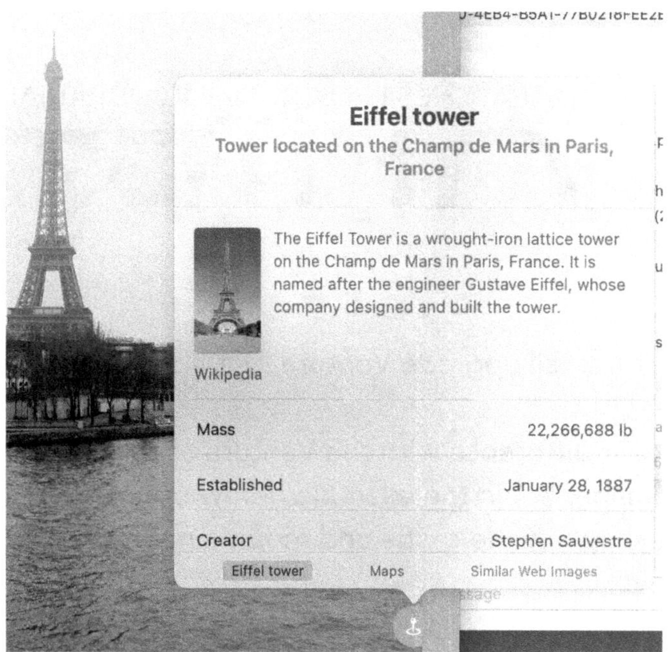

In the photo below of an audiobook, it will show the name of the book, the author (hey, look! It's my pen name!), a description, and where to buy it.

That's pretty smart, right? But it gets smarter! It also recognizes text. You can highlight words in a photo the same way you would any-where else—just drag your mouse over it! So if you have a book cover, like in the example below, you don't have to type the name to look it up. You can just highlight it, and copy and paste it! Just right click and select Copy from the menu (or press Command+C on your keyboard).

## MAPS

Maps got a small upgrade Ventura, but it still functions largely the same.

The biggest difference with the Ventura update is buildings now have more shape. So, in the example below of an amusement park, you can see the shape of the castle and mountain. This is only available in some regions.

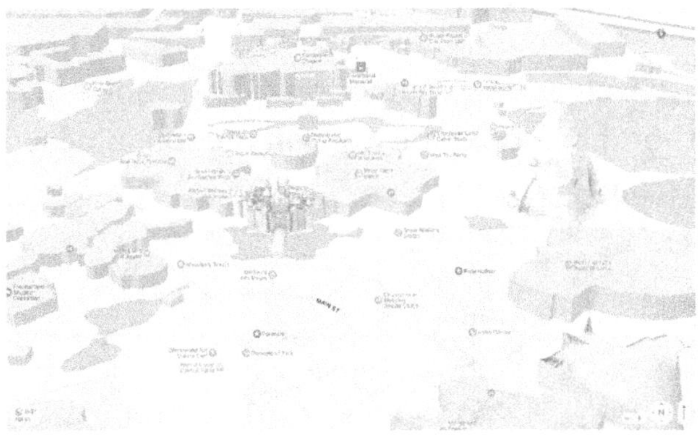

Some, but not all, cities also have more in terms of lanes on the road; if the city has been configured, you'll be able to see more details on lanes to help you navigate through the city and know what lanes to be in. If you don't see this detail, it's because the city has not been set up yet.

# CONFERENCING

Presenter Overlay and Reactions make your video conferencing experience more enjoyable and interactive!

### How to Use Presenter Overlay

It used to be when you were in a Zoom or Teams meeting sharing your screen, the participates would just see your presentation. With Presenter Overlay, they can see either a small round box with your video feed, or a large version of you infront of the screen.

Let me show you what I mean. In zoom, here's what the small version would look like with presenter overlay turned on.

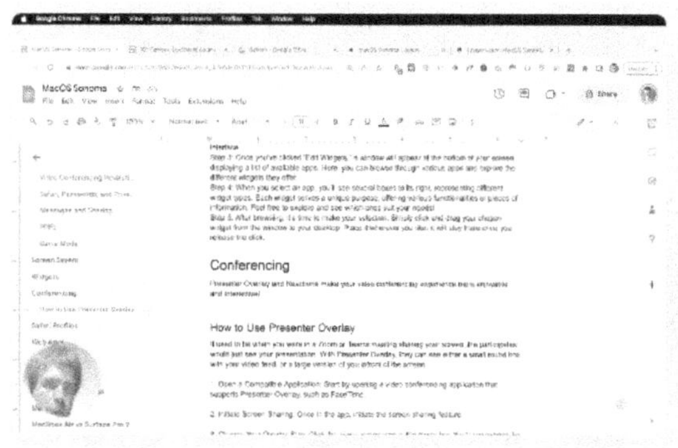

And here's what the large one would look like.

How do you do this? Let's learn:

1. Open a Compatible Application: Start by opening a video conferencing application that supports Presenter Overlay, such as FaceTime, Zoom, or Teams.

2. Initiate Screen Sharing: Once in the app, initiate the screen sharing feature.

3. Choose Your Overlay Size: Click the share screen icon in the menu bar. You'll see options for Small or Large under Presenter Overlay. Selecting one of these will give you a preview of your video layered over the screen. Here's how it would look in Zoom.

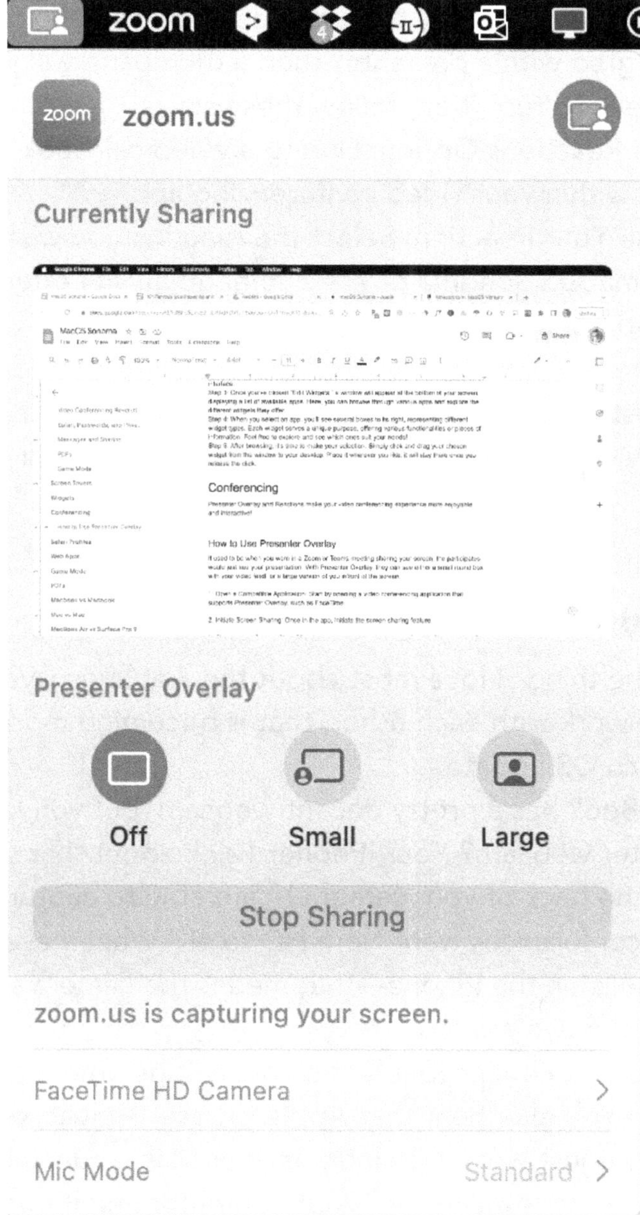

4. Position Yourself: In Large mode, you will appear in front of the content. In Small mode, you'll be in a resizable, movable bubble on the screen.

5. Personalize Your Presentation: This innovative feature allows your audience to see both you and the content, adding a personal touch to your presentation.

How to Use Reactions

Reactions is an easy way to respond to what someone is saying. If you like or agree with a presenter then a thumbsup will just that reaction on screen. To turn it on, follow these steps.

1. Locate Reactions Option: During a video call, look for the Reactions option within your video conferencing app.

2. Choose Your Reaction: Select the reaction you wish to display in your video. macOS Sonoma offers cinematic-quality effects like balloons, confetti, and hearts.

3. Gesture or Click: You can set up gesture-triggered reactions and use hand gestures, like giving a thumbs-up, to display them. Alternatively, simply click on the reaction to showcase it in your video.

## CONTINUITY CAMERA

One of the things I love most about the Apple ecosystem is how well devices work with each other; that is becoming more and more true with each OS update.

The MacBook has a pretty decent webcam. But you know what has an even better webcam? Your iPhone! Think about that stunning camera lens on the back of your camera being able to capture you. Suddenly, your conferences went from HD to 4K! What's even nicer is now, Center Stage is on the iPhone—that means the camera stays focused on you as you move around.

A feature that cool probably requires a huge amount of setup, right? Nope! You ever hear that Apple phrase, "It just works"? Well, this feature…it just works! (as long as your Mac is running OS Ventura) All you have to do is make sure your computer and iPhone are on the same wireless network.

Let me show you how it works in Zoom. Here's how I look on my MacBook without my iPhone:

Not bad. But now I go to the video tab in Zoom and select my iPhone as the camera. You should see any available webcam listed. One will be the name of your iPhone followed by "Camera"; that's the one you want.

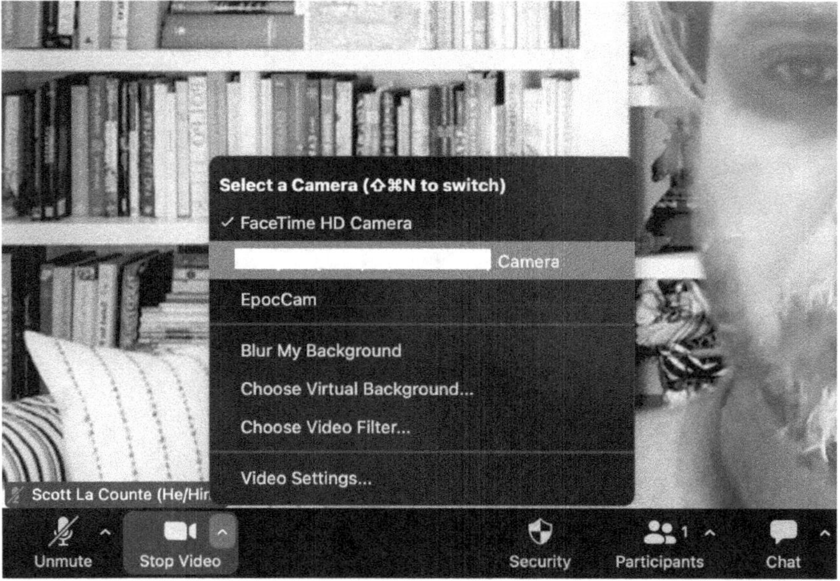


You'll hear a little bell-type noise, then after a second or two, your iPhone's camera will appear.

The difference is pretty crazy; my office doesn't have great lighting, but when I switch to my iPhone for meetings, the image not only looks clearer, the lighting looks flawless.

The example above is Zoom, but the feature works on most video conference apps (FaceTime, Microsoft Teams, etc.).

There are all kinds of ways to mount a camera to make this happen, but the way Apple has promoted is with the Belkin mount, which is $29.99 and called "iPhone Mount with MagSafe for Mac Notebooks".

It's very small and clips easily to the back of your phone, and then slips on your MacBook.

# [6]

# APPS

This chapter will cover:
- Phone calls
- Contacts
- Message
- FaceTime
- Photo Booth
- Calendar
- Reminders
- Notes
- iTunes
- App Store
- Siri

Now that you know about how Mac works (and how to find cat memes), I'm going to talk about the pre-installed programs.

## PHONE CALLS

Apple products really work best with other Apple products; that's even truer with Catalina, where you can sync your iPhone account to make phone calls (both video and regular) and send messages right from your Mac. Additionally, you can even use your iPhone's data connection to get the Internet on your laptop on the go—this is especially handy while travelling if you don't want to pay for Wi-Fi spots that charge for access (just keep in mind that your data connection does have monthly limits and using a computer can go through those limits very quickly—in other words, this probably isn't something you want to do to stream Netflix movies).

## CONTACTS

Unless you are a business person, having contacts on your computer might not seem necessary; here's the advantage of it—it syncs with your phone. So having a contact on your computer will carry over to your other mobile devices. To use it, go to your Launchpad, then click the icon.

If you're signed into iCloud, then you should see dozens of contacts already. To create a new contact, click on the (+) button at the bottom of the main window. On the next screen add all the info you want—it can be as much or as little as you desire. Some contacts may only need a website address, others might have mailing address—it's entirely up to you how much information you add. You can also edit a contact by finding their name, then clicking on the Edit button. If you want to delete someone, then find their name and hit Delete on your keyboard (you can also delete by clicking on their name with two fingers).

## MESSAGE

When you use Messages from your Mac to send messages just keep in mind that it's kind of like instant messaging for Mac users—that means it's designed to work with Mac products...nothing else.

### *Setting Up Message*

1. To set up Message, click the Messages icon to launch it.
2. If you were already logged into iCloud on the Mac, you will automatically be logged into Message.
3. If you'd like to change this account or haven't yet logged in, select Messages > Preferences on the top menu bar.
4. When the Accounts dialogue box comes up, click on the Accounts tab.
5. In the left-hand window, you will see Message. Select it.
6. The following screen will prompt you to enter the email address and password associated with iCloud. Do so and click the blue Sign In button to complete the setup process.

### *Setting Up Other IM Clients*

While Message is made for Mac products, you can use it for other messaging services like Google, Yahoo, and AOL.

To add other instant messaging (IM) clients to Messages:

1. Open up Messages if it isn't already running.
2. On the top menu bar, click Messages > Add Account.

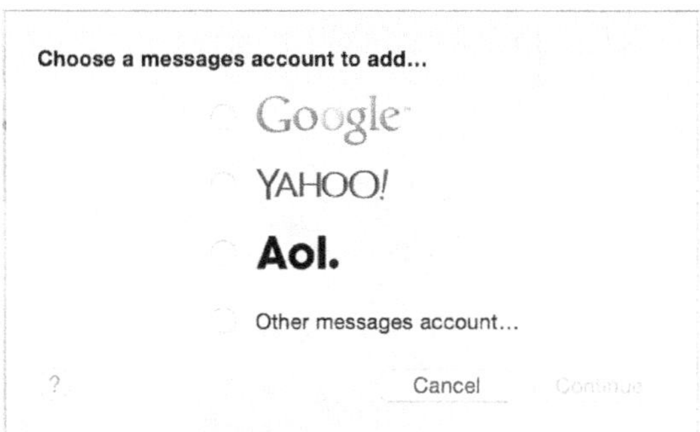


3. Select the type of account that you'd like to add, such as Gmail or Yahoo, and select Continue.
4. You will be prompted to enter the appropriate email address and password, and click the Set Up button to finish.

So now that it's set up, how do you send a message?

### *Start New Conversation*

1. Before we begin, take a look at the entire Messages screen. It should be totally empty with no conversations. On the left sidebar it will say No Conversations. This is where you will be able to change between different conversations with people by clicking on each one. On the right-hand side, you will also see No Conversation Selected. Here is where you will be able to type new messages and read everything in whatever conversation is currently selected. If you have an iPhone (or any phone for that matter), it will be like the screen where you read your text messages.
2. To create a new conversation with someone, click the Compose new message button located at the top of the left sidebar, next to the search bar. It should look a little pencil inside of a square.

When you get a message, if your sound is enabled, you'll get a little chime.

### *Tapbacks*

If you've used Stickers on the iPad and iPhone, you might be disappointed to see that feature has not yet arrived on MacOS. There is one feature from iOS: Tapbacks. Tapbacks let you respond to a message to indicate you like what the message says or that you agree with it. To use it, right-click (two-finger click) on any message and select your response.

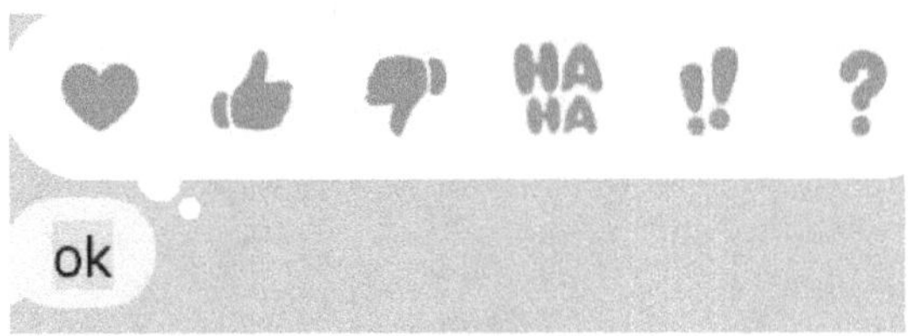


### PINNING MESSAGES

If you text a lot, then it might get a little cumbersome replying. The way Messages works is the most recent conversations go to the top. This mostly works well, but you can also pin favorites to the top.

In the example below, my wife is pinned to the top of the conversations. Even though other people have written to me more recently, she will always be up there (unless I remove her). That makes it easy to reply.

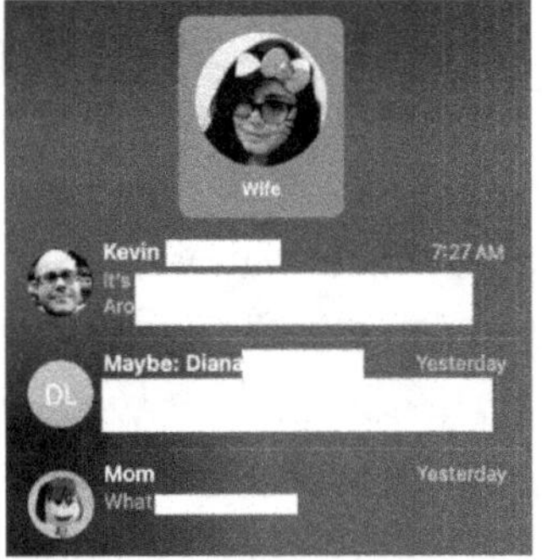

To add or remove someone from the top, drag / swipe with your mouse over the message, then tap the pin.

If you want to remove them, right click the message, and select unpin.

You can have several people pinned to the top. Personally, I find three is good, but you can add even more.

## MESSAGE TAGGING

If you have used messaging programs like Slack, then you are probably all too familiar with tagging someone in a conversation. Tagging gets the person's attention and starts a new thread within the conversation.

So if you are in a large text message exchange, then when you tag someone, everyone can read it, but everyone is not notified. So it's a little less obtrusive.

To tag someone in a conversation, just put an @ in front of their name when you reply.

## REPLYING TO MESSAGES

Obviously, you can reply to a message by typing the message in the box and pressing return on your keyboard. But that only replies to the last message. What if the message is several threads up? Or what if it's a group and you want to reply to one particular message from a specific person?

To reply to a message that's higher up, right click over that message, and then select reply.

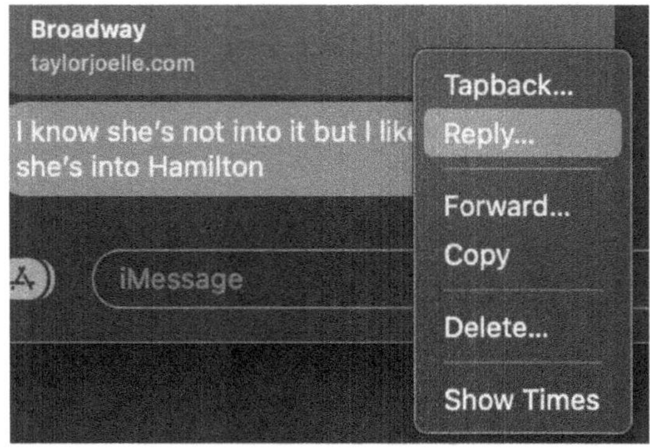

When you do this, the message will show up with a reply underneath it.

It will also show up as the last message sent but with an arrow notifying the user that you've replied to something in particular.

### SENDING PHOTOS

When you send groups of photos, Messages will lay out photos of less than three vertically. Tap them to make them bigger.

If you send more than three photos, then they'll stack on top of each other, and you swipe through them.

### EDIT AND UNSEND MESSAGES

Did you make a typo in a message? Or maybe you regret sending it all together. You can unsend a message and edit it…kind of. There's some important caveats here. One, it has to be a message you have recently sent–not one from several hours ago. Two, the person on the other end of the message needs to have the current OS running. Three, the other person also gets notified that the message was either unsent or edited. So don't think you can tell the person you never said that.

To use it, right click on the message, then select the option that you want. If you don't see the option, then too much time has past.

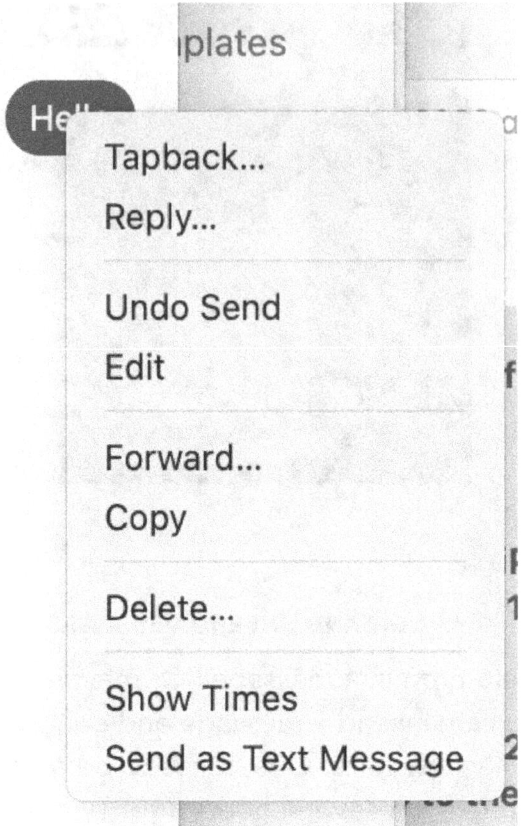


## FACETIME

FaceTime allows you to connect with friends and family using your computer's built-in camera.  I've heard people say they are so worried that someone is watching them through their webcam that they cover it with tape. When FaceTime is in use (i.e. when the camera is on and people can see you) a bright green light comes on—so you don't have to worry about people spying on you…if you don't see the light, then the camera is off.

The app can be launched by clicking on Launchpad > FaceTime.

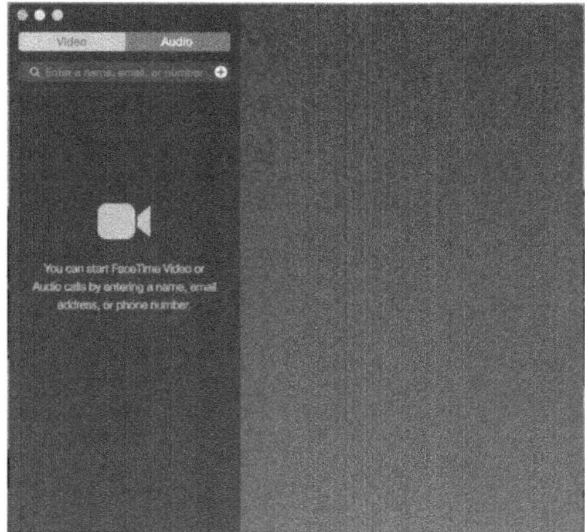

On the left side you can enter a person's name if they are in your Contacts, or a phone number.  For FaceTime to work, the other person must also have an Apple device, and accept your call.

You can also use FaceTime audio. This lets you call someone without the camera—it's essentially a Wi-Fi phone call.

## USING FACETIME TO KEEP FAMILY TOGETHER

How do you keep people together when they are apart? This is something Apple has thought deeply about. FaceTime on the Mac looks better than ever. Later in fall 2021, you will be able to watch movies together, listen to music together, and even troubleshoot device problems by sharing your device screen. It's called SharePlay. Unfortunately, some of these features are coming later in the fall, so this instructional guide cannot include them at this writing.

To get started, open the FaceTime app from your launchpad.

You have two options: Create Link or New FaceTime Call. Creating a link will let someone who doesn't have a Mac or Apple device join in on the call.

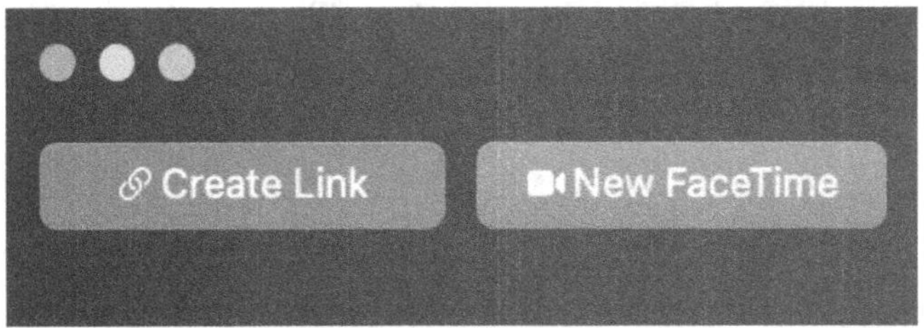


The Create Link button will give you a sharable link that you can give out to people. So they can open it inside Chrome on a Windows computer.  Just tap the copy button and paste it wherever you want people to see it. You can also tap Add Name to give it a name.

If you prefer to call someone directly, then tap the green New FaceTime button and type in their name.

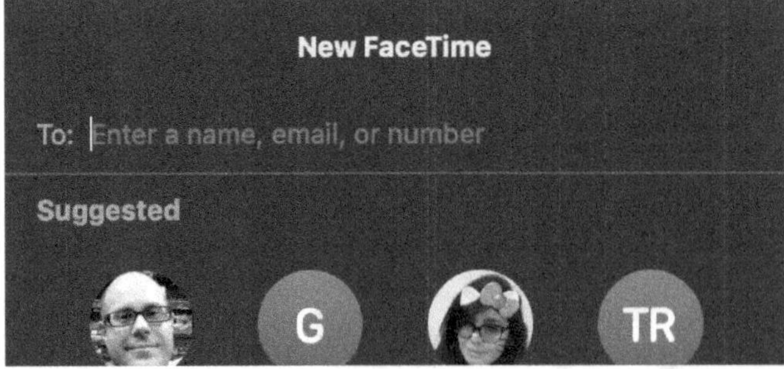


Your preview box is in the lower corner, but it can be moved anywhere on the screen by tapping and holding it, then dragging.

If you make this preview box larger, there's one option available to you. On the bottom center is a small image icon; tap that and it will blur or unblur your background.

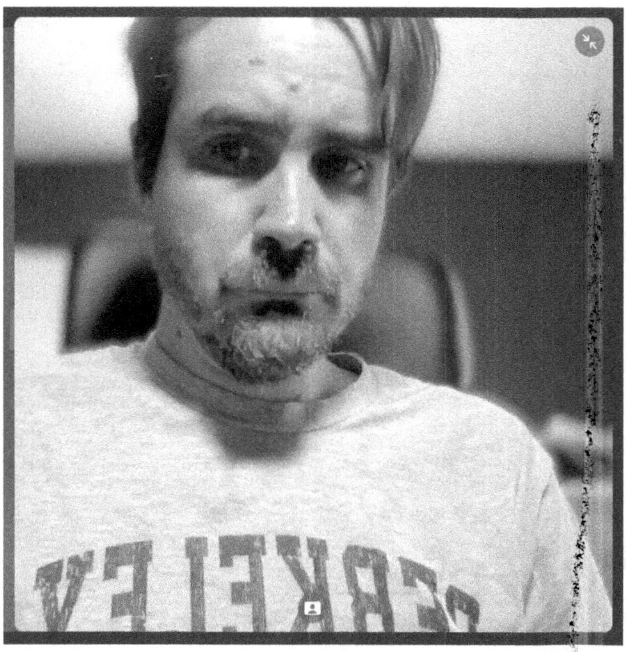

If you use FaceTime on your iPhone or iPad, then you'll notice several options are missing—such as adding effects. Mac does not support those as of this writing.

Over in the bottom left corner there's a few other options—the first is the left pane hide / show icon; this reveals a left sidebar where you have access to admitting people into the video call. Next to that is the mic (click to mute yourself), video (click to turn your video off), and X to leave call.

If someone joins your call, then click the left pane icon, then click the green checkmark icon. From here you can also add people and grab the link one more time to share it.

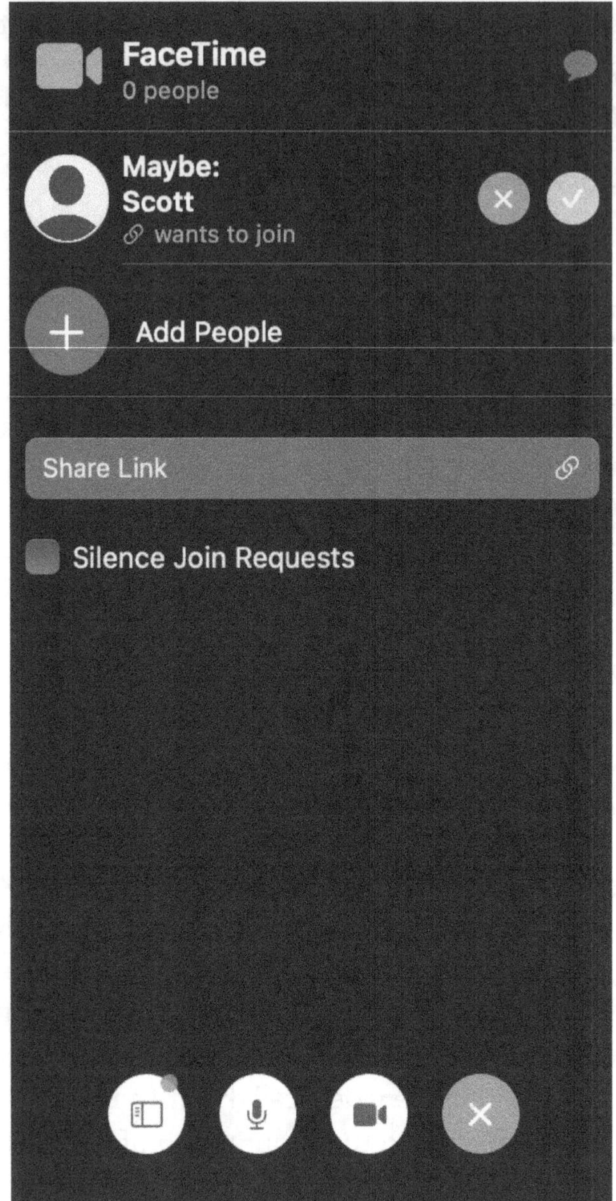


## CALENDAR

Calendar is another feature that can be synced to your iCloud account—so as long as you're using the same account, then everything you put in your calendar from your computer will also show up on your iPhone and iPad. You can also sync the calendar to other ones you may be using online like Google or Yahoo.

To get started with it, go to your Launchpad in the Dock and click on the Calendar icon.

At the top of the application window from left to right you have the standard stoplight buttons, Calendars, New Event (+), several different views including Day and Month, and the Search bar.

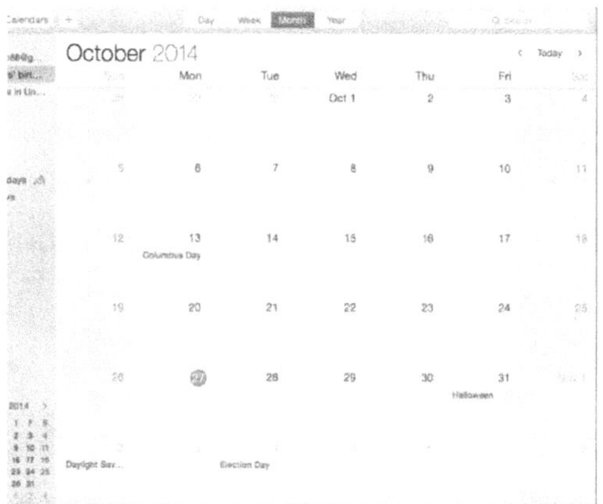

*Syncing Calendars*

If you already use a calendar with iCloud, Google, Yahoo, or any other provider, you can sync it up with the Mac Calendar application.

1. In the top menu bar click Calendar > Add Account.
2. Like you did with Mail, you'll be prompted to enter your name, email address, and password.

Once you finish the setup process your events from that calendar should automatically populate in the Calendar window. If you have multiple accounts with separate calendars, you can filter through them by clicking on the Calendars button in the toolbar, and checking or un-checking the boxes next to the appropriate calendars.

*Changing Views*

You can change the calendar view between Day, Week, Month, or Year by clicking on the corresponding button in the toolbar.

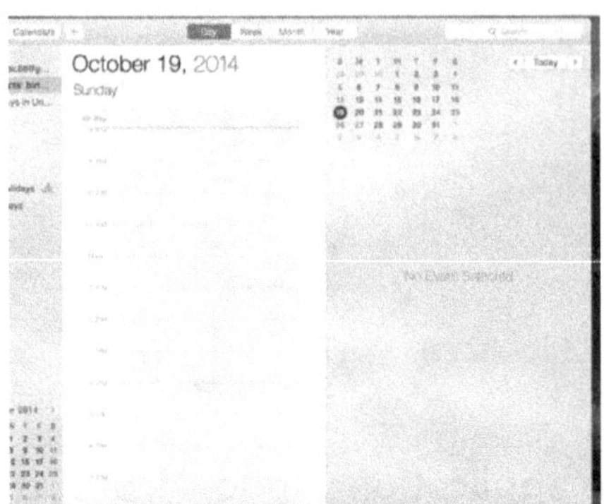

Day will display all of that day's events, broken down by hour.

Week will show you the whole week at a glance, and displays blocks for events so you can easily see when you have events, and if you have any upcoming free time.

The Month view will probably be your default view if you just need your calendar to remind you about bill payments and due dates, or don't have too many appointments each month but they are scattered through the month.

## REMINDERS

As the name implies, the Reminders application is used to remind you of things—and, as you might have guessed by now, it can be synced using iCloud to the Reminders app on your iPhone or iPad.

The app lets you create lists for things like groceries or anything else on your mind; you can also use the app to schedule when things are due—like paying a bill by the 15th of the month. It can even be set to remind you every time you leave or arrive at your home to turn your home alarm on or off.

You can create shared lists so others in your network can also add things to the list.

To get started, open the app by clicking on the Launchpad icon, then selecting it from the list of apps.

Creating a list is still very simple. Tap Add List from the lower right corner of your screen.

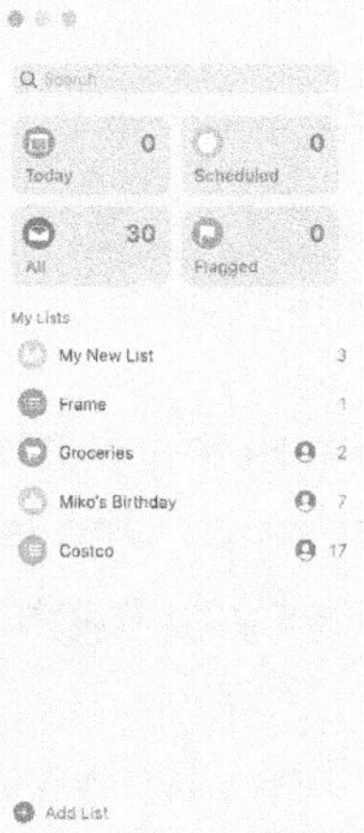

Once you create your first list, you can start adding to it by tapping the '+' button in the upper right corner. This lets you add the item as well as set when it's due and even include images and attachments.

If you tap the ⓘ at any point, you'll be able to add more details (such as a due date or even what location to remind you at—you could, for example, have it remind you when you get to the grocery store).

Tap Return on your keyboard to add another item.

To share a list, right-click (two-finger click) the name and add a person that you want to share it with.

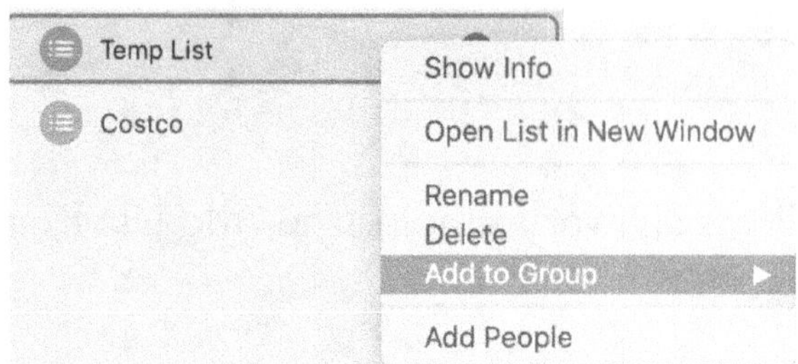

This option also works to remove a list.

## MAIL

You may be used to checking your email in your browser. There are a few advantages to emailing through an app. One is instant notifications when mail comes; another is features you might not get in browser-based mail.

If you want to try an app, then there are plenty you can choose from: Airmail, Outlook, Spark, Canary Mail (some are free, some are not).

For this book, I'm going to cover only one app: Apple Mail.

### Mail Crash Course

To get started, go to your Launchpad and click the Mail app.

Next, it will ask you to sign into your email provider. The steps vary depending on the services you use, but it will walk you through each step.

Once you have your mail set up, you'll immediately start seeing your inbox fill up with all the messages from that account. Don't see it? Go to "Get New Mail" under Mailbox in the top menu.

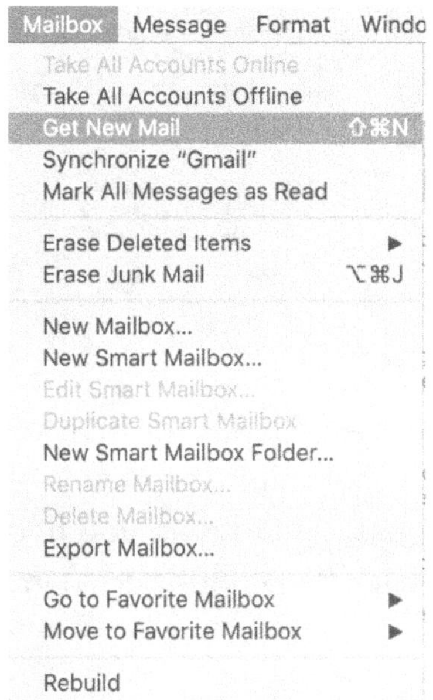

The app should look pretty familiar to you because most the features from your browser mail are there.

A few features you should know about:

Block – If there's someone you don't want to hear from, then block them. To do so, open the email from them, click on their name, and select Block Contact from the dropdown. If only blocking people in real-life was that easy!

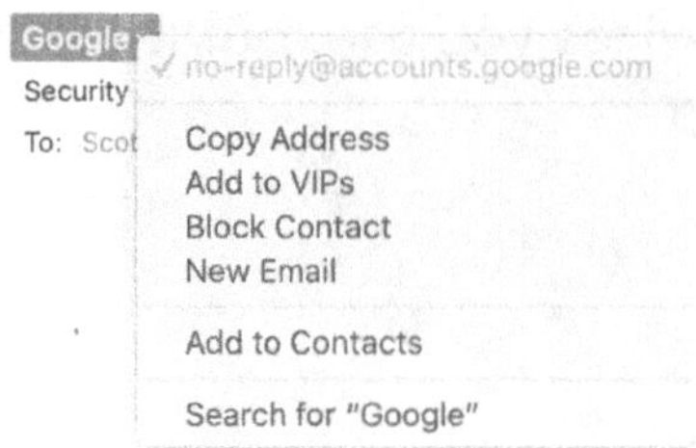

When you right-click (two-finger click) on a mail message, you also have a few options.

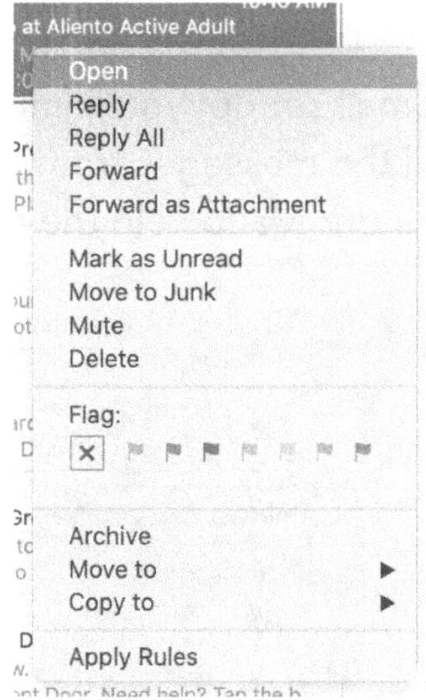

If you have ever used email before, then you will know what Reply, Reply All, etc., do. One that might be new is "Flag." Flag lets you color coordinate different messages to help you find them more easily.

You can also right-click (two-finger click) in the side menu to get more options.

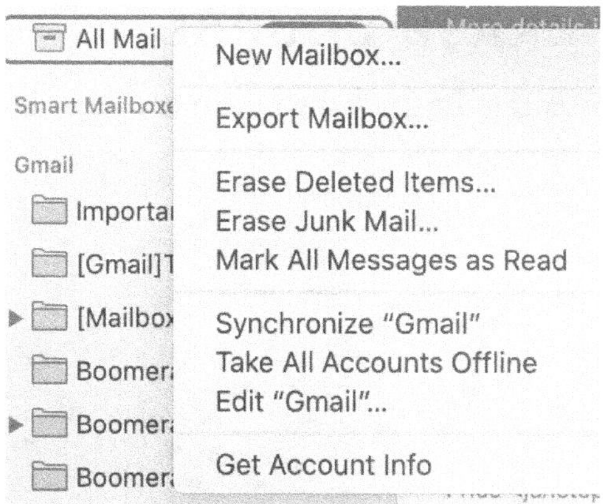

# LOCATION BASED REMINDER

If you want to create a reminder that is location-based (i.e. "when I leave work, remind me to call wife") then follow the steps above.

Click the Information icon next to the reminder (the "i" with a circle).

This will bring up a few extra options. One says, "remind me" with a checkbox for "At a location"; click that checkbox. Next, enter the address, and select if you want the reminder when you get there or when you're leaving there.

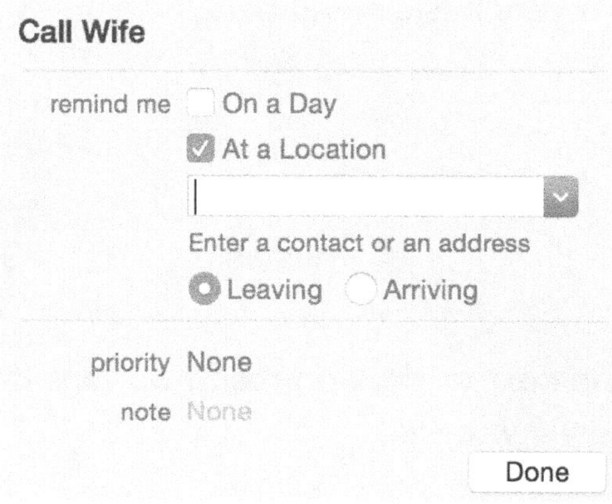

# THE NOTES CRASH COURSE

To open it, go to the Launchpad icon on your Dock and click the Notes icon.

Notes, like most of the apps in Catalina, syncs to your iPhone and iPad as long as you are logged into the same iCloud account.

Unlike word processing editors that you may be used to, there is no fancy ribbon or menu bar with lots of features. There's a side bar with a list of all your notes (across devices if you use an iPhone / iPad sync'd to your Mac).

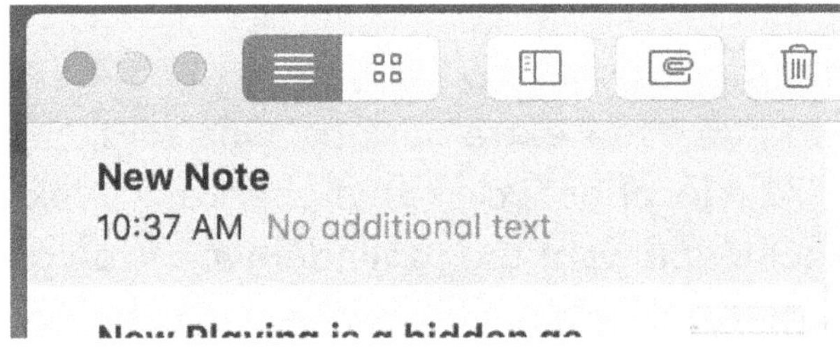

On the top is a very basic menu bar.

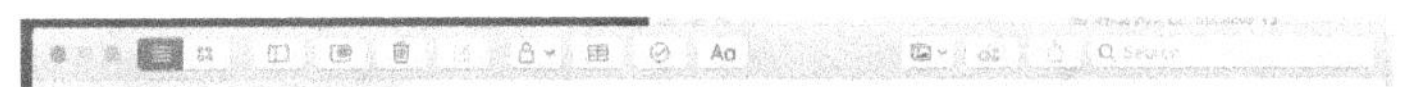

## VIEWS

The first option next to the app resize options (the red / yellow / green dots) is the view toggle.

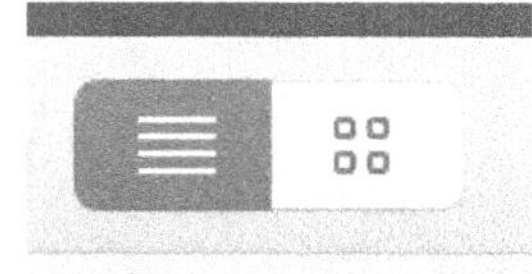

This toggle switches between a list view of your notes and a thumb-nail view (see below).

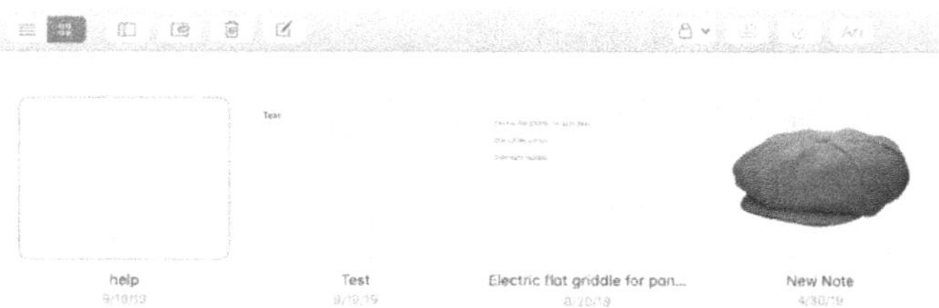

If you are in list view, then you only need to click the Note one time to open it; if you are in thumbnail view, then you will need to double click it.

## FOLDERS

The next button is for creating folders.

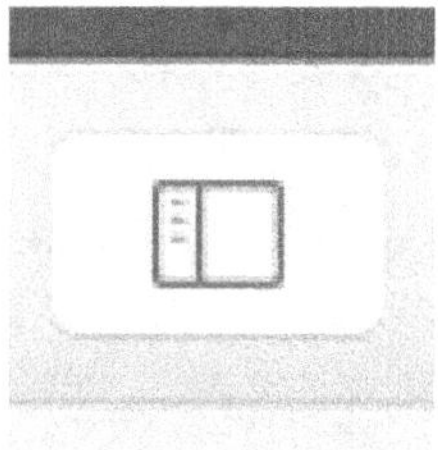

This brings up a list of all your folders (if any).

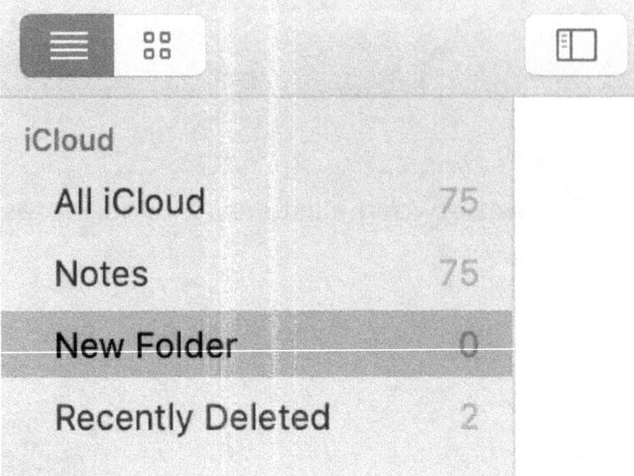

If you don't have one yet, then click New Folder at the bottom of the window.

To rename, delete, or add people to the folder, click the three dots with the circle around them.

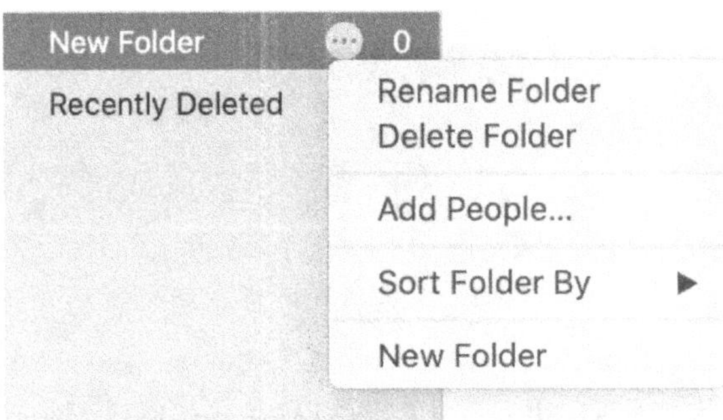

Finally, to add a note to a folder, click it from the side, and then drag it into the desired folder.

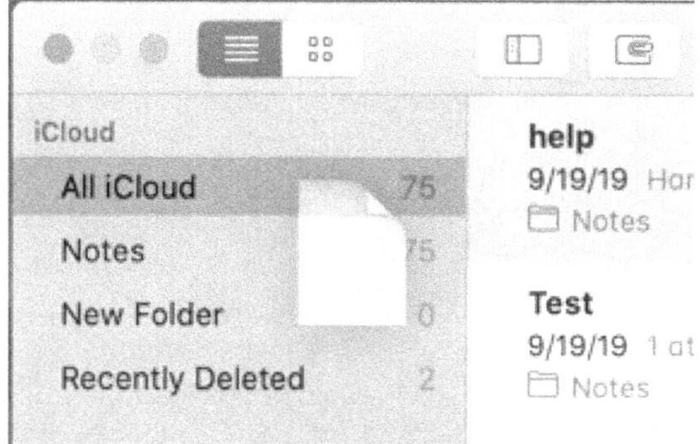

Once you are done, click the view button again to hide the folders panel.

## VIEWING ATTACHMENTS

The next option looks like the button to attach things; that's not correct. It's the option to view all the attachments you have added into notes. When you click on it, you can sort by all the different attachment types (Photos & Videos, Scans, Maps, Websites, Audio, and Documents)

When you double click an attachment, it opens a preview of it (it does *not* open the note which it's found in). If you would like to see the Note that it is in, then right click to bring up the option menu and click "Show in Note."

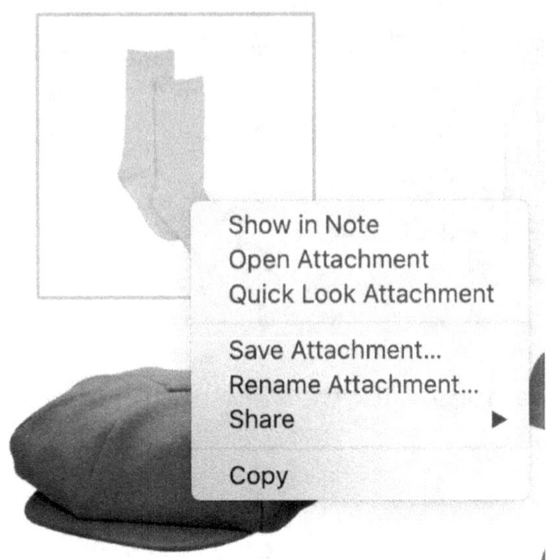


## DELETE NOTE

The next option is pretty straightforward. It deletes the note that you have currently selected.

## CREATING A NOTE

Next to the delete button is the "Create a Note" button, which, as you can expect, creates a note. When you open your note, the left panel will have the name of the note with a time stamp, and the right will have an empty text area to write in. The title of the note will change once you start typing text; the first line of text is the title of your note. You cannot rename the title; if you change the first line of text in the note, then the title is changed automatically.

## LOCK NOTE

The security on Notes may not seem quite as robust as other word processors, but there is a very resourceful Lock feature that helps keep private notes secure and for your eyes only. To use it, click the Lock icon.

This will bring up a dialog box that asks you to add a password. Now anytime you want to open the Note, you'll need a password. If you forget your password then you will not be able to access your Note, so be careful!

**Create a password for all your locked notes.**

Password:

Verify:

Password Hint:

IMPORTANT: If you forget this password, you won't be able to view your locked notes. Learn more...

Cancel    Set Password

## CREATE A TABLE

You can also add Tables to your Note. Personally, I would stick to adding tables into other word processing suites, because this is one feature a bit more cumbersome than other tools out there. But if you want to try it out, click the Tables icon.

This adds a very small table to your note—just two rows and two columns.

To add a row or column, click the three little dots on top of the column or to the left of the row, then click what you want to add. You can also delete it using this method.

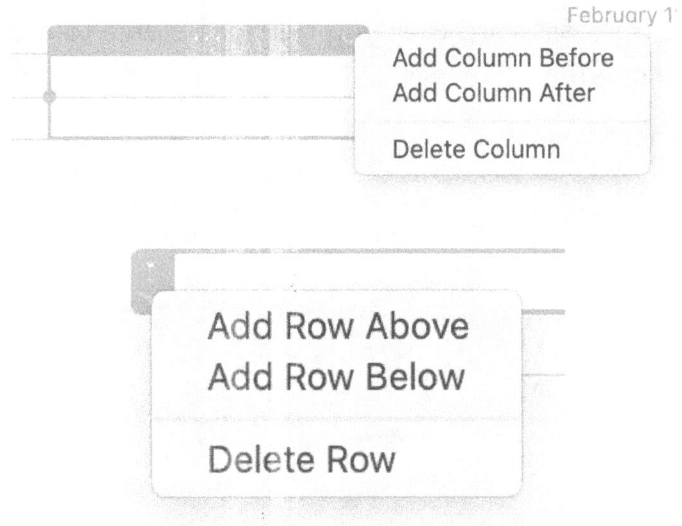


### CREATE A CHECKLIST

If you are using Notes to create a shared list between people (or just a list for yourself), click the Check icon.

This turns each line of text into a list. Hitting return on your keyboard will create a new list item; hitting return twice will take it out of list mode and return it to normal typing.

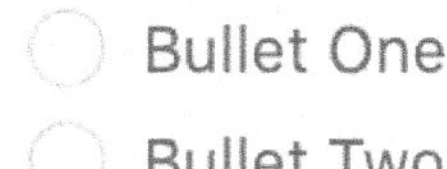


You can click inside any of the circles and check an item off. If you made a mistake, then just uncheck it again.

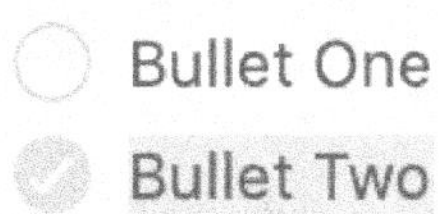


You can also move a list item up or down by right clicking it, then going to "Move List Item."

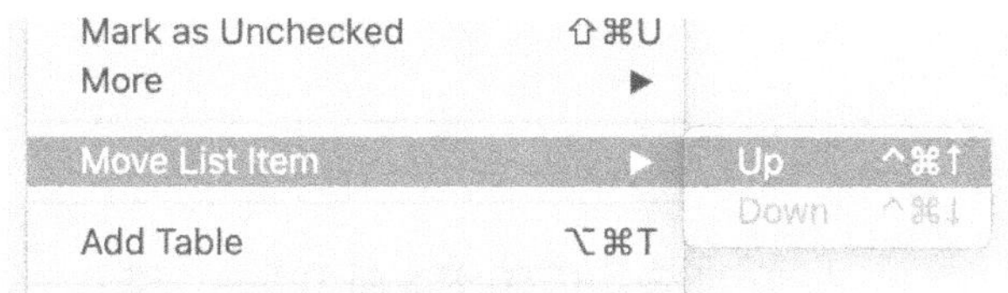


By right clicking, you can also go to More and check off all items (or uncheck all items).

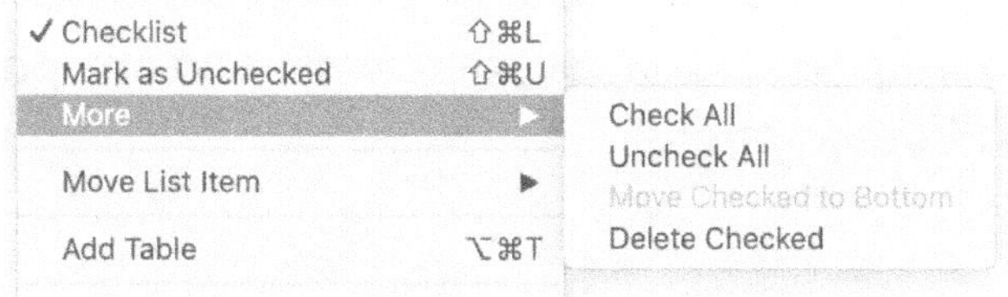


### ADD A STYLE

While you can't do as much to the format as you could in other word processors, Notes does have basic styles. To access them, click the Aa icon.

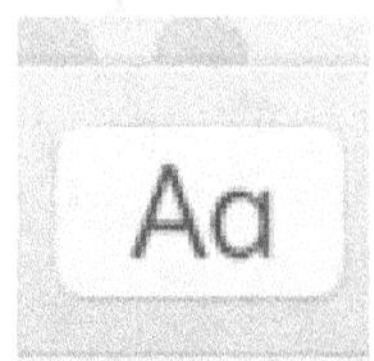

This gives you a drop-down of all the possible styles available.

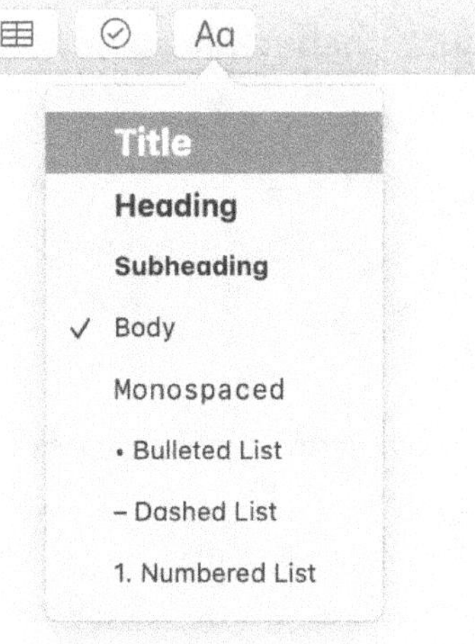

### ADDING SKETCHES AND IMAGES

One of the many areas Apple has always really shined is with syncing between devices. Using Notes for Mac with your iPhone, you can add in sketches or take photos.

To get started, go to the photos icon. This brings down a drop down of all your options. You can, of course, add any photo on your Mac with the Photos option.

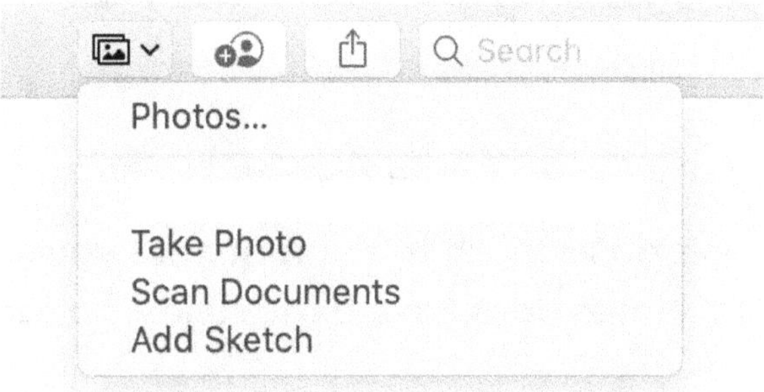

Using the next three options (Take Photo, Scan Documents, Add Sketch) will bring up an image that asks you to connect to your phone to complete the tasks (make sure you are on the same network).

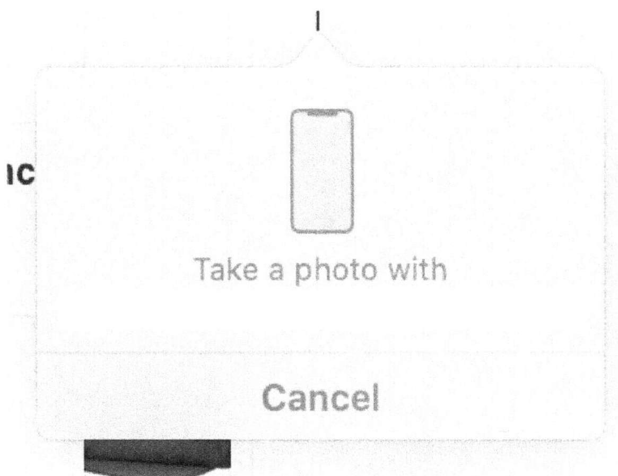


When you add a sketch, you draw it on your phone.

Once you hit done on your phone, it will automatically appear in Notes for Mac.

### ADDING COLLABORATORS

If you want to add others to your note, click the icon with the person and +.

Next click "Note 'New Note'".



It will ask how you want to add them. Through messages, a link, Air-Drop, etc.

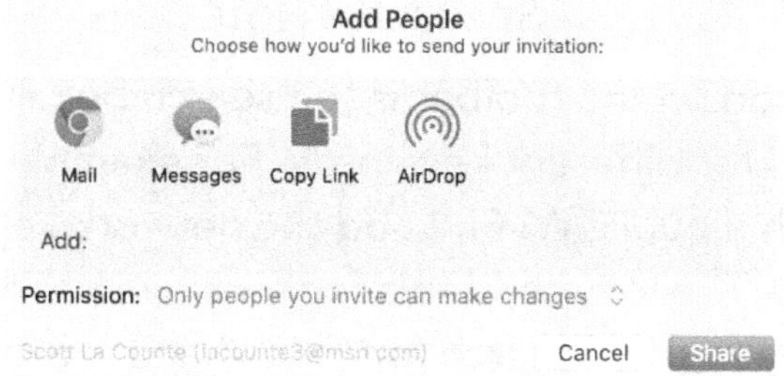

When you're ready, click share, but before you do, click the Permissions drop-down and make sure it's set up the way you want. You can either let the note be view-only for others or you can let them make changes.

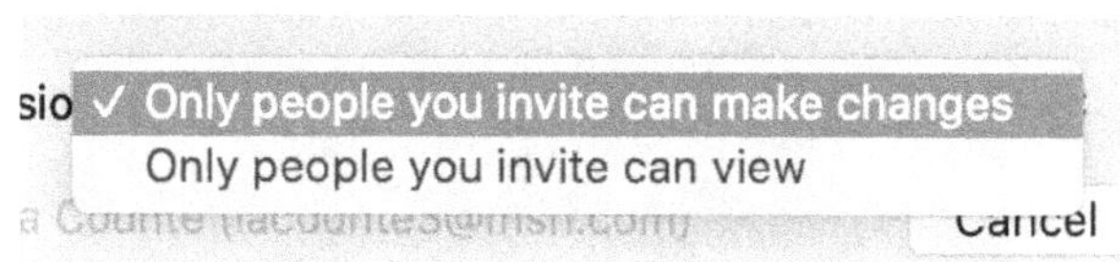

### SHARING NOTES

If you want to share the note without adding the person to the note, click the share icon.

Next, pick how you would like to share the note.

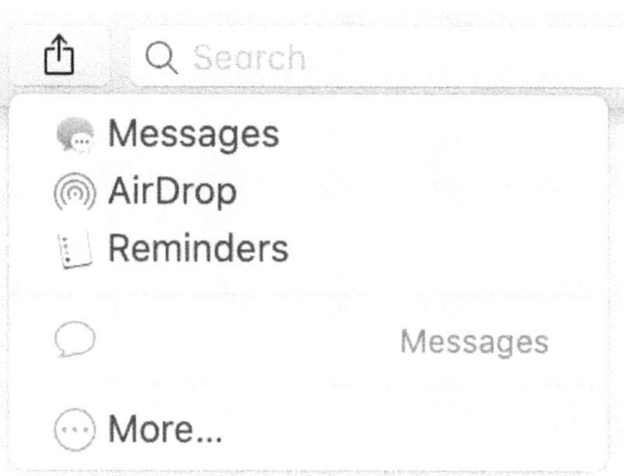

## SEARCHING NOTES

The last option on the toolbar is the search box. This lets you search all of your notes for different keywords. For example, whenever I go somewhere with a public Wi-Fi, I add the network key to a Wi-Fi password note (I don't recommend this for sensitive passwords); whenever I need to quickly find it, I search for "WiFi" and it comes up immediately.

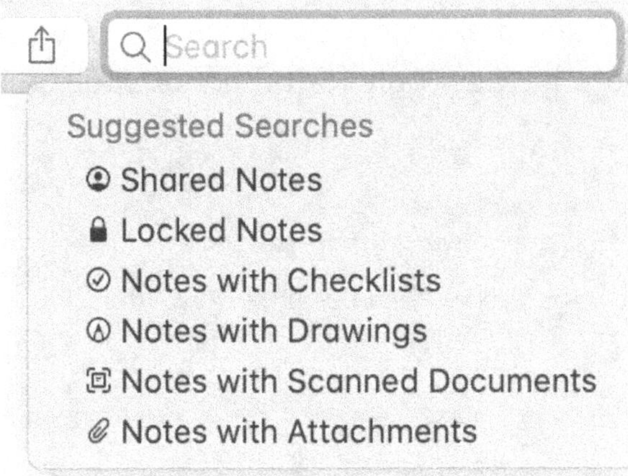


## EXPORTING NOTES

Now that we've seen all the features on the toolbar, let's go up one level to the top menu bar. Everything you did in the toolbar, you can also do there; there are also, however, a few extra features.

The first is exporting a Note as a PDF. That's found under File > Export as PDF.

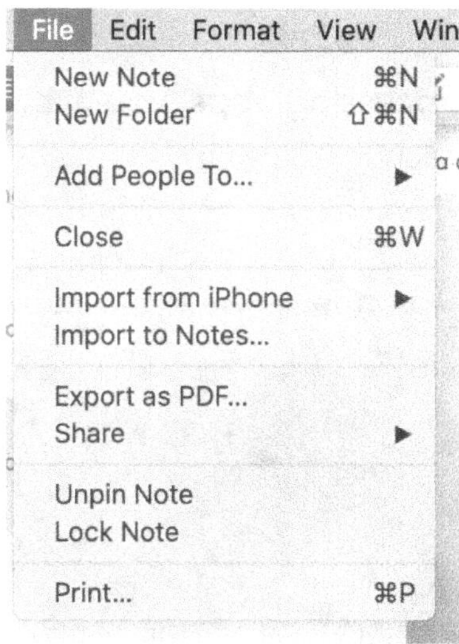

Above Export is the Import option; personally, I find it easier just to share a note from another device, but if you have a copy somewhere and have a reason to import it, then you would go here.

### PINNING NOTES

Pinning notes is a very basic, but useful feature; when you click on a note and then select to Pin it from File > Pin Note, it sticks it at the top of all your notes to make it easier to find.

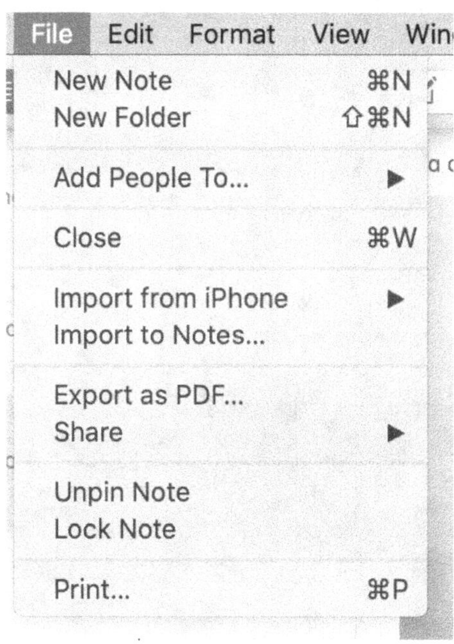

## ATTACHING FILES

Unlike many word processing apps, you can actually attach files to Notes. Go to Edit > Attach File.

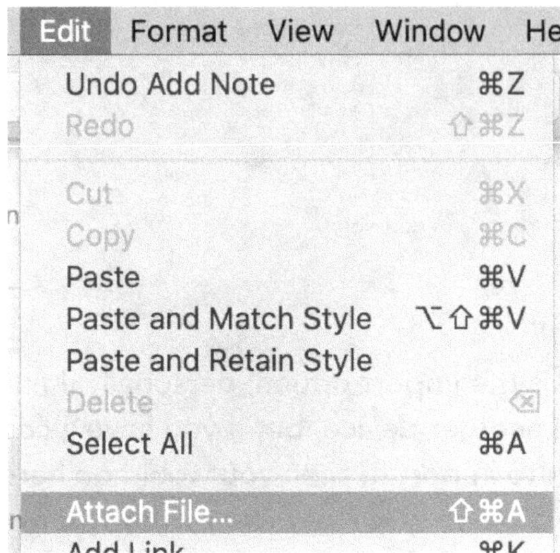

## SPELL CHECK

Like any word processing software, there is a spell checker buried in the top menu. You can start spell check by going to Edit > Spelling and Grammar. By default, it checks spelling / grammar as you type.

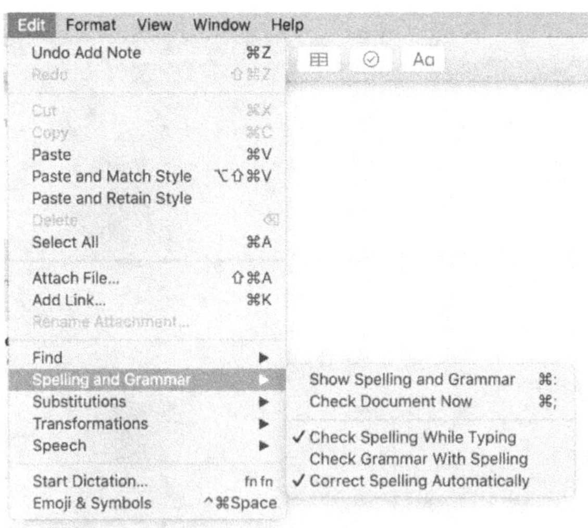

## FONT FORMATTER

Finally, while changing the font color / type is not quite as simple as Pages or Word, it is still possible. Go to Format > Font.

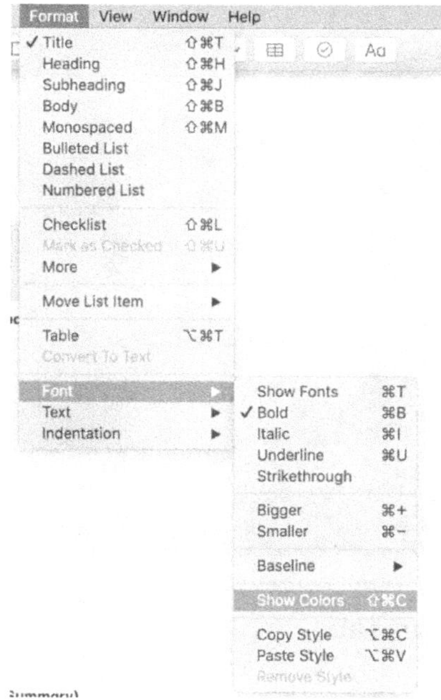

## QUICK NOTE

Quick Note lets you quickly jot things down as you work. How does it work? It depends on how you want it to work! To get it to work, you have to first create a shortcut to access it.

Go into LaunchPad and open System Preferences.

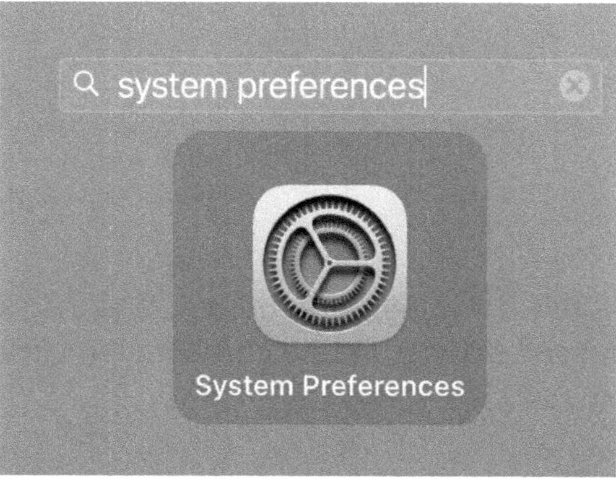

Next, click on Desktop & Screen Saver.

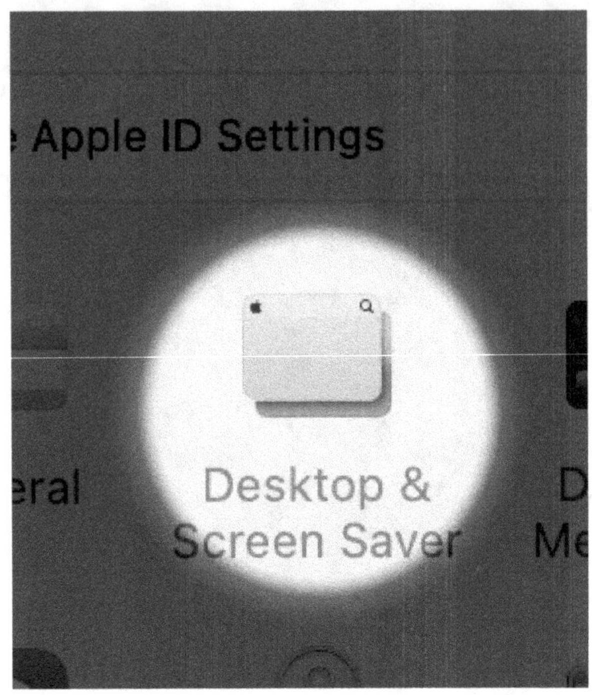


Click the Screen Saver tab.

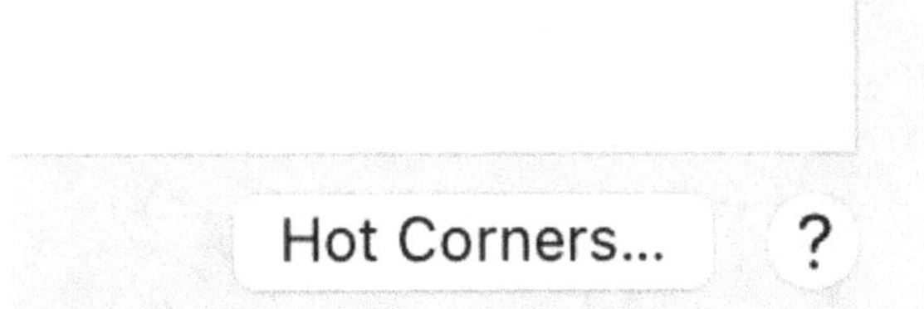


In the lower right corner is a button that says Hot Corners. Click that.



Hot Corners tells the operating system when you go into a corner, you want it to do something. Find a corner, then click the drop-down and select Quick Note.

The corner is now activated. I picked the upper left corner. When I move my mouse up there, a tiny box appears. To open the Quick Note, I have to click that box.

Your note should now be opened. It will sync across any device you are signed into with the same iCloud address.

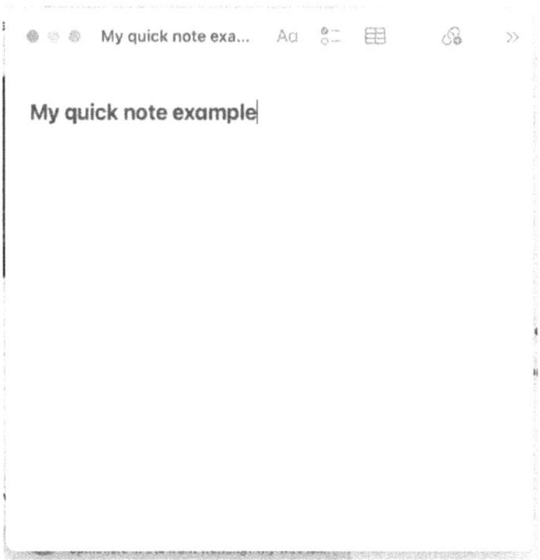

## APP STORE

The App Store is where you'll be able to download and install many different applications that have been developed specifically for use with a Mac computer.  These apps will do everything from add new functionalities and make your life easier, to providing a fun way to waste time and play some games during downtime at work.  Keep in mind that for the App Store to be functional, you need to be connected to the Internet.

To be clear, apps purchased on the App Store only run on Macs; if you have two Macs, you can download it on both if you have the same account. But you cannot download them on your iPhone or iPad. So, if you are wondering why a game you downloaded on the iPhone or iPad is not available free on your Mac, that's why. Mac apps are developed using an entirely different framework.

Open the App Store by selecting it either through the Dock or Launchpad.  The App Store's home page will greet you, showing you the latest and greatest in the world of apps.

At the top you will see different sections: Featured, Top Charts, Categories, Purchases, and Updates.

The Featured, Top Charts, and Categories tabs will show you apps that can be downloaded, but organized in different ways.  Featured will show you Best New Apps, Best New Games, Editor's Choices, and collections of different apps that work great together.

Top Charts shows you the best of the best when it comes to available apps, and is broken down by Top Paid, Top Free, and Top Grossing.  On the right side, you can also browse through Top Apps broken down by category, in case you wanted to refine your search.

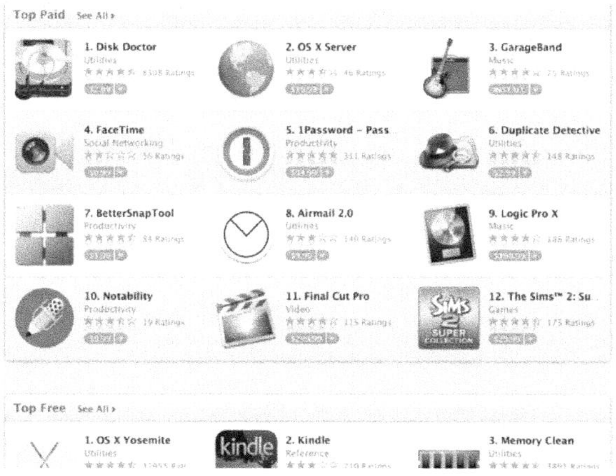

Categories further breaks down your app hunting into different categories like Business, Education, Reference, Productivity, Medical, Entertainment, and Games.

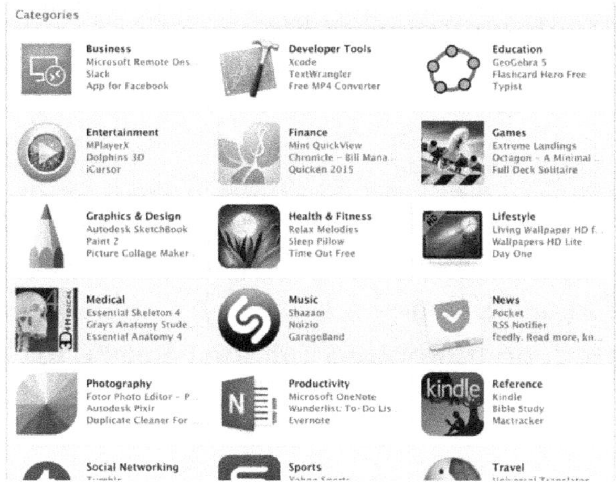

Choosing a category will bring up more selections and the right side will be filled with even more categories.  For example, selecting the Business category will bring you to the main Business apps page where the hottest apps are listed.  On the right side, smaller categories like Apps for Writers, App Development, or Apps for Designers can be selected.  It doesn't matter what category of apps you are currently under; the list remains the same in the right half.

Purchases and Updates are where you can go to view past App Store downloads.  The Purchases title can be a bit misleading, because your free apps will also appear here.  In the Updates section, you can view which apps need to be updated to the latest version.  If you have multiple apps that need updating, you can choose the Update All button and it will go down the entire list.

## PHOTOS

Photos has been around on the Mac for quite a while. In OS Catalina, however, it got a bit of a facelift that closer resembles the experience on the iPad and iPhone.

To get started, go to Photos from the Launchpad.

If your Mac is synced to your iPhone, then your photos are synced as well. No need to move them over. If you don't have an iPhone or you have other photos that you'd like to add that weren't taken on an Apple device, then you can go to File > Import.

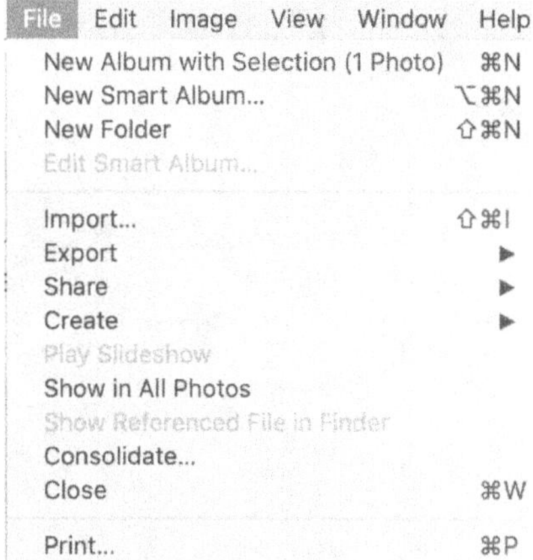


There are a few options to check out in the top menu. The first is the bigger / smaller slider.

This lets you adjust the thumbnail preview size of your photos.

Next to that is the Years / Months / Days / All Photos option, which lets you pick how photos are grouped.

If you have a photo selected, you can click the "i" and see information about the photo (what camera was used, resolution, ISO, file size, and more).

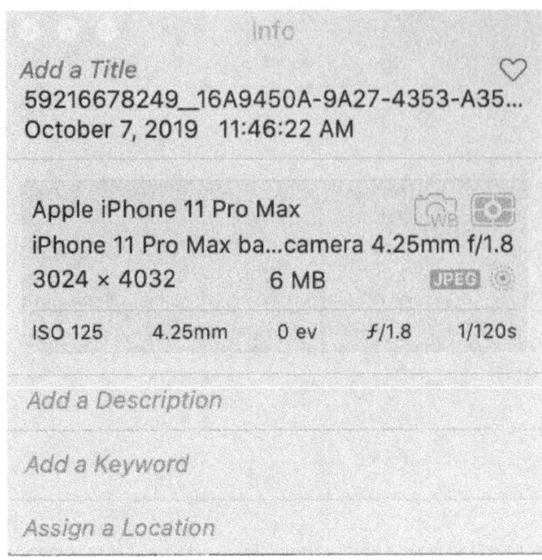


Next to information is the option to share, favorite, rotate, or search for images.

Search is pretty smart—you can search by the names of people or by the location it was taken.

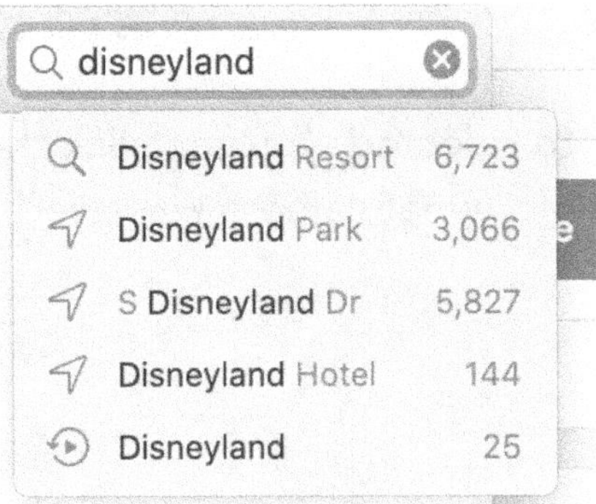


On the left menu, you have the option to view specific photos—photos with people, for example.

If you go into Memories, you can watch slideshows of past photos (Apple's AI groups these together). To watch the slideshow, right-click (two-finger click) on the memory you want to see.

Under Albums in the left menu, you can right-click to create a new Album.

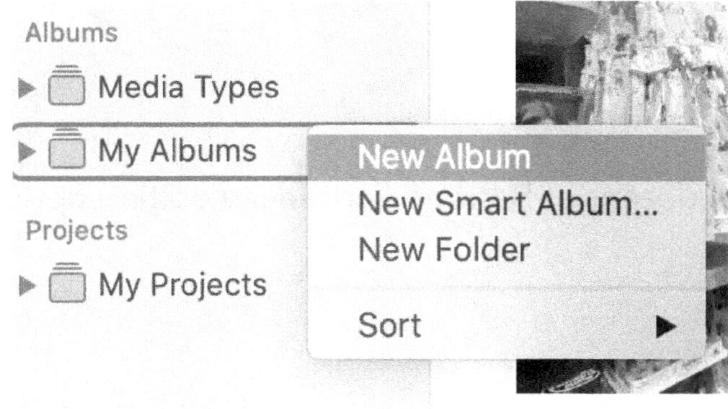

If you select New Smart Album, then you can create an Album based on a defined filter you select.

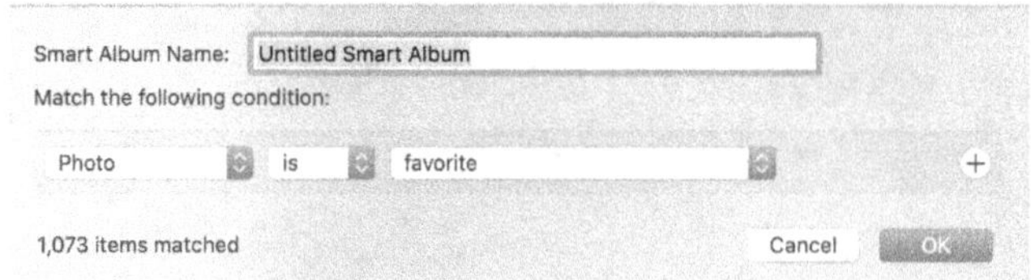

Once you create an Album, then you can right-click on any photo and add it to that Album.

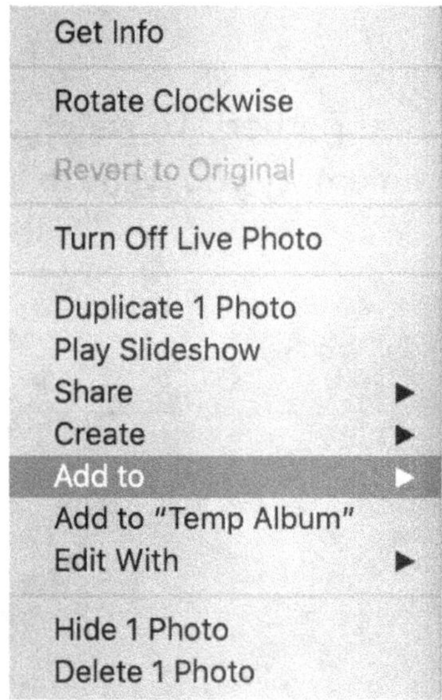

When you double-click on any photo, you can edit it. In edit mode, there's an option to auto edit, which adjust the lighting based on what the AI thinks is correct.

There are dozens of basic and advanced editing options.

There are three main sections when doing edits (accessible in the top menu): Adjust (lighting corrections), Filters (pre-defined photo filters), and Crop.

# SIRI

If you've used Siri on the iPhone, iPad or Apple Watch, then you'll be right at home with this feature. Siri is built into the Dock. To use it, just click the Dock icon.

HINT: There's a shortcut key for bringing up Siri: hold the Command key and Spacebar.

Siri is great for asking general questions, but it also works for doing more involved tasks. Here's a few examples of that:

Drag and Drop Images – Ask Siri to find you photos of something; it will confirm if you want web images or images on your hard drive. It will bring back photos and you can click and drag them into documents, emails, and lots of other things.

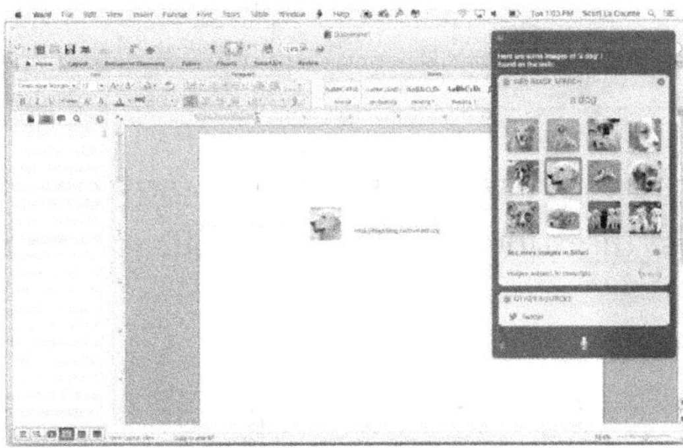

Locating Files – Siri works much like the finder…except easier. You can tell Siri to find a specific file, or you can tell Siri to find you all files opened last week, or virtually anything else.

Personal Assistant – Siri is great at doing tasks for you. You can ask Siri to email someone, read text messages, or make an appointment in your calendar. Just ask and see what happens!

If you'd like to change Siri's settings (change the voice from female to male, for example), then go to the Launchpad, open System Preferences, then click Siri.

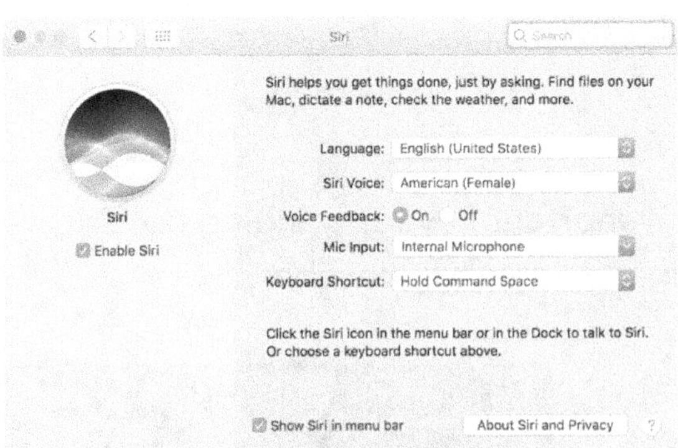

# [7]

# APPLE SERVICES

## INTRODUCTION

It used to be a few times a year Apple would take the stage and announce something that everyone's head exploded over! The iPhone! The iPad! The Apple Watch! The iPod!

That still happens today, but Apple also is well aware of the reality: most people don't upgrade to new hardware every year. How does a company make money when that happens? In a word: services.

In the past few years (especially in 2019) Apple announced several services—things people would opt into to pay for monthly. It was a way to continue making money even when people were not buying hardware.

For it to work, Apple knew they couldn't just offer a subpar service and expect people to pay because it said Apple. It had to be good. And it is!

## ICLOUD

iCloud is something that Apple doesn't talk a lot about but is perhaps their biggest service. It's estimated that nearly 850 million people use it. The thing about it, however, is many people don't even know they're using it.

What exactly is it? If you are familiar with Google Drive, then the concept is something you probably already understand. It's an online storage locker. But it's more than that. It is a place where you can store files, and it also syncs everything—so if you send a message on your iPhone, it appears on your MacBook and iPad. If you work on a Keynote presentation from your iPad, you can continue where you left off on your iPhone.

What's even better about iCloud is it's affordable. New devices get 5GB for free. From there the price range is as follows (note that these prices may change after printing):

- 50GB: $0.99
- 200GB: $2.99
- 2TB: $9.99

These prices are for everyone in your family. So, if you have five people on your plan, then each person doesn't need their own storage plan. This also means purchases are saved—if one family member buys a book or movie, everyone can access it.

iCloud has become even more powerful as our photo library grows. Photos used to be relatively small, but as cameras have advanced, the size goes up. Most photos on your Mac are several MB big. iCloud means you can keep the newest ones on your phone and put the older ones in the Cloud. It also means you don't have to worry about paying for the phone with the biggest hard drive—in fact, even if you have the biggest hard drive, there's a chance it won't fit all of your photos.

## WHERE IS ICLOUD?

If you look at your MacBook, you won't see an iCloud app. That's because there isn't an iCloud app. To see iCloud, point your computer browser to iCloud.com.

Once you sign in, you'll see all the things stored in your Cloud—photos, contacts, notes, files; these are all things you can access across all of your devices.

In addition, you can use iCloud from any computer (even PCs); this is especially helpful if you need to use Find My Mac, which locates not only your computer, but all of your Apple devices—phones, watches, even AirPods.

## BACKING UP YOUR COMPUTER WITH ICLOUD

The first thing you should know about iCloud is how to back up your computer with it. This is what you will need to do if you are moving from one Mac to another.

If there's no iCloud app on the computer, then how do you do that? While there is no native app in the traditional sense that you are used to, there are several iCloud settings in System Preferences.

Open the System Preferences; at the top you will see your name and profile picture; click that. That brings up the option to manage iCloud.

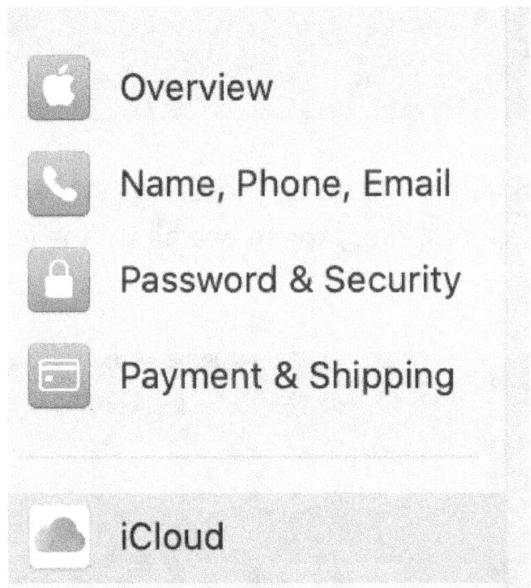


## ICLOUD DRIVE

To see your cloud files, open the Finder app; on the left menu, there is an option for the iCloud Drive.

You can use iCloud Drive to create and move folders just like you would in the Finder app.

# APPLE MUSIC

Apple Music is Apple's music streaming service.

The question most people wonder is which is better: Spotify or Apple Music? On paper it's hard to tell. They both have the same number of songs, and they both cost the same ($9.99 a month, $5 for students, $14.99 for families).

There really is no clear winner. It all comes down to preference. Spotify has some good features—such as an ad-supported free plan.

One of the standout features of Apple Music is iTunes Match. If you are like me and have a large collection of audio files on your computer, then you'll love iTunes Match. Apple puts those files in the Cloud, and you can stream them on any of your devices. This feature is also available if you don't have Apple Music for $25 a year.

Apple Music also plays well with Apple devices; so, if you are an Apple house (i.e. everything you own, from smart speakers to TV media boxes, has the Apple logo), then Apple Music is probably the best one for you.

Apple is compatible with other smart speakers, but it's built to shine on its own devices.

I won't cover Spotify here, but my advice is to try them both (they both have free trials) and see which interface you prefer.

### APPLE MUSIC CRASH COURSE

Before going over where things are in Apple Music, it's worth noting that Apple Music can now be accessed from your web browser (in beta form) here: http://beta.music.apple.com.

It's also worth noting that I have a little girl and don't get to listen to a lot of "adult" music, so the examples here are going to show a lot of kid's music!

The main navigation on Apple Music is on the side menu:
- For You
- Browse
- Radio

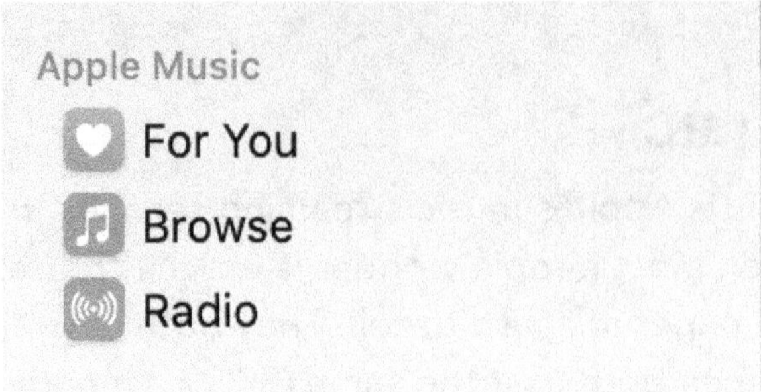



There's also a Library below this of what you have downloaded.

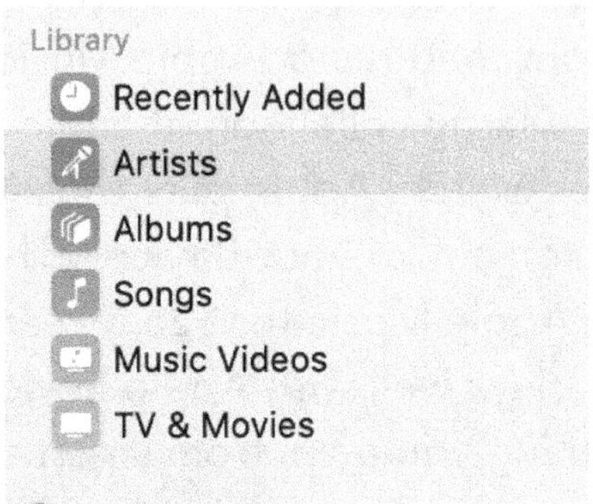



## LIBRARY

When you create playlists or download songs or albums, this is where you will go to find them.

You can change the categories that show up in this first list by tapping on Edit, then checking off the categories you want. Make sure to hit Done to save your changes.

## FOR YOU

As you play music, Apple Music starts to get to know you more and more; it makes recommendations based on what you are playing.

In For You, you can get a mix of all these songs and see other recommendations.

In addition to different styles of music, it also has friends' recommendations so you can discover new music based on what your friends are listening to.

## BROWSE

Not digging those recommendations? You can also browse genres in the Browse menu. In addition to different genre categories, you can see what music is new and what music is popular.

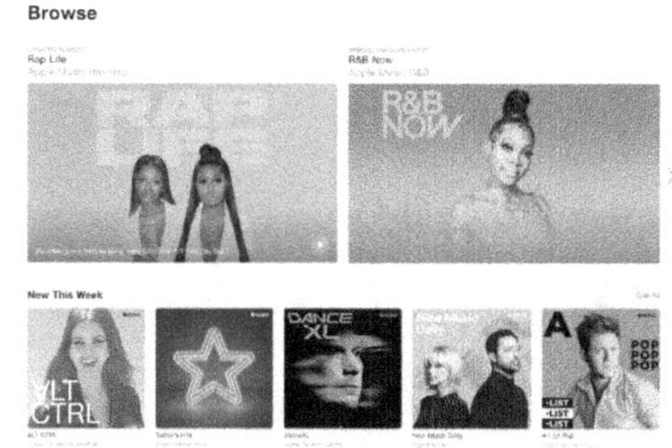

## RADIO

Radio is Apple's version of AM/FM; the main radio station is Beats One. There are on-air DJs and everything you'd expect from a radio station.

While Beats One is Apple's flagship station, it's not its only station. You can scroll down and tap on Radio Stations under More to explore and see several other stations based on music styles (i.e. country, alternative, rock, etc.). Under this menu, you'll also find a handful of talk stations covering news and sports. Don't expect to find the opinionated talk radio you may listen to on regular radio—it's pretty controversy-free.

### SEARCH

The last option is the search menu, which is pretty self-explanatory. Type in what you want to find (i.e. artist, album, genre, etc.).

### LISTENING TO MUSIC AND CREATING A PLAYLIST

You can access the music you are currently listening to from the top of your screen.

Right-clicking (two-finger clicking) on the album on this brings up several options. One is to take you to the album, which shows a full screen view.

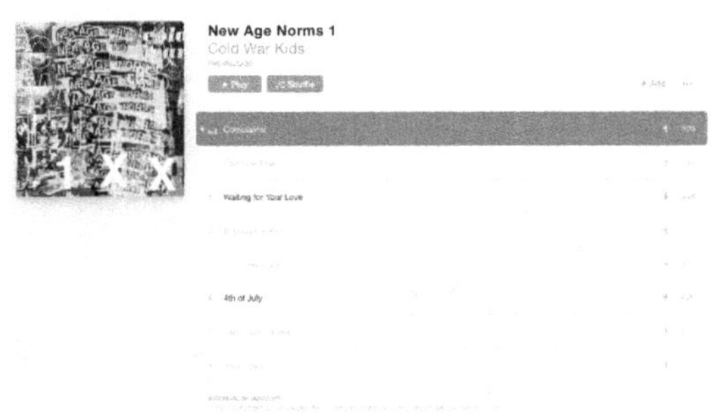

Clicking on the chat-like button will show you the text from what's playing.

To the left of that is the option to select where you want to play the music. For example, if you have a HomePod and you want to listen wirelessly to the music from that device, you can change it here.

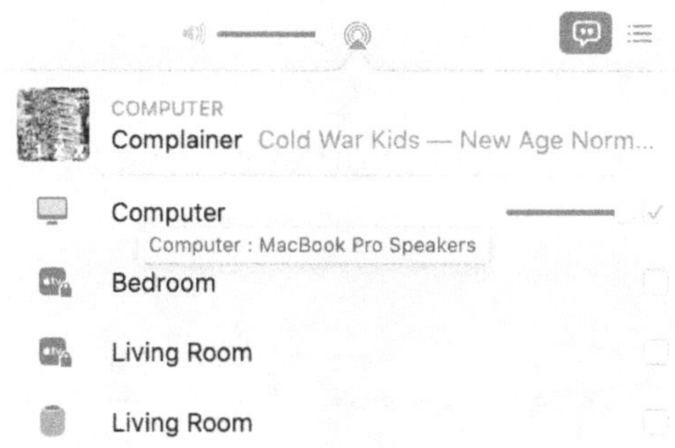

The option on the far right shows the next song(s) in the playlist.

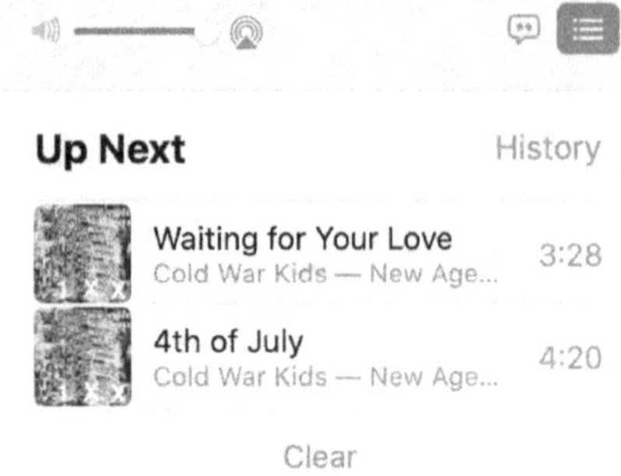

If you want to add a song to a playlist, then right-click the song and select the playlist (or create one).

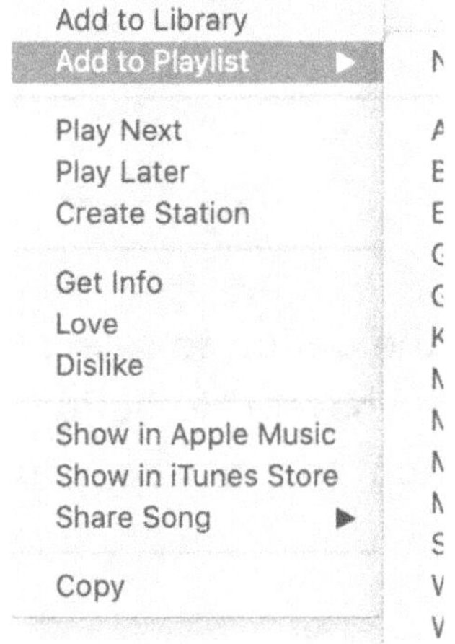



At any point, you can tap the artist's name to see all of their music.

In addition to seeing information about the band, their popular songs, and their albums, you can get a playlist of their essential songs or a playlist of bands that they have influenced.

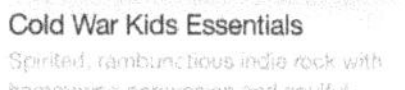

If you scroll to the bottom, you can also see Similar Artists, which is a great way to discover new bands that are like the ones you are currently listening to.

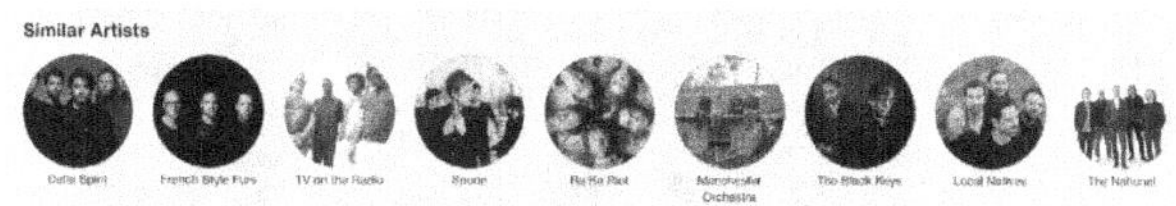

## TIPS FOR GETTING THE MOST OUT OF APPLE MUSIC

### *Heart It*

Like what you're hearing? Heart it! Hate it? Dislike it. Apple gets to know you by what you listen to, but it improves the accuracy when you tell it what you think of a song you are really into...or really hate.

### *Download Music*

If you don't want to rely on wi-fi when you are on the go, make sure and tap the cloud on your music to download the music locally to your phone. If you don't see a cloud, add it to your library by tapping the plus, which should change it to a cloud.

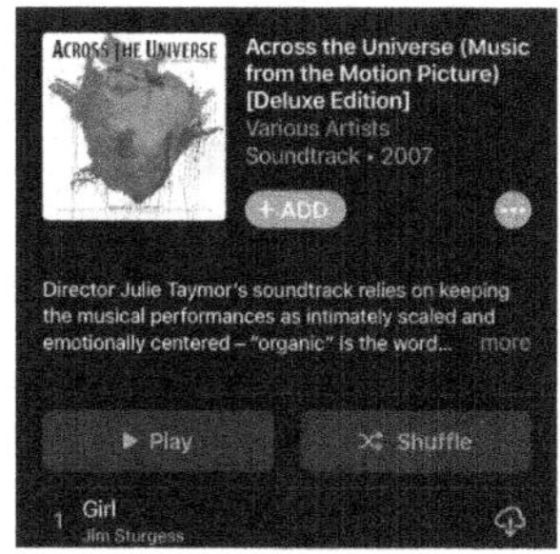

## *Hey Siri*

Siri knows music! Say "Hey Siri" and say what you want to listen to, and the AI will get to work.

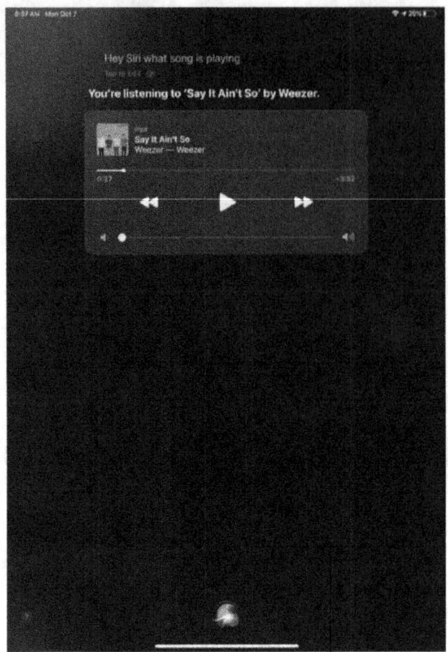

# [8]
# HOW TO CUSTOMIZE THINGS

This chapter will cover:
- System preferences
- Adding social networking and other accounts
- Controlling sound
- User groups
- Screenshots
- Photo continuity
- Accessibility
- Privacy / security

So now you know the basics; you should be able to work your way around the desktop with ease and use all the basic programs comfortably. But it still doesn't feel quite…you. It still has all the default settings, colors, gestures, and backgrounds. Sure it's a cool computer, but now let's make it feel like your computer.

# SYSTEM PREFERENCES

All of the main settings are accessed in System Preferences which is essentially the Mac equivalent of Control Panel on a Windows computer. So to get started, let's get to System Preferences by clicking Launchpad, then clicking the System Preferences icon.

You can also get there by clicking on the Apple in the upper left corner of the menu and clicking System Preferences.

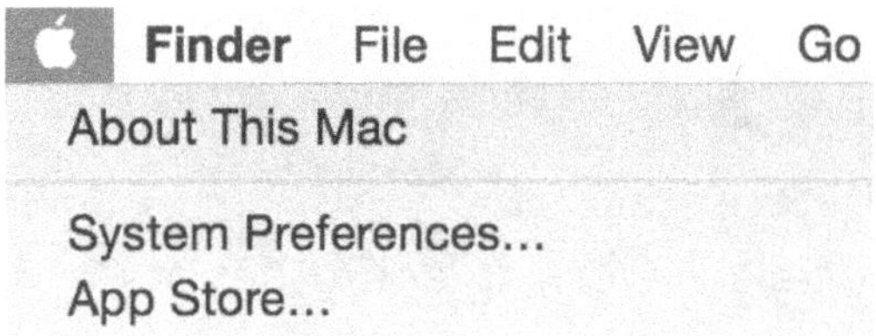


Once the app opens, you'll see there are lots of things that you can configure.

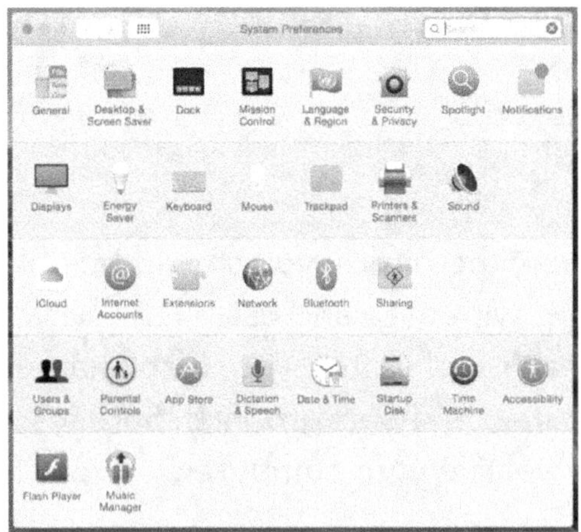

*General*

Let's get started with the first option: General. Under General, you can:

- Change the appearance of the main buttons, windows, and menus by selecting either Blue or Graphite.
- Choose the highlight color.
- Change the top menu bar and Dock to dark colors.  This option works well with dark wallpapers.
- Set scroll bars to display automatically based on mouse or Track-pad, only when scrolling, or always on.
- Select the default web browser.
- Here is where you can allow Handoff to work between your Mac and iCloud devices (some older Macs don't support this feature).

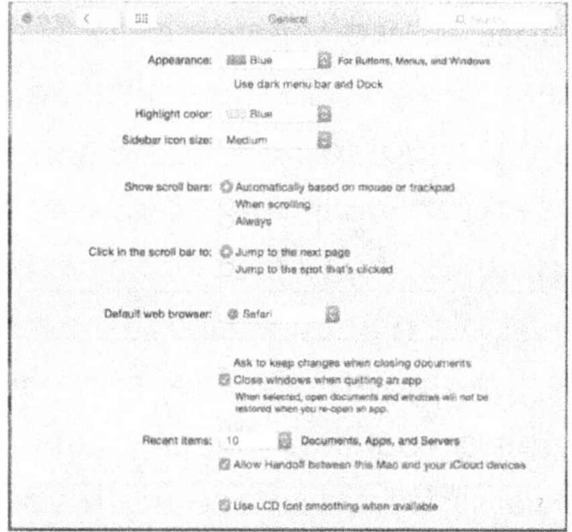

At any time, you can get back to the main System Preferences page by clicking on the button with 12 tiny squares. You can also hit the Back button, but if you are several menus in, you may have to hit the Back button several times.

*Desktop & Screen Saver*

The Desktop & Screen Saver section will help you change perhaps the most visually noticeable thing on your Mac—the desktop wallpaper.  Along the left sidebar you will see several different dropdown options: Apple, iPhoto, and Folders.

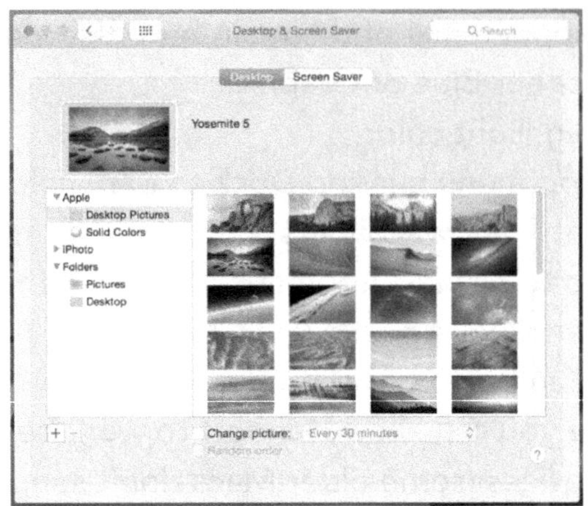

At the bottom, you will be able to change the picture every so often, and you can choose how often you'd like a new image to refresh. The images that show up in the right-hand window will be the ones that get scrolled through during refreshes.

To change your desktop wallpaper to one of the great-looking images provided by Apple, or if you just want to browse the available choices, click on the Apple name. A bunch of colorful, high-resolution images will populate the right-hand side, and you can scroll through the list to find something you like. Clicking on an image will change your wallpaper to that particular selection. If you're a plain Jane and prefer to keep things really simple, you can also select Solid Colors to find an array of potentially yawn-inducing plain wallpapers.

Selecting iPhoto will let you scroll through your photos, allowing you to select a cherished memory as your wallpaper.

The Folders option will let you choose between added folders where more image files might be lying in wait. If you save lots of images to your desktop, you might want to add the Desktop folder here so you can include those images as would-be wallpapers.

### Adding and Removing Folders

1. To add new folders and image collections, click on the '+' button located at the bottom of the left sidebar.
2. When the window comes up, search for the folder that you'd like to add.

3. Once you find the desired folder, click the blue Choose button to confirm the changes.
4. To remove a folder, highlight the folder that you'd like deleted and then click the '–' button to remove it.

*Screen Saver*

To set one up, click on the Screen Saver button at the top of the Desktop & Screen Saver window.

The left sidebar will have more options than you probably need when it comes to different ways to display your pictures.  Some great ones you will probably like are Shuffling Tiles, Vintage Prints, and Classic.

On the right side you can see a preview of what your screen saver will look like.  In this part of the window you can also select a source: National Geographic, Aerial, Cosmos, Nature Patterns, and Choose Folder if you have a particular folder of images you'd like to use.  If you'd like to shuffle the order in which images appear, check the box next to Shuffle slide order.

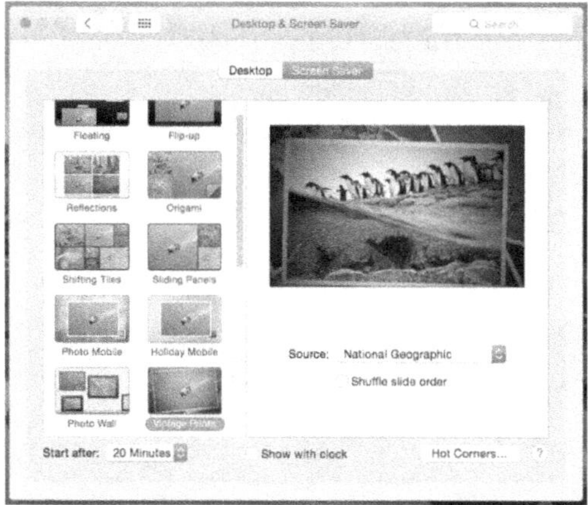

At the very bottom of the window you can choose the length of time before the screen saver starts.  You'll also be able to pick if you'd like to display the clock or not.

*Dock*

There isn't a lot you can do to the Dock and most of these settings are self-explanatory. For the most part the settings just make things a little more…animated. Magnification, for example, makes an app icon larger when you hover your mouse over it.

One option I will point out, however, is the option to automatically hide and show Dock; all of these settings are a matter of taste; I personally choose to hide the Dock for two reasons: one, it gives you more screen space, and two, it lets you use the Dock while you are in a full screen app.

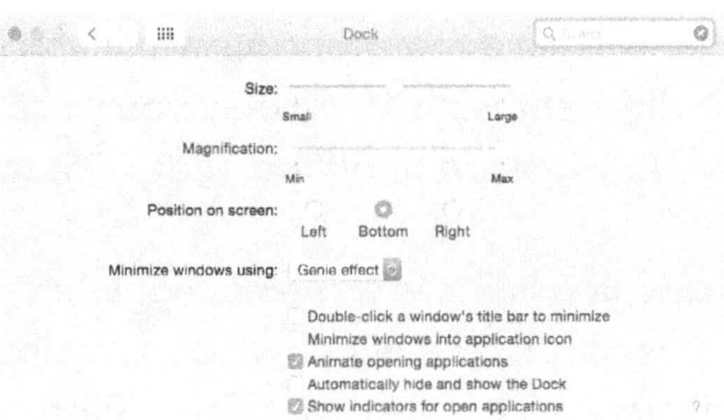

## Mission Control

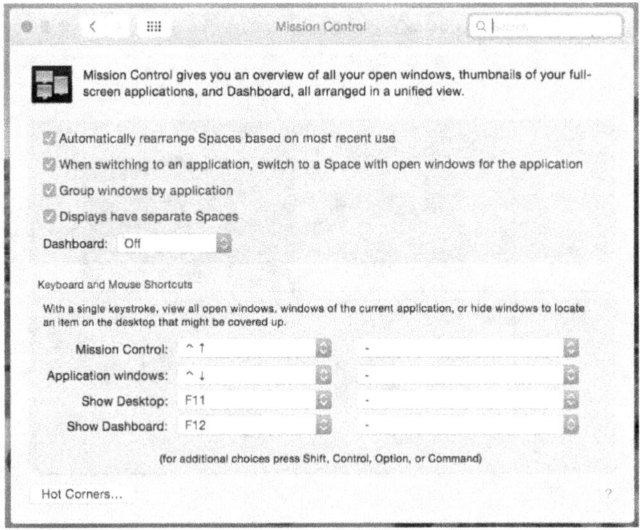

Mission Control is where you can set different parts of your screen to do different things. What do I mean by that? For example, you can set up a shortcut so that every time you move your mouse to the far upper right corner, your desktop is revealed. You can also set up shortcut keys on your keyboard. Mission Control is really about helping you make simple tasks quick.

*Social Networking, Mail, Contacts and Calendars*

When you use Twitter, Facebook and other apps, you may be used to just going to a website. On a Mac, you can add them into your computer's information, so you don't need to login; this also lets you get notification pop ups when you have new messages, likes, etc.

*Adding Accounts*

To add accounts, go to System Preferences on your Dock (the gears icon) and select Internet Accounts. From here, you can add accounts that haven't already been migrated, including iCloud, Exchange, Google, Twitter, Facebook, LinkedIn, Yahoo!, AOL, Vimeo and Flickr. Adding accounts here will start populating Catalina's native Mail, Contacts, Reminders and Calendar apps, and add options to your Share button.

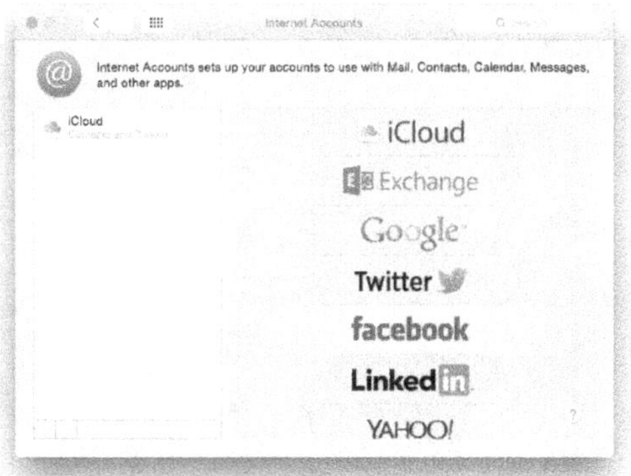

Note: You can also add accounts within the Mail, Contacts, Calendars, and Reminders apps by opening each app and clicking File > Add Account.

*Twitter, Facebook, LinkedIn, Vimeo and Flickr*

Catalina OS supports deep Twitter, Facebook, LinkedIn, Flickr and Vimeo integration. To get started, simply sign in to your account(s) from System Preferences > Internet Accounts. Select Twitter, Facebook, LinkedIn, Flickr, or Vimeo, and then enter your username and password. From now on, you'll be able to use that account with the Share button throughout Catalina and receive notifications in your Notifications Center.

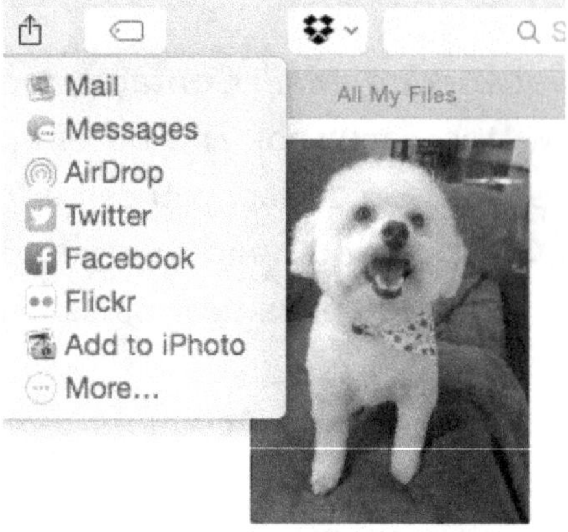


IMG_0030.jpg

# SOUND

As the name implies, the Sound menu is where all changes related to sound effects and sound in general can be modified.  There are three tabs that you can switch between.

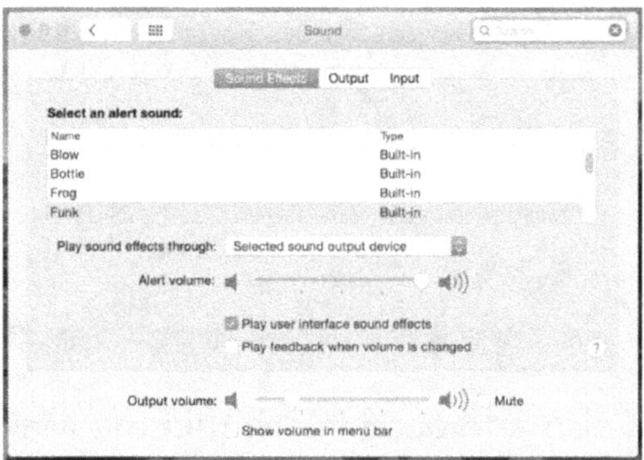


*Sound Effects*

The Sound Effects tab is where you can select an alert sound from the many different built-in options. By default, the following dropdown menu should be set to Selected sound output device to play the chosen sound effects through your standard speakers.

The next two checkboxes let you turn sound effects on or off for the user interface, and for volume control.

Lastly, you'll be able to adjust the output volume of your speakers.  This will affect the loudness of everything from sound effects to music that's currently being played through the computer.

*Input & Output*

The input and output tabs are both very similar. Each will let you change the device for sound input or output (speakers or microphones), as well as adjust sound settings. In the output tab, you can adjust the slider to move the balance left or right, and in input, you can change the microphone's input volume and enable or disable the built-in noise reduction feature in case you frequently use your Mac's microphone in busy cafes.

# USERS & GROUPS

If your Mac is for family use and a couple of people will be using it, then this setting will come in handy.

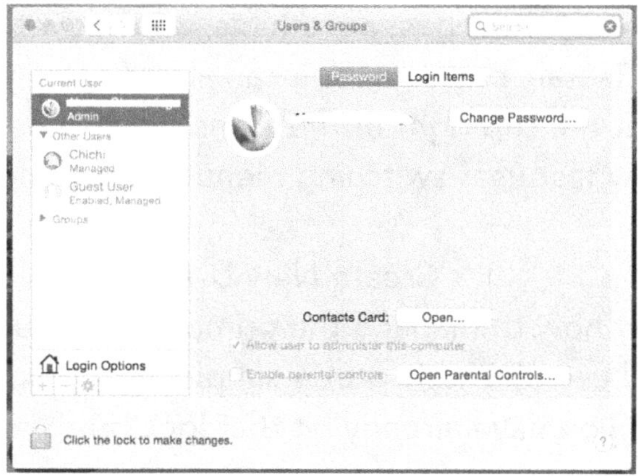

Along the left sidebar all existing users and groups (if you have any) will be laid out for you. To make a change to an existing user, first you need to choose the "Click the lock" icon and unlock it; unlocking lets you change settings to the user. You will also be asked for your password at this time—this is all a safety measure to ensure that if you accidentally left your computer unattended, someone couldn't come along and lock you out of your own machine.

Below are a few things you'll be able to do with each user. Depending on the type of user it is (admin, guest, child, etc.), some of the settings won't be available.

- Selecting the admin user account will let you change the login password, open up the Contacts card and enable parental controls. Clicking the Login Items will allow you to change the applications that start running automatically each time you log in. There has to be at least one admin user.

- Any other created users that you make will have options to enable parental controls, change password, or turn that account into another administrator account that has full control of the Mac.
- By default, you will see a guest user set up.  If it's selected, you can choose to disable the guest user from being available as a login option.  You can also set parental controls and allow guest access to your shared folders.  If you do choose to keep the guest user, keep in mind that there will be no password required, and all information and files created during that session will be deleted upon logging out.
- At the bottom of the left sidebar there is another option, called Login Options.  This is where you'll find different options such as automatic login, show password hints, and show the Sleep, Shut Down, and Restart buttons.  You can also display your full name or user name at the top right of the menu bar by checking the box next to Show fast user switching menu and making a selection.

### Create New Users

So you know how to manage the primary user, but what about creating additional users? That's pretty simple. Just follow these steps (and make sure you have already hit that lock button to unlock the option).

1. Click on the '+' button.
2. From the New Account dropdown menu, choose from the following options: Administrator, Standard, Managed with Parental Controls, or Sharing Only.

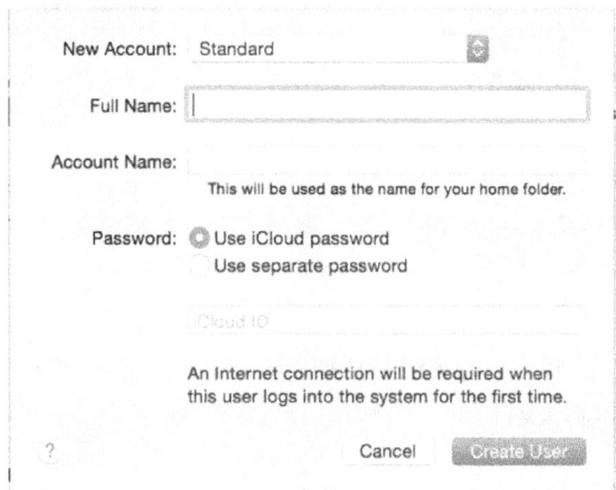

3. Fill in the Full Name and Account Name fields. These don't have to be real names. Mickey Mouse can have a user name if you want.
4. You can choose to have the new user log in using an existing iCloud account and password, or create a whole new password.

5. If you selected Use iCloud Password, you will be prompted to enter the associated iCloud ID.
6. If you instead choose to opt for a newly-created password, you will be asked to enter it twice to verify it.
7. Once finished, click the blue Create User button. If you chose to use an iCloud ID, you will be asked to enter the password. If you made a new password, you don't need to do anything else.

### *Removing Existing Users*

Just because you added a user, that doesn't mean they're there forever. You can delete them at any time. But remember, deleting them deletes all the settings they've set up—so if you create that user again, everything will be gone.

1. To remove current users, select the user that you'd like to delete.
2. With that user highlighted, click on the '–' button.
3. A prompt will appear asking if you are really sure you'd like to remove the user from the computer.

4. You can also choose from one of three radio buttons: save the home folder, leave the home folder alone, or delete the home folder.
5. Once you've made a decision, click the blue Delete User button to confirm your choice and make the changes happen.

### Creating Groups

If the computer is being used in a place where there are dozens of users (a classroom or library, perhaps), then creating a group would be a good option for you.

1. At the bottom of the left sidebar, click the '+' button.
2. From the New dropdown menu, select Group
3. In the Full Name field, create and enter a name for your group.
4. Click the blue Create Group button to confirm.
5. The new group will be created, and you will be able to check boxes next to each existing user to designate who will be a part of this group.  If you have existing groups, you can also select entire groups to be a part of yet another group.

## GAME MODE

Designed to enhance your gaming experience, Game Mode optimizes CPU and GPU usage and minimizes latency with wireless devices like controllers and AirPods when a game is launched.

### WHAT IS GAME MODE OFFER?

Historically, Mac has been somewhat sidelined by serious gamers due to its lack of hardware customization. However, the transition to Apple silicon has amped up performance levels, especially for gaming. Game Mode is Apple's response to this historical critique, aiming to boost the gaming credentials of the Mac by enhancing video framerates and graphics settings and reducing device latency.

### HOW GAME MODE WORKS

Game Mode, when activated, gives top priority to the game in play, relegating background apps to lower priority.

### ACTIVATING AND USING GAME MODE

Activation is simple - Game Mode kicks in automatically when a game is launched, with a notification and a game controller icon appearing in the menu bar to indicate its activation. It is important to note that the game must be in full-screen mode for Game Mode to operate. It pauses if the game is played in a window.

If you wish to deactivate Game Mode, click the game controller icon in the menu bar; you'll find the option to turn it off and on again here. Note, if you deactivate Game Mode and exit the game, you'll need to manually activate it when you reopen the game.

### GAME MODE COMPATIBILITY AND SETTINGS

Game Mode is compatible with any game, according to Apple.

# SNAP THIS

Screenshots on MacOS have always been pretty simple and straightforward. Shift-Command-3 to take a screenshot of your entire screen and Shift-Command-4 to take a screenshot of a specific area of your screen.

These commands still work, but Apple took it up a notch and allows you to edit the screenshot—if you've taken screenshots on iOS, then the experience is probably familiar to you.

As soon as you take a screenshot, you'll see options for what you can do next in a small popup at the bottom right of your screen. These options will take you to a Markup window where you can add annotations, shapes, text, and more.

In addition to these options, MacOS has added a new command: Shift-Command-5. This opens up a screenshot interface with several options such as capture entire screen, selected window, or a selected portion. The last two options are new: record the entire screen or record a portion of it.

## CONTINUE THAT PHOTO WHERE YOU LEFT OFF

One thing Apple has done really well with their devices is continuity—the idea of stopping on one device and picking up where you left off on another. For example, you could stop a movie in the living room on Apple TV and continue watching it on your Apple TV in the bedroom. Or you could get a text on your Apple Watch and reply on your phone. It's all very intuitive and just works.

This concept of using on one device and picking up on another now extends to the camera. With OS Catalina, you can take a picture on your iPhone or iPad and have it automatically sent to your Mac and into the photo editing app of your desire.

If the Mac app supports the feature, then you'll see it under Edit in the menu area; there will be a new option that says "Insert from Your iPhone or iPad" with the option to Take Photo or Scan Documents.

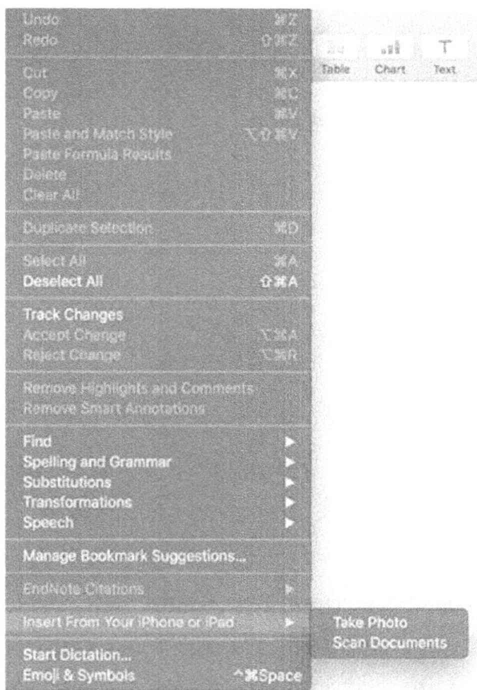


Once you snap the photo on your phone or tablet, it will automatically appear in the document.

## PARENTAL CONTROLS

If kids are using your computer, then Apple has Parental Controls to help you make sure the kids don't get into trouble. It's a pretty powerful app, but it does have a few limits—if you want ultimate protection, then there are also several paid apps like NetNanny (www.netnanny.com). Parental Controls is also good for guests—if you don't mind if people use your computer, but you only want them to use the Internet and have no access to anything else, then you could set it up like that.

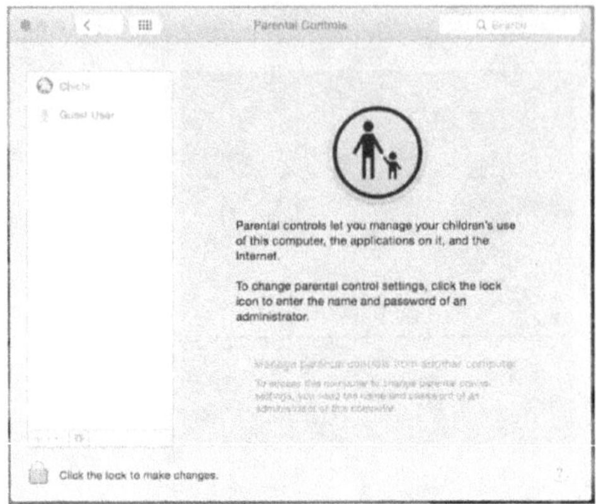

To use Apple's Parental Controls, first make sure you have created a user account for your child. Next go to System Preferences and Parental Controls.

If the padlock on the lower left corner is locked, then click it to unlock it and type in your password.

You can now set up parental controls for each child user. You can make it as restrictive as you want. The first tab lets you pick what apps they can use. You could block all apps except games, for instance. The next tab lets you control web usage. By default, Apple will try to filter out adult content. If this is a young child, then a better option might be picking the web pages they can access—you could, for instance, block every Internet website except Disney. The next tab is People. This lets you select who they can email and message—you could limit them to only emailing parents and grandparents, for instance. The second to last tab lets you pick time limits. You can pick when they use the computer and for how long. And finally, the last tab lets you turn off the camera so they can't do video chatting, allows you to hide profanity from the dictionary, etc.


## SIDECAR

What's Sidecar? It's basically using your iPad as a second screen alongside your Mac.

Using your iPad as a second Mac screen is nothing new. Popular apps such as Duet have been doing this successfully for years.

Apple has finally taken note and decided to release a feature called Sidecar that lets you wirelessly use your iPad as a secondary Mac screen; it's just like using AirPlay on your phone to show YouTube on your TV. So long apps like Duet, right? Not exactly.

Before moving into how to use Sidecar, let me first mention what Sidecar is not: a rich app full of pro features. It does one thing very well: shows your Mac screen on your iPad. Apps like Duet are compatible with iPhone and iPad and also work with cross OSes—so you can also show your Windows device on your iPad. But personally, one thing I find lacking on Sidecar is touch. I expected to be able to tap the iPad screen and launch apps and folders. That wasn't the case. It was for display purposes only...unless you have an Apple Pencil. Sidecar feels like it was made to entice people to buy an Apple Pencil. With an Apple Pencil, touch suddenly becomes possible. There's probably a good reason for this—the Apple Pencil is more precise and has more gestures than your finger.

So now that you know a little about what it isn't, let's look at how it works.

First, make sure your MacBook (yes, this is only compatible with MacBooks—sorry Windows users) is up-to-date with the latest OS (Catalina).

Second, make sure your iPad is turned on, in standby mode, and on the same Wi-Fi network (if not, you won't see the next step).

Third, go to the menu in the upper right side of your MacBook and click the rectangular box for AirPlay.

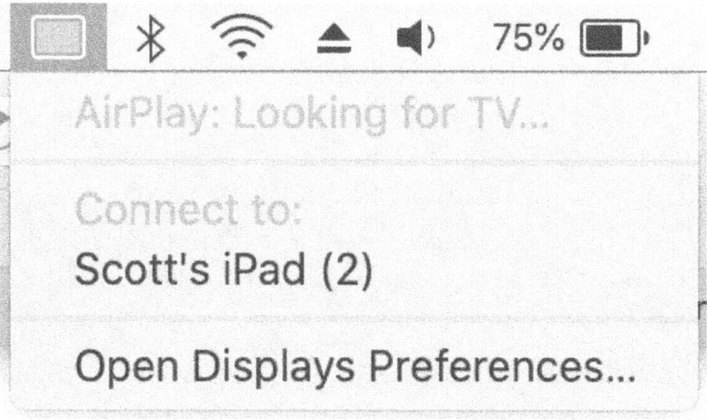


That's it! Kind of. Your MacBook should now be showing on your iPad. It will look a little like this:

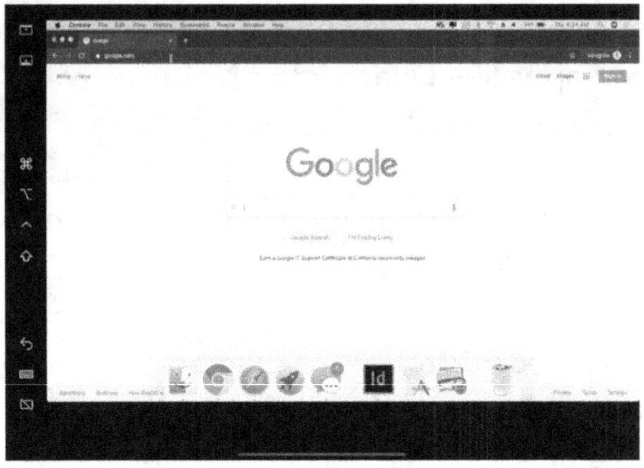

So what do I mean "kind of"? There are still a few more settings you should know about. Click that AirPlay box in the right corner again and you'll see even more options.

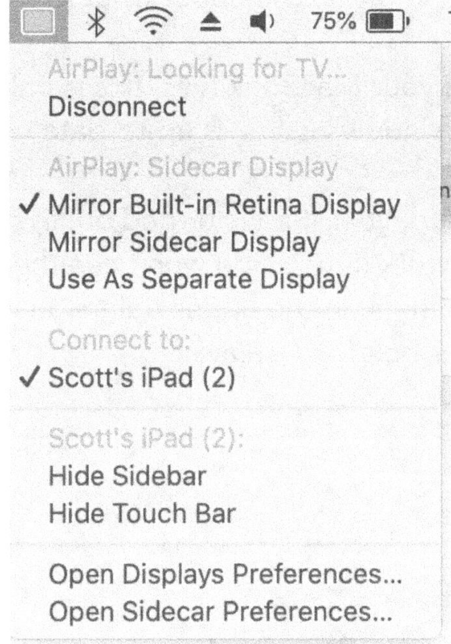

What are all these options? Use As Separate Display (vs the two Mirror options) turns your iPad into a second screen—so you can have another Mac app running on your display instead of just showing whatever is on your MacBook. The two Hide options get rid of the boxes you see on your iPad to make it a bit more full screen.

Finally, Open Sidecar Preferences will give you a few additional options. You can, for example, pick to show the menu bar on the right instead of left.

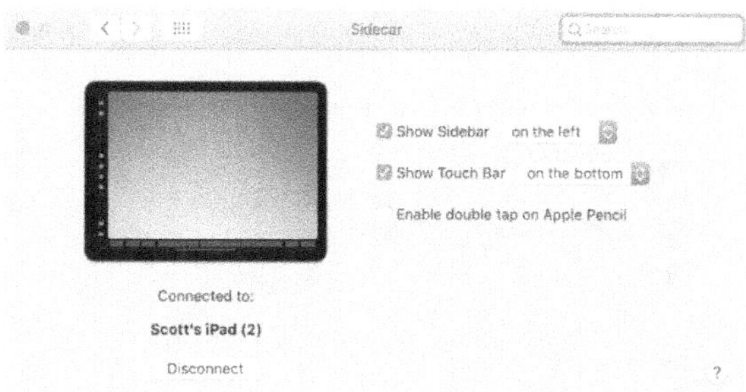

You can disconnect from Sidecar by either tapping on the box with the line through it on your iPad or going to the AirPlay button on your Mac and disconnecting.

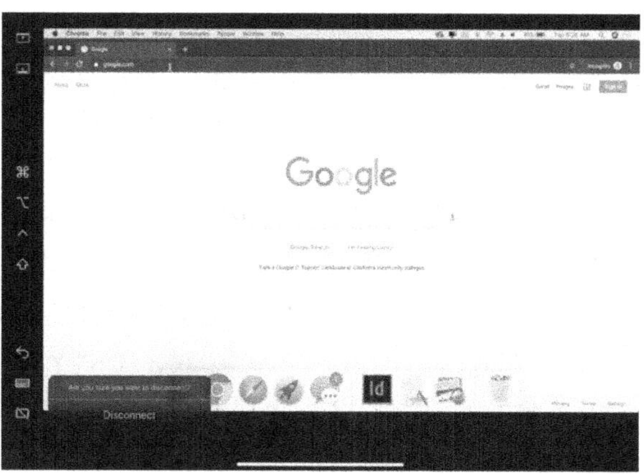

# PRIVACY AND SECURITY

If your computer is in a place where other people can get to it, or if you are just generally concerned about your privacy being violated, then head on over to Privacy and Security in the System Preferences.

*Creating Strong Passwords*

Strong passwords are the first line of defense against potential hackers (or smart children!); a strong password is not something like "password"; a strong password has letters, numbers and even symbols in it. It could be something like this: "@mY_MACb00k."

You can use the Password Assistant to test how strong your password is.

When Keychain loads, you will be able to view the entire list of accounts that are already synced to Keychain. If you would like to change the password for an account that already exists, find the account and double-click on it.  If not, click on the '+' button at the bottom to add a new account.

When the new window comes up, take a look at the bottom.  There will be a field for password, and at the right of it will be a small key icon.  Click the key icon to open up Password Assistant.

From Type you can select Manual (create your own), Memorable, Letters & Numbers, Numbers Only, Random, and FIPS-181 compliant.

Suggestions will automatically populate, and you can scroll through several different suggestions by using the dropdown menu.

Adjust the length slider to make the password longer or shorter.  Any password you create will meet at least these requirements to be considered fair.

As you generate a password, the quality indicator will change to show you how safe and complex a given password is.

*Firewall*

Another line of defense you can add is a firewall, which protects you from unwanted connections to potentially malicious software applications, websites, or files.

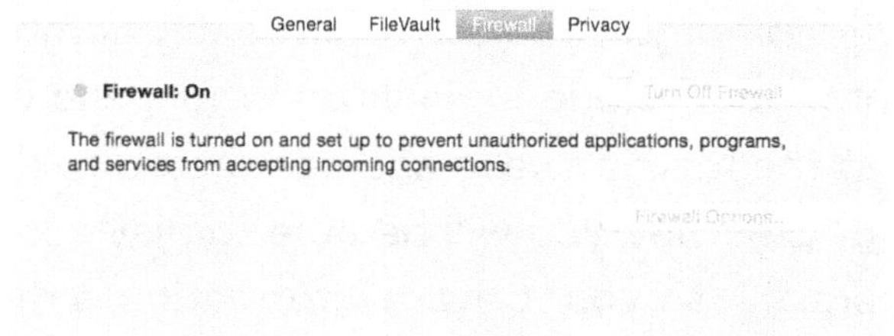



To enable the firewall that comes with your Mac, go to System Preferences > Security & Privacy and select the Firewall tab.  Before you can make any changes, click on the lock icon in the bottom left corner and enter your administrator password to continue.

*Find My Mac*

Just like your iPhone or iPad, Mac comes with a handy feature called "Find My Mac" which lets you find your computer if someone steals it or you just misplace it; you can also wipe its hard drive clean remotely.

To enable Find My Mac, go to System Preferences > iCloud and check the box next to Find My Mac.  Your location services must also be turned on, so go to System Preferences > Security & Privacy > Privacy > Location Services and make sure Enable Location Services is checked on.

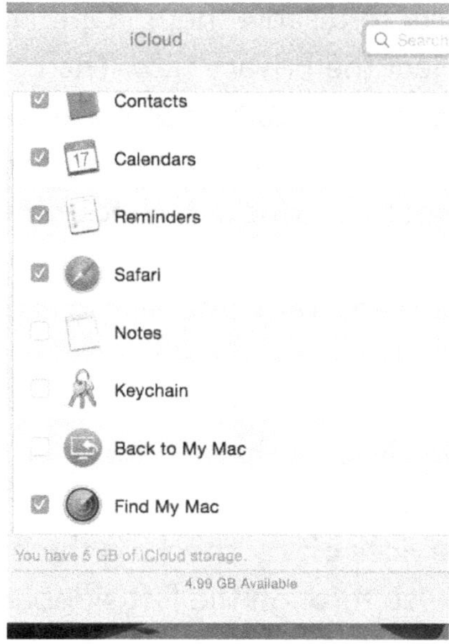

To track your computer, you can log into any computer and visit iCloud.com, enter your iCloud login information, and click on Find My Mac. As long as the Mac is awake and connected to the Internet through Wi-Fi or Ethernet, you will be able to play a loud sound, lock it, or completely erase it so your private information is removed.

### Privacy

Apple knows people worry about privacy; they have lots built in to help you control what can (and can't) be seen.

### Internet Privacy

If you'd like to clear your search and browsing history, there are two ways to do it: either by clicking on Safari > Clear History and Website Data or History > Clear History and Website Data. Both can be found on the top menu bar. When the window comes up, you will be able to choose how far back you want the clearing to reach. Once you make a selection just press the Clear History button to make the changes final.

Cookies allow websites to store data and track certain things, like what other websites you visit during your Internet session, or what kind of products you tend to look at the most. This information is mostly used by advertisers to better target ads for you, but the option is always there if you'd like to disable them. Open up Safari, go to Safari > Preferences, then select the Privacy tab. The cookie options range from allowing all websites to store cookies to blocking all websites. You can also allow cookies only from the most frequently visited websites. If you prefer not to be tracked, check off the box at the bottom that says Ask Websites To Not Track Me. Some websites will not function as you may want them to by disabling this feature.

### Application Privacy

The other part of privacy is through installed applications. Go to System Preferences > Security & Privacy and click the Privacy tab. You can shut Location Services off by checking the box next to Enable Location Services. Browse through the left sidebar and you'll be able to customize permissions. If you don't want any apps to access your contacts or calendars, here is where you can block some or all programs from that information.

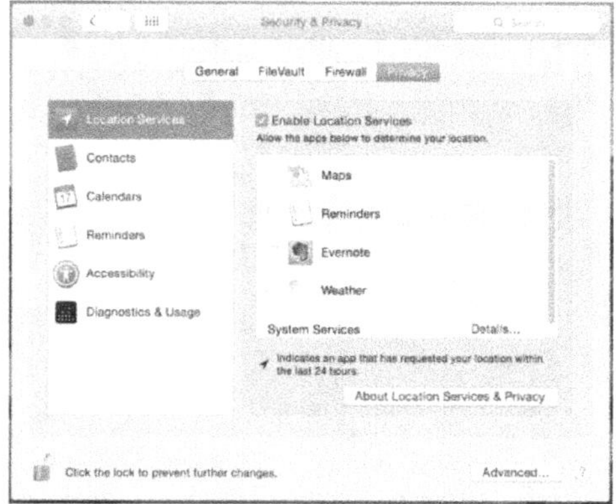

## Screen Time

Screen Time might be something you are familiar with. It's been on iPads and iPhones for a while. It comes to MacOS with the Catalina update. What is it? It's a productivity setting that lets you restrict how long you can use certain apps (games for instance). It's highly customizable, so you can set one app like Word to have zero restrictions, but another one like Internet to have limits.

Screen Time isn't an app in the traditional sense; it's an app within your system settings. To use it, go to System Preferences, then click Screen Time.

This launches a new window that tells you how much time you've been on your computer.

You can set up a passcode by clicking on options at the bottom of the window.

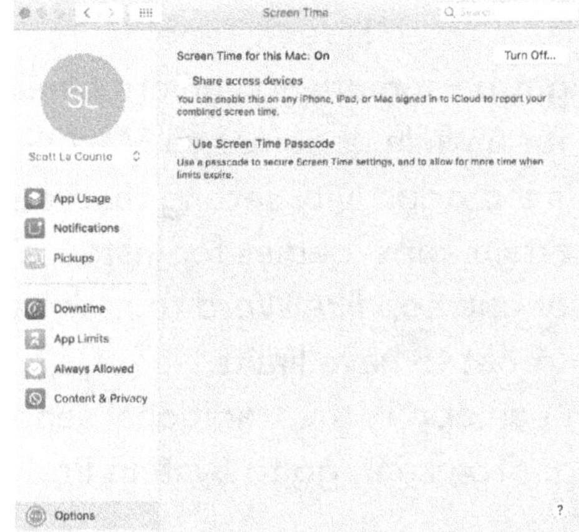

App Limits is where you can start restricting certain apps. Click the '+' in this section.

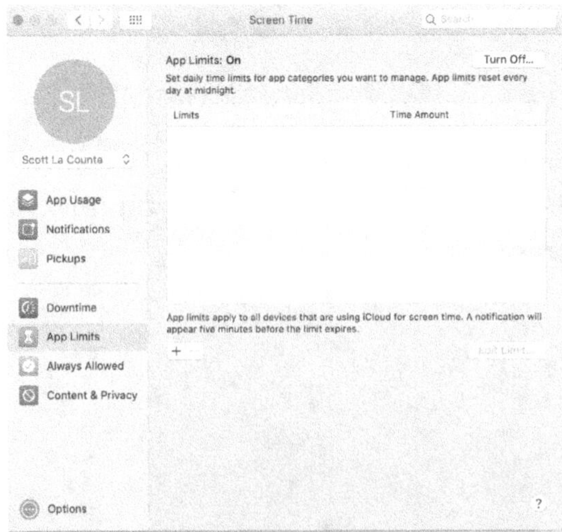

From here select the app (or kinds of apps) that you want to limit.

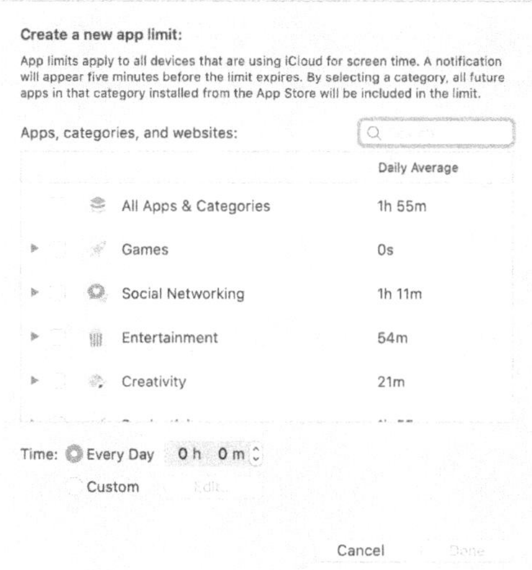

At the bottom, you can say how much time you want to set the limit to.

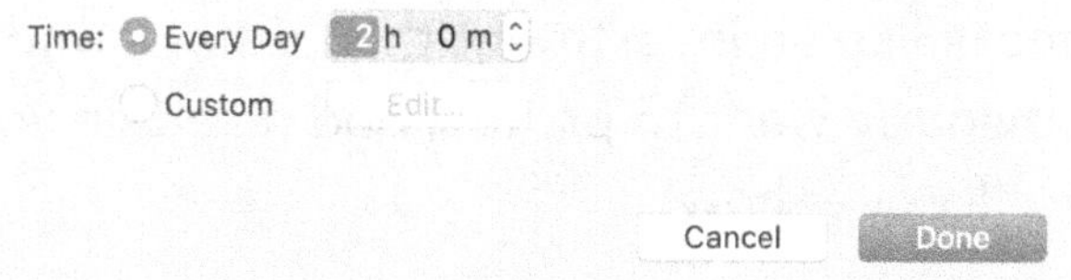

Under Always Allow, you can select apps that have no restrictions.

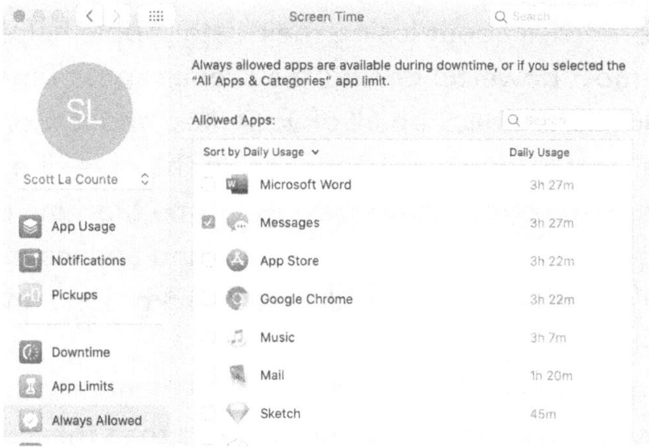

[9]

# KEEP IT RUNNING SMOOTHLY

Macs feel more like an investment than other computers; with that in mind, you obviously want to protect and maintain your investment. In this chapter, I'll cover how.

## TIME MACHINE

Everyone worries about losing their data; Apple helps you out with one of their most powerful behind-the-scenes apps: Time Machine.

Time Machine will back up all of your files, applications, and settings with minimal configuration or headache. In the case of a catastrophic event such as hard drive failure, having a Time Machine backup can allow you to quickly recover all of your data and applications, and even all of your settings (such as your desktop background and even the specific location of icons on your desktop).

You will need to buy an external USB or Thunderbolt hard drive. It is recommended to buy a drive that is larger than the current used space on your computer. For example, if you have used 100 gigabytes of space on your computer's hard drive, you should buy at least a 120-gigabyte hard drive.

You can also purchase an additional Time Machine Airport Capsule that does all of this wirelessly.

To get started, plug the hard drive into your computer and Time Machine will start automatically. It will ask you if you would like to use the drive as a Time Machine Backup Disk. Choose Use as Backup Disk.

If Time Machine does not start automatically, go to Finder > Applications > Machine, and click Choose Backup Disk. Select your new hard drive.

After you specify the drive to use as a backup, Time Machine will automatically begin backing up your data.

## SOFTWARE UPDATES

If you want your computer running smoothly then make sure you update regularly; updates are free and come once every couple of months. They fix minor bugs and sometimes add things to correct vulnerabilities that might make your computer open to viruses.

MacOS X, by default, will prompt you when updates are available, and you need only to click "Update" and enter your password in order to run the updates. Sometimes, in the case of major updates, you will need to restart your computer to complete the update. You can click Not now if you would like to delay the updates until a more convenient time.

# INDEX

# ABOUT THE AUTHOR

Scott La Counte is a UX Designer and writer. His first book, *Quiet, Please: Dispatches from a Public Librarian* (Da Capo 2008) was the editor's choice for the Chicago Tribune and a Discovery title for the Los Angeles Times.

He has written dozens of best-selling how-to guides on tech products.

He teaches UX Design for U.C. Berkeley.

You can connect with him at ScottDouglas.org.